YOUNG and HOMELESS in HOLLYWOOD

YOUNG *and* HOMELESS
in HOLLYWOOD

Mapping Social Identities

Susan M. Ruddick

Routledge
New York & London

Published in 1996 by

Routledge
29 West 35 Street
New York, NY 10001

Published in Great Britain in 1995 by

Routledge
11 New Fetter Lane
London EC4P 4EE

Copyright © 1996 by Routledge

Printed in the United States of America

Library of Congress Cataloging-in-Publication Data

Ruddick, Susan M.
    Young and homeless in Hollywood: mapping social identities / Susan M. Ruddick
       p.   cm.
    Includes bibliographical references and index.
    ISBN 0–415–91032–3 — ISBN 0–415–91031–5 (pbk.)
    1. Homeless youth—California—Los Angeles. 2. Homeless youth—Services for—California—Los Angeles. 3. Hollywood (Los Angeles, Calif.)—Social conditions.
I. Title.
HV4506.L67R83   1994
362.7'08'6942—dc20   94–21839
                                            CIP

To my parents

Contents

List of Figures

ACKNOWLEDGMENTS

I am indebted to many people for broadening my horizons in the research and writing of this book. Ever the dialectician, Ed Soja has provided me with thought-provoking and often productively unsettling commentary, while at the same time giving me enough space to find my own argument. Michael Storper's insightful critique cut to the kernel of what I was trying to say, and his support and feedback has been crucial throughout the project. Peter Marris has shown me (although I haven't always managed) the beauty of saying things simply. Both he and Eric Monkonnen provided helpful feedback on an early draft of the work. Jennifer Wolch and Michael Dear gave me practical support far beyond the call of duty.

As a friend and fellow traveler through the program at GSAUP, Robin Bloch expanded both my practical and theoretical perspective on youth subcultures, and provided intellectual inspiration (and humor) on a wide range of issues. Talmadge Wright's work on the spatial strategies of homeless people in Orange County sustained me in the knowledge that we were working on parallel tracks. Katherine MacMahon supported my interest in the semiotic side of life and taught me on the more practical side, that the only way to break a writer's block is to apply the seat of the pants to the seat of the chair.

On the issue of youth gangs, which became a counterpoint to the study of homeless youth, I am indebted to Mike Davis for getting me started in a collaborative project. Working with him taught me a great deal about crafting an argument. Marjorie Robertson fanned the flame from afar, sending me articles on California's juvenile penal system while I was in Germany. Thanks to her also for information about her own work on homeless youth in Hollywood. Michael Zinzun's inspired dedication and commitment to inner city youth made it impossible to think about the issue solely in academic terms.

While I was in Germany, Jost Müller and Klaus Ronnenberger shared insights from the German debate on politics and space. Both helped me in different ways to fuse the presence/absence of Hollywood with the absence/presence of Frankfurt. Deborah Redman's gift of *Less than Zero* provided the inspiration on youth and modernization, and Sabine Brock's careful commentary on an early draft of that chapter helped me hone my argument. In Toronto, I would like to thank Kim England for turning an eagle's editorial eye to a final version of the introduction, and to Linda Hershkovitz for her comments on chapter five. Laura Van de Bogart did the painstaking work of formatting footnotes and bibliographic material and Jane Davies, in the cartography lab of the University of Toronto helped by transforming my cartographic scribbling into readable maps. In Germany, Connie Eichhorn gave me "a room of my own" for my moveable feast of Post-its and papers so that I could finish up the project, as well as an insightful discussion about Judith Butler and the politics of difference which helped me think through my conclusion.

While I was in the field in Los Angeles, young homeless people, service providers, local political actors and planners provided hours of interview time and information. In particular, I would like to thank Dale Weaver, Greg Carlson, and Mindi Levins for the hours of their time that they gave, discussing the dynamics of service provision. John Kaliski provided me a very thoughtful interview in the most hectic of circumstances. Steven Flusty is living proof that some of the so-called "ordinary practitioners" of the city have a far-from-ordinary grasp of their own spatial practices. His insights enriched the manuscript immeasurably. Sheryl Madonna braved the streets of Los Angeles from Venice Beach to Skid Row (both depicted on the cover) and back through Hollywood with

Acknowledgments

her camera to capture the most elusive tactics of young homeless people on celluloid. Her photos appear on the cover and throughout the book. Special thanks to Anne Sanow and Adam Bohannon at Routledge for careful and painstaking editing.

Finally, I would like to thank Roger Keil. His careful editing of an entire draft of my manuscript helped to make the document readable, but his love and support made it possible.

INTRODUCTION

    The last evening of my most recent trip to Los Angeles was April 29, 1992. I spent it in the newly gentrified and eminently successful Santa Monica Mall on Los Angeles's wealthy Westside. It was the evening of the Rodney King verdict, and rumor had it that there would be some trouble in town, but no one in the mall seemed to think much of it. The place was crowded with the typical array of tanned beachgoers, smartly dressed office workers stopping off for a drink, and a few homeless people whose passage through the mall with their shopping carts seemed exactly synchronized with the exit of two "bike police"—the latter clad in sporty shorts and lemon yellow alligator shirts, scanning the mall for "undesirables." As darkness fell, a handful of homeless (white, male) youths gathered at the south end of the mall under a topiary, part of the new, upbeat, design features of the mall—a leafy dinosaur, spouting water from its mouth. The youths were dressed in the latest heavy metal gear, with black-painted fingernails, tattooed, strumming newly composed tunes on guitars to the delight of my three-year-old. When I was out of earshot, they confided to one of my friends that they lived in a squat, spent their time on the streets, and survived most recently by selling their blood. To me (in my social role as "mother" perhaps) they claimed it was all a ruse, an act to support their music image—that tattoos were for show, the squat an invention—they actually led quite normal lives, lived in apartments, drove big cars. They began to play a song they thought would appeal to my son—"The Child and the Beast"—but we never got to hear the end. My husband waved me across the mall to a local restaurant/wine store/deli which offered, among other things, Moët & Chandon at thirty-two dollars a bottle. Inside, on the overhead TV screen, the riots had begun.

The scene is seared into my brain with the clarity of a hologram. It was, in capsule form, the expression of a problem which has dogged me for five years now: on the one hand, the absence/presence of "homeless youths"—there, in the new social space of the mall, inscribed into the new public space of the city, yet there only by virtue of their invisibility, by their ability to appear as something else; on the other hand the presence/absence of "youth gangs," exorcised from this public space, and from virtually all the new spaces of the city, yet continually evoked within them, in this instance as part of the "mob" that erupted in violence following the Rodney King verdict.

Both the "youth gangs" to be found among rioters on the TV screen, and the "homeless youth" on the stone ledge of the fountain in Santa Monica Mall represent two new social *imaginaries* (collective mythologies) that have been constructed in Los Angeles over the past fifteen years. My book deals properly with only one—homeless youths. Yet it is impossible to think of one without thinking of the other.

As Berger notes in *The Look of Things*, "It is scarcely possible to tell a straight story in sequentially unfolding time. And this is because we are too aware of what is continually traversing the story-line laterally. . . . Such awareness is the result of having to take into account the simultaneity and extension of events and possibilities."[1] Laclau has expressed a similar sentiment elsewhere when he talks about the *radical contingency of the social*—the maintenance of identity that depends, not on any *a priori* law of history, but on its immediate relation to a constitutive outside, a set of contingent social practices against which and in relation to which we all define and redefine ourselves. In this sense, the imaginary "homeless youth" was constructed and is being constructed against the imaginary "youth gangs" as one of its many constitutive outsides. In my book I try to explore the one, with the other as an ever-present backdrop. But this gets too far ahead of my argument.

2

Introduction

The substantive focus of my book—the development of services for homeless youth in Hollywood, California (no doubt patronized by the youths I met in Santa Monica Mall)—could be read as the continuation in a long tradition of the good and charitable works of women. With this topic in hand, I join a venerable "community of women reformers," beginning with child-savers of the turn of the century such as Jane Addams and Ellen Gates Starr, founders of Hull House. The qualities of my topic give me entry into this community: it appropriately "tugs at the heartstrings," it is suitably domestic in its referent, and it is appropriately focused on victims as opposed to militants. However, my intentions in choosing this topic (acculturation aside) were different ones. My fascination with the topic was largely theoretical. Homeless youth pose a challenge to a series of theoretical premises that have become fashionable within critical theory, but are all too often agreed upon by fiat. These include the transformative possibilities of agency in the structure/agency dyad; the role of space in the constitution of social subjects; the role of symbolism and culture as material forces which produce their own effects, rather than as epiphenomena which reflect predetermined meanings. Admittedly, some of these connections between my chosen empirical object and the theoretical questions that continue to intrigue me were clarified only in the course of research and writing. But I felt them early on in the selection of the topic, although I was able at the time to express this only by taking a bungee jump between epistemology and ontology—mumbling that my topic was "not really about homeless youth," but "had more to do with the construction of the social." In hindsight, there were four major issues that I wanted to explore.

First of all, I wanted to test the premise that *agency matters*. My "object" was, fittingly, those people who are denied agency in all but the most banal forms: adolescents. Adolescents, in the common view, are generally considered too old to be ascribed the power of "nature"—we do not look on their activities with awe and wonder, the way we do those of small children. Yet adolescents are generally considered too young to be reasoned actors in the sense one might consider adults. When it comes to any form of sustained and serious agency, adolescents are depicted as awkward, simpleminded—"stupid and contagious." They live in a state where agency is continually denied them, as a recent grunge rock song suggests.[2]

Secondly, I wanted to test the premise that *new social subjects are created and create themselves in and through the social space of the city.* What better test case than a subject which denies itself, which hides itself, a subject which presents itself to you as something other than it is (or at least than you believe it to be), a subject whose "true identity" remains hidden, sequestered from view? Homeless youths fit this criteria. Homeless youth, I was warned, could not be trusted—they would tell you what you wanted to hear or something calculated to shock. They had an overwhelming desire to please, and a limitless capacity to deceive. The purpose of my investigation, however, was not to surface the "true story" of homeless youth, in the spirit of a Charles Loring Brace, bringing back my photos and taped interviews from the uncharted inner space of Hollywood's squats. The purpose was rather to investigate whether and how the control of public social space might play a role in privileging one story over another, in creating and sustaining a social imaginary.

Thirdly, I wanted to investigate *the material power of symbolism* in the creation and maintenance of social identity in and through space. The two sets of literature dealing with this issue that are most appropriate to my topic are literature on oppositional youth subcultures, and literature on the role of space in the marginalization of the homeless. The first deals with the role of symbolism and culture in maintaining and transforming social identity, the second with the role of marginal space in maintaining and transforming social identity. The problem is that they never quite meet in the middle. The literature on oppositional youth subcultures says little about space itself as a medium of subcultural and symbolic production. Space is a container where subculture "takes place." The literature on the homeless has much to say about the role of space in confirming cultural identity, in this case the marginal status of homeless people, but here space and its symbolic meaning are pregiven. Marginal status is predetermined and confirmed by marginal space, never transcended. Homeless youths, again, presented an interesting challenge. In California, they had been able to sustain an image which negotiated between the Scylla of "the homeless" and the Charybdis of youth as "the dangerous classes." Unlike other marginalized youth and other homeless people, they had developed a social identity which confronted their stigma.

Finally, my choice of homeless youth, and in particular homeless youths in Hollywood from the mid-1970s to the mid-1990s, grew out of a conviction of the need to focus on something concrete and specific "in all its humble individuality and materiality." This choice of empirical object was itself an act of theorizing. I am not uninterested in "larger" questions of space and social subject, but I believe we are at the limits of what can be said, operating exclusively at the level of metatheory, about new forms of marginality, and worse, we are in danger of seizing upon those we perceive to be in the most extreme positions of marginality with the view that they can somehow "speak" for the others, or reveal dynamics of marginalization and resistance that are common to all. The study of specificities is much more than and something other than simply the exploration of "outwardly apparent or contingent forms of an essential reality."[3]

In this case, the choice of homeless youth was a tactical one. In a rush to claim the "theoretical high ground" of difference, one strategy appears to be to chose the "most marginalized" of our sisters. In trying to come to grips with marginality and difference, one might reason that if the white, middle-class male is the "marked" representative of the species, the black, working-class female is the "most unmarked," and should be the starting point for all discoveries about "difference." The danger here lies not in the choice of object, but in those studies which conclude that black, working-class women might come to stand for "all" difference. Race is not always black, and gender is not always female. And to take black, working-class women to "stand for difference" is to risk drawing a thick straight line between the marked and the nonmarked of the species, in a simple polarity of marginalization and resistance that obliterates the specific histories and geographies of struggles of marginalized people and, more importantly, the space- and time-contingent strategies they use, to challenge their difference in some times and places or even to seize difference in others, including those of black, working-class women themselves. It is to risk missing the space-time-contingent character of social identity.

To this end I chose empirical investigation rather than theoretical exposition as a mode of inquiry, but with the full conviction that to identify a social subject is *itself* a theoretical act and not an empirical one. In choosing empirical investigation, I have integrated my theoretical concepts into the analysis. These are addressed more fully in the concluding chapter. For now I will provide the reader with a road map of my argument.

Why was it necessary to construct an image of homeless youth? In the first chapter, I address this question by situating the appearance of homeless youths on the streets of North American cities in the context of a wider breakdown in concepts of adolescence and juvenile delinquency as hegemonic, modern notions about acceptable and unacceptable youthful behavior. Drawing on the works of social historians, I examine arguments advanced in the early 1970s, in the wake of campus and ghetto riots of the 1960s, that adolescence itself was a social construction, which crystallized in America around the turn of the century and became dominant in the 1920s. Under contemporary processes of modernization, many social forms deemed normal during the modern period are once again being called into question, including adolescence, specific gender roles, and the nuclear family. In the 1960s this took the form of a challenge to hegemonic notions by a cultural avant-garde, and by numerous political and social movements. By the 1970s however, this was a crisis within the hegemonic forms themselves. There are certain parallels in the current period with the social ferment of the *fin de siècle*, and much to be learned from the way social historians related changes in social forms of the family and adolescence to processes of industrialization and class reproduction. I take issue, however, with the role social historians accord to the space of the modernizing city in the development of new concepts of social life and social behavior. For these social historians, the environment invoked in the proper socialization or rehabilitation of adolescence was simply a mask, concealing larger imperatives of social control. For me, this space was a constitutive medium, not a mask but a *means* by which they constructed an ethos of appropriate behavior.

The first chapter provides some clues to the first line in the story of homeless youth—that of a fundamental restructuring of conceptions of youth and adolescence. The second chapter, to return to Berger, looks at the simultaneous development of images of the homeless and scholarly attempts to explain their marginalization. Here I examine contemporary works on the geography of homelessness, and the role that space is assumed to play in this marginalization. While this literature adequately captures the process by which the homeless are marginalized, it accepts almost without question the label of stigma, missing important ways that homeless people, through the use of space, challenge preconceptions about themselves. This is crucial if we are to begin to understand how homeless youth (and service providers) have managed to construct a sympathetic image of themselves—especially when many of the activities they reportedly engage in could link them through a chain of equivalences to their inner-city counterparts, "the dangerous classes." How have service providers managed to break this chain of equivalences? Before addressing this question I

Introduction

examine, in Chapter Three, many of the tactical uses the homeless have made of space in Los Angeles to challenge stigmatization, to be recognized as citizens, as political actors, as campers, as couples—any range of selves that transcend the "simple fact" of homelessness.

Chapters Four through Seven address the historical and geographical shifts in concept and context of runaway and homeless youths: from their placement in juvenile halls and county camps with "other juvenile delinquents" until the mid-1970s; to their affiliation with the punk squatting subculture, following deinstitutionalization and in the absence of state intervention until the early 1980s; and finally to their assimilation into services and shelters, with the destruction of a punk squatting subculture and the growth of services in Hollywood, California. It is clear that these youths were unequal partners in struggles around the control of space and definition of self. But through their agency, through their tactical inhabitation of space, they made some gains nonetheless; in forcing a recentering of services from Los Angeles County to the Hollywood area, which had until the early 1980s attempted to decenter them throughout the county; in forcing further relocation of services once they were within the Hollywood area and, equally important, in influencing the organizational ethos and programmatic content of programs simply by forcing them to operate *in a different space*. Service providers, for their part, were able, in their use of space in Hollywood, to recuperate the concept of troubled youth as juvenile delinquents who might be rehabilitated. This impulse towards rehabilitation was all but destroyed in the wake of deinstitutionalization. Chapter Seven addresses the final moment of stabilization of service network and social imaginary of homeless youth in Hollywood. This moment was the incorporation of service providers into the local growth coalition, a move which linked homeless youth and their services to the emergent symbols of growth and modernization of the area. Here I examine the ways that local service providers both negotiated the latent and territorial interests of the local community, and themselves came to stand for "the community," acting as a pivotal support in a reconstituted local regime that had threatened to split over issues of growth and redevelopment. The principal point here is that, by negotiating the social and symbolic meaning of the space of Hollywood, service providers were able to integrate themselves within a new, local, social configuration of growth which would ensure their place and the place of youths in Hollywood for the foreseeable future. In this way they were directly engaged in the reconstitution of a social identity through a new (albeit local) political imaginary.

It would perhaps be comforting at this point to conclude with some sweeping statement about the stabilization of a social imaginary that homeless youths in Hollywood represent, or to speculate about the attempts of service providers to use Hollywood as a base point to reach out to other communities and introduce services for youth who would otherwise be ignored by the juvenile system until they "turned up" in youth gangs. The riots in 1992 introduced an unstable element into the tenuous stability between self and space and the social imaginary constructed for homeless youths in Hollywood. The destruction of commercial space in Hollywood along Hollywood Boulevard has sent tremors through the local community, and has raised questions about the presence of youths in the area and the meaning of services in the area for the community. Whether this will result in the development of yet another social imaginary which includes both homeless youth and youth gangs, and, if so, which of these will become the organizing principle of the other, remains to be seen.

1

YOUTH AND MODERNIZATION

I had this dream, see, where I saw the whole world melt. I was standing on La Cienega and from there I could see the whole world and it was melting and it was just so strong and realistic like. And so I thought well if this dream comes true how can I stop it you know? How can I change things, you know? So I thought if I like pierced my ear or something, like alter my physical image, dye my hair, the world wouldn't melt. So I dyed my hair and this pink lasts. I like it. It lasts. I don't think the world is gonna melt anymore.

—Ronnette, a character in
Bret Easton Ellis', *Less than Zero*

Ronnette was a pink-haired, roller-skating, Los Angeles punk. She divided her time between the Beverly Center (a new, major, enclosed mall located a few miles to the southwest of Hollywood, and not incidentally, a final nail in the coffin of Hollywood's commercial decline) and Danny's Oki Dog (a ratty hamburger joint which, for almost twenty years before its closing in 1990, was a hangout for squatting punks, runaways, homeless youths, prostitutes, drug dealers, and all forms of Hollywood flotsam and jetsam).

Perhaps when Ellis created Ronnette, he was not thinking about her experience as part of a larger crisis of modernization. But her musings resonate with the same crisis of meaning that Berman describes in the experience of modernity:

> To be modern is to experience personal and social life as a maelstrom, to find one's world in perpetual disintegration and renewal, trouble and anguish, ambiguity and contradiction: to be part of a universe in which all that is solid melts into air. To be modernist is to make oneself somehow at home in this maelstrom . . . to grasp and confront the world that modernization makes, and to strive to make it our own.[1]

And they resonate with the writings of an earlier scholar of youth and modernization, Jane Addams, who, at the turn of the century, noted:

> We cannot expect young people themselves to cling to conventions which are totally unsuited to modern city conditions, nor yet be equal to the task of forming new conventions through which this more agglomerative social life may express itself.[2]

It is no accident that Jane Addams's musings about youth[3] emerge in the context of turn-of-the-century Chicago—at that time, arguably the site of a paradigmatic urban and societal transformation—while Ellis's contemporary novel, dealing with all manner of youthful anomie, is a product of Los Angeles of the 1980s—a current site of formidable urbanization.[4] Indeed, a subtext connecting Addams, legendary founder of Hull House and a central agitator for the juvenile court system, and Bret Easton Ellis, a new star in the growing constellation of young "brat-pack" writers, is in the crises in the social construction of youth in its various forms *during different periods of accelerated modernization*,[5] and the struggle to find the social and spatial expression of new forms *in* and *through* the city.

This role of the city, not simply as the context or product of accelerated modernization, but as a medium through which one shapes one's experience, has been overlooked by many scholars on the subject, save Raymond Williams, who argues:

> Modernism can be located not on the "inside" of its self-validating ideologies nor in the "outside" of a political

trauma on the order of 1848, but in the *intermediate* zone of urban experience, in solution not as a precipitate, in a "structure of feeling" that has not yet assumed the relatively formalized shape of aesthetic doctrine or political act.[6]

The story of homeless youths in Los Angeles County that has evolved in the past two decades can be seen, using Berman's view, first and foremost *as a construct of, and constructive of responses to, contemporary modernization.* Berman argues for a "broader more inclusive idea of modernism," which recuperates the role of the "underclass" because it "reveals solidarities between great artists and ordinary people,"[7] and which focuses on "the environments and public spaces that are available to modern people, and the ones they create and the ways they act and interact in these spaces to attempt to make themselves at home."[8]

Traditional definitions of modernism focus strictly on strategic programs in arts, literature, and science. A new, more incorporative perspective includes a variety of responses: such as social movements, a range of sociocultural responses of the underclass—which Berman suggests have remained unacknowledged sources, pilfered or sampled for these strategic programs; or even, in Pinkey's most radical and elusive redefinition, the intermediate zone of urban experience, in solution not as a precipitate, in a "structure of feeling" that has not yet assumed the relatively formalized shape of aesthetic doctrine or political act. Larry Grossberg takes a similar position in insisting that contemporary debates on postmodernism can account for the power and place of emergent social and cultural practices only if they take into account their articulation into everyday life.[9]

But the connection between homeless youth and contemporary modernization provides more than additional insights into (Berman's) redefined modernism. This connection helps to explain how a broad range of young people living on city streets came to be understood as "homeless youths," rather than as prostitutes, gang-bangers, drug dealers, panhandlers, or other labels connected to any of the practices these youth engage in. Social space and social subject were constructed interdependently. By the early 1990s, the image of homeless youths *qua* homeless youths has become, almost without exception, one of the victims of both dysfunctional families and duplicitous urban environments—an image which organizes common perceptions about their day-to-day life.

There are several ways that one might refer to this image, for it signals something more than simply a symbol or referent which has come to stand for homeless youth. Barthes, for instance, uses the term *myth* to indicate a process of inflexion whereby a concept becomes naturalized, and symbol and referent collapse into one another. He attributes to myths a specific geography: a region or place of origin from which they "ripen and spread."[10] Benjamin suggests that particular places of representation, such as the arcade, come to be burdened with particular meanings.[11]

Similarly, *social imaginary*, a term used by Lefebvre,[12] signals an image that exists within the popular imagination or unconscious: social, because the process which produces it is societal rather than individualized, and imaginary, rather than symbolic, because it indicates not a state of signification but a condition of possession[13] —the distinction between the symbol and the object to which it refers becomes collapsed, confused, conflated.[14] The *imaginary*, far from reflecting the object to which it seems to refer (be it a social, political, or other imaginary) is, in fact, *produced* by the discourse that surrounds it.[15] It is constituted by a context that exists outside of it. Moreover, as with Benedict Anderson's concept of the nation as an imagined community, the imaginary is a concept shared by members who are unknown to each other, yet who live in the image of communion. The imaginary is a contested concept, incomplete, negotiated, existing "only to the extent that (it) can play a part in people's discourses, in short . . . to make a way of human being, a form of life possible."[16] And yet the emergence of an imaginary tends to halt this process, in so far as it comes, in the minds of those who use it, to "stand for" the object to which it in fact, simply refers. Laclau and Mouffe refer to this process in terms of the hegemonic constitution of a particular social identity, whose development cannot be explained as the logic of a single social force, but acquires meaning, rather, through sets of contingent social logics, a range of partial concentrations of power which themselves acquire meaning in relational context. What one must infer in their discussion is the inherently spatial nature of this process, the geography in and through which the imaginary is constituted.

In this sense, as a naturalized concept, as the expression of a series of partially constituted processes, the term *homeless youths* has come to function as a social imaginary.[17] The question remains as to how this imaginary came into being.

Youth and Modernization

SOCIAL HISTORIES OF YOUTH AND MODERNIZATION

Social histories of youth and modernization provide an initial frame within which one can understand the social subject "homeless youths," and their service networks, as a response to contemporary modernization—in short, a kind of modernism. But as Raymond Williams notes, "it should no longer be possible to present these specific and traceable processes as if they were universals . . . . The formulation of modernist universals is in every case a productive but imperfect and in the end fallacious response to particular conditions of closure, breakdown, failure, frustration."[18] Theories that link youth and modernization are no exception. Each phase of modernization has been characterized by a different dominant interpretation of "youth," "modernization," and the link between the two.

Modernization is not only subject to a specific temporality but to a spatiality as well. In spite of broad, transnational similarities, both experiences and representations of youth differed (and continue to differ) in significant ways between nation-states, as Gillis's comparative social history of youth in Oxford, England, and Göttingen, Germany, reveal. Gillis's appreciation of the importance of geography is largely unconscious, as suggested by the title of the work, *Youth and History*.[19] My own study of homeless youth is set within the larger experience of youth at different periods of modernization in the United States, although observations by Gillis are drawn in where they are more generally applicable.

In the United States, the Parsonian interpretation of youth and modernization which dominated sociology through the 1950s and early 1960s was, in a sense, the theoretical bulwark to a specific social form of youth—adolescence—which became hegemonic after the turn of the century. For Parsons and his followers, youth in industrial society was (although they did not state it this way) the quintessential moment of modernism—"a dynamism or the delirious multiplication of the possibilities of self."[20] Youth culture was the means of easing the transition from the security of childhood in the family to full adulthood, a transition which in industrial society was made precarious by the separation of family and work. This view was undifferentiated by race, gender, or class, as later critics were to note.[21] In the wake of the inner-city riots and student unrest of the 1960s, social historians Joseph Kett, Anthony Platt, and John R. Gillis launched an implicit critique of this view, and set out to reposition class at the center of analysis.[22] Gillis, for example, characterizes the works of Parsons and his followers this way:

> They wrote of a singular youth culture, whose uniformity
> reflected the universalistic values of what they perceived
> to be a tightly integrated society without significant class,
> ethnic or sexual divisions. . . . Adolescence itself was the
> axis on which individual and social progress turned. It was
> the point in the life-cycle when particularist identities
> were dissolved and universalistic habits and values assimi-
> lated. It was the time in the life of the individual when he
> or she was least encumbered by the legacies of class,
> ethnicity, and gender and most capable of casting off
> the past and embracing the future. . . . Young people
> were perceived as the one group capable of transcend-
> ing outmoded identities, unburdening themselves of history
> and its legacies.[23]

It is worth examining their substantive and theoretical contributions at some length. Each differs somewhat in its emphasis.
Kett focused more on the differentiated material basis of class practices, Gillis on the variety of cultural forms appropriated by each
generation of youth, and Platt on the wide range of child-saving
institutions that emerged to support adolescence. But they all asso-
ciate successive phases of accelerated modernization with
changes in the social form of youth, a form which was not simply an
undifferentiated passage between childhood and adulthood, but
a differentiated practice of the reproduction of classes. As class
practices shift, these authors argue, so do conceptions of and
modalities of treatment for youthful misconduct and youthful
cultures attempting to accommodate these shifts. These social historians could not anticipate that deinstitutionalization of juvenile
correction systems in the 1970s would result in a rising number of
street youths, but if we extend their argument, it becomes clear
that the rise of homeless youth is both a symptom and constitutive
element of contemporary restructuring of the transition from childhood to adulthood.

YOUTH IN PREMODERN AND MODERN TIMES—
FROM "PRECOCIOUS YOUTHS" TO "DELINQUENT ADOLESCENCE"

The thesis that adolescence was invented as a response to
turn-of-the-century modernization had gained widespread curren-
cy in many disciplines by the mid-1970s. Some scholars, such as

Youth and Modernization

Musgrove, continued and deepened the theses of "youth-and-modernization" theorists of the 1950s and early 1960s, with their emphasis on generational-based conflicts and a relatively cohesive "youth culture." This argument was critiqued somewhat obliquely by critical British sociologists, who insisted on the class basis of concepts of adolescence, delinquency, and deviance,[24] but it was most boldly stated and fully explored by Platt, Kett, and Gillis. While they did not always share the same terminology, the authors argued that *adolescence* —defined as a tightly age-graded phase of the life cycle revolving around puberty—was essentially a *modern* construction and was identifiably different from the *premodern* experience of a more loosely bounded and variable transition defined as *youth*.[25] Keniston argued that a postmodern form of youth was imminent, although Gillis noted, rightly, that the youth Keniston described remained primarily middle-class. Precise dating of the shift from youth to adolescence varies somewhat. Differences depend partly on whether one focuses on the earliest class practices reproducing *adolescence as a social form*, the subsequent emergence of the *concept of adolescence* which indicated the practice had become a self-conscious one, or *attempts to generalize adolescence* as a social form through a wide range of institutions, broadly designated as *child-saving* institutions, which included youth workers involved in both public and private institutions and the penal system.[26] But it is generally agreed that the concept of adolescence (as distinct from the set of class practices associated with adolescence) first appeared in the mid-1800s. The term *adolescence* began to supersede the "less precise" term *youth*, when adolescence was democratized around the turn of the century—a kind of *fin de siècle* for youth. One must realize, however, that "youth" appears as a less precise transition only when one holds adolescence as the norm. As Joseph Kett notes, semi-dependence of youth in premodern times was marked by a more complex alternation between precocious, adultlike independence and the demands for childlike subordination than was the case for adolescence in modern times.[27]

Both the concept of adolescence and the institutions designed to support and sustain it became generalized after the turn of the century, largely because of the efforts of child-savers, who fought to establish a separate juvenile court, to institute anti-child-labor laws and compulsory education, and to create a wide variety of leisure institutions which reinforced adolescent socialization.

Platt, Kett, and Gillis shared an underlying objective of *dena-turing adolescence* and the behaviors associated with it, as a phase of life inextricably linked to *biological* maturation—a view initially propounded by Stanley Hall, at the turn of the century or later (when culture rushed in to fill the vacuum left by a discredited biology) as a phase organized around a distinctive, uniform, and ubiquitous youth culture[28]—the Parsonian model mentioned above. Hall stood conceptually and chronologically poised between two centuries, particularly in his saltatory theories of adolescence. The theory proposed a radical change which was assumed to occur at the time of puberty—and therefore to require careful institutional management—and it contained vestiges of the earlier idea of adolescent religious conversion around the time of "the change" which was more common to a premodern period.

In contrast to this rather self-contained view of adolescence, Platt, Kett, and Gillis linked the concept of adolescence, and behavioral expectations associated with it more firmly with a par-ticular set of class practices. They argued that the principal main-stay of a broad, and largely unconscious, acceptance of adoles-cence as a necessary and natural stage of youth was a newly emergent middle class which depended on extended periods of education to ensure the upward mobility of their children. Adolescence as an enforced stage of immaturity was not a universal experience, but rather a hegemonic social norm, which was not actually practicable for all classes, and reflected, rather, the reproductive imperatives of white-collar middle-class families. Gillis makes the most forceful argument:

> The new white-collar class came into existence precisely at the time when new social attitudes towards youth were being generated . . . the mode of upward mobility of this group was no longer the time-honored ladder of the trades and private enterprise, but education, at first secondary, but later university as well. Little wonder that so much of the anxiety about the years 14 to 18 was expressed in the organizations and agencies that were patronized by members of this class.[29]

It was, therefore, a change in the real, material conditions of youth within the new white-collar class (as Gillis calls them) that precipitated the shift in definition of acceptable youthful behaviors. White-collar families could no longer tolerate precocious behavior on the part of their youths. To do so would risk the upward mobility of these youths and their reproduction as the new "occupants," as it were, of the space for white-collar workers. The concept of adolescence legitimated the new behavioral imperatives of this class. The concept of juvenile delinquency (compared to that of precocity) expressed a reduced range of tolerance for experimentation with other forms of class behavior by the sons of white-collar families.

Once adolescence was established by the authors as a class-based strategy for social reproduction, it was possible to reinterpret the institutions and programs developed by child-savers both as an attempt to extend the socializing norms of adolescence to working-class youth, and to protect both middle-class and working-class youth from what were, in essence, working-class behaviors. Behaviors which were essentially considered *precocious* and even valued in the premodern period became devalued, even considered dangerous, and labeled *delinquent* in the modern period.

Precocity was an attribute revered in the 1820s and 1830s, when youths were encouraged to "strike out on their own at an early age" and had its most stark expression in the acceptance of child-aged religious leaders. Underlying the notion of precocity was the idea that youths who adopted "adult behaviors" at an early age might become very successful. As a result, youthful attempts to ape adult behaviors were not punished by law, but rather, generally encouraged. Conversely, youthful criminal behavior was measured by adult standards. Platt argues that nineteenth-century American criminologists tended to emphasize the nonhuman qualities of criminals, suggesting they were part of a dangerous class who stood outside the boundaries of morally regulated and reciprocal relationships. By the turn of the century, however (with the exception of a brief resurgence in the 1930s), criminals were considered to be environmentally created, rather than having criminal qualities that were biologically inherited. Child criminality was deemed "reversible." [30]

With the onset of industrialization, however, the impulse to "strike out on one's own" did not open the possibility to early adult success, but rather became the prerequisite to finding "dead-end" work in the factories. *Juvenile delinquency became the* doppelgänger *of adolescence*. Notions of *precocity* were replaced with those of *delinquency*. Delinquency was considered a common danger faced by all adolescents in a process of biological and physical maturation peaking, some youth workers felt, at the onset of puberty.

As Gillis notes:

> It was no accident that what the public came to regard
> as juvenile delinquency became the focus of attention
> precisely at the time when pressures to universalize
> adolescence were first being felt; for despite their
> apparent dissimilarities, the two were related. *The very
> traits that stigmatized certain youth as delinquent—
> namely precocity and independence of adult authority—
> were precisely the opposite of those embodied in the
> model adolescent. . . .*
>
> The same group instrumental in "democratizing" norms of
> adolescence created an aggressive anti-social image of
> the modern juvenile delinquent . . this is not to say they
> invented juvenile crime, . . . but the criminal of Dickens'
> time had been more closely associated with a class than
> an age group . . . By the 1890s however delinquency was
> beginning to be seen not as an attribute of
> precocity, but of immaturity. *Adolescence itself was iden-
> tified as a cause of delinquency and thus all
> children, regardless of class, were deemed vulnerable to
> deviance unless carefully protected.*[31]

As Kett notes, theories of delinquency went through a range of
deterministic incarnations. These include associating delinquency,
at various times, with physical characteristics such as head shape
(Cesare Lombroso), or with environmentally stimulated pathologies
such as the lack of playgrounds or "social disintegration" of urban
areas.[32] Nevertheless, they shared a fundamental difference from
earlier views of criminality and misbehavior: attention shifted from
specific criminal infractions of youth to the motivating factors
"producing" the delinquent—which included a range of departures
from decorous behavior.[33]

These social histories situate the origins of the juvenile-care
system in a fundamental shift in class practices—from a tolerance
or even promotion of behaviors considered precocious, to the
redefinition of these behaviors as delinquent. With the advent of the
juvenile court at the turn of the century, juvenile crime was no
longer understood as a class practice, in the sense that juvenile
criminals were viewed as part of the "dangerous classes," but
rather as resulting from the improperly managed maturation of
young offenders. One could now draw a continuum from
delinquency to criminality. This attitude reflected a general consensus about principles underlying the juvenile care system. What

Youth and Modernization

Kett characterizes as the modern period for adolescence has an approximate parallel in the juvenile-justice system: the modern period of adolescence coincided with the "socialized era" of the juvenile-justice system.[34] The underlying principles of this system are captured in the writings of Judge Mack of the Chicago court, who, in 1907, argued in the *Harvard Law Review* that:

> The judges of juvenile court in exercising jurisdiction, have in accordance with the most advanced philanthropic thought, recognized that the lack of proper home care can best be supplied by the true foster parent (the state). . . . to find out what (a youngster) is physically, mentally and morally, and then if it learns that he is treading the path that leads to criminality, to take him in charge, not so much to punish as to reform, not to degrade but to uplift, not to crush but to be developed, not to make him a criminal but a worthy citizen.[35]

And, until recently, these principles have been sustained. *Kent v. United States*, for instance, argued successfully:

> The theory of the District's Juvenile Court Act, like that of other jurisdictions, is rooted in social welfare philosophy rather than in the *corpus juris*. Its proceedings are designated as civil rather than criminal. The Juvenile Court is theoretically engaged in determining the needs of the child and of society rather than adjudicating criminal conduct. The objectives are to provide measures of guidance and rehabilitation for the child and protection for society, not to fix criminal responsibility, guilt and punishment. The State is *parens patriae* rather than prosecuting attorney and judge.[36]

As conceptions of juvenile delinquency began to replace precocity, the "path to criminality" became broadly defined indeed, including a range of cultural behaviors which were associated with the lower classes, and which were not considered criminal offenses for adults. These "status offenses" might consist of smoking, habitually attending billiard halls, or any wide range of behaviors that might lead to idleness or a lewd or immoral life.[37] Social historians argued that the juvenile-justice system appeared to operate independently of class bias, but essentially smuggled bias back into the interior of the system under the guise of specifically frowned-upon (class-based) behaviors. The jettisoning of status offenders from the system of juvenile care through deinstitutionalization—a process which set the immediate preconditions for homeless youths—signaled a breakdown in consensus about juvenile delinquency, and left wide open attitudes towards and treatments of homeless and runaway youths.

HOMELESS AND RUNAWAY YOUTHS—
IMAGES IN HISTORY/ IMAGES OF HISTORY

It would be tempting at this point to move directly to the select historical record of homeless and runaway youths and sketch out the way that these works might be mapped onto the framework proposed by Kett, Platt, and Gillis. Kett treats the theme in passing throughout his work, and there are many parallels in the attitudes held towards "street" youths and general attitudes towards youthful misconduct during different periods. In fact, waves of homeless and runaway youths appear to be "produced" by successive waves of modernization, and Lipschutz even suggests that "runaways and vagrants were largely responsible for the birth of the child-saving movement."[38] By this account, far from being an epiphenomenon, runaways were at the very center of the progressive response to turn-of-the-century modernism and the construction of ideas of youthful behavior and misconduct.

But to note that shifts in attitude towards homeless and runaway youth paralleled shifts in conceptions of youthful misconduct tells us very little about how these attitudes came to be constructed, and gives the misleading impression that social forms of modernization follow almost automatically from the material processes of modernization—that the former could simply be read off the latter.

Part of the current attempt to construct an image for contemporary homeless and runaway youths, which is being undertaken through critical reviews of their image in history, contradicts such simple determinism.[39] Contemporary scholars writing on the historical evolution of images of homeless and runaway youths reveal more about an uncertain present than an imprecise past—or as Fraser and Nicholson might say, their critiques speak to the ways they themselves are infected by the historicity and contingency from which they claim immunity.[40]

What is striking about the reviews undertaken by Marjorie Robertson, Rivlin and Manzo, and Lipschutz, is that they argue that the real dynamic underlying the constitutive reality of homeless and runaway youths throughout history, and often "hidden from history," has been the prevalence of family neglect and abuse that provoked their running. This is not to say that the authors' perceptions are false, nor that abuse and neglect are insignificant issues. But it rather begs the question as to how in some historical periods this discovery surfaced as an organizing principle, and in other historical periods it was submerged. More important, it begs the question in the current period as to how neglect has come to be the organizing principle for the understanding and treatment of 'homeless and runaway youths, yet denied other juveniles such as youth gang members.

Rivlin and Manzo focus on popular images of these youths which dominated the latter half of the nineteenth century, and construct the problem between the reality of homeless youths and competing representations of them as one of a recurring tendency to "unselfconscious moralism," in the face of serious political, social, and economic crisis. "Youthful street vagrant," "street-wandering children," "young outcasts of metropolitan life," "street adventurers," "street lads," "*enfants perdus*," were the milder terms. But they were also called "petty thieves," "pickpockets," "young sharpers of the city," "begging imposters," "street sinners," "thieves-at-heart," and "young barbarians." In 1869 an article by an official of the Children's Aid Society described young homeless boys as:

> "enjoying the idle and lazzaroni life on the docks living in the summer almost in the water, and curling down at night, as the animals do, in any corner they can find . . . this is without a doubt in the blood of most children—as an inheritance, perhaps from some remote barbarian ancestor—a passion for roving."[41]

Why some child-savers of the period were able to leap outside of this moralism while others did not is not made clear, but implicitly becomes a question of morals over moralism—or, to continue with the argument of Fraser and Nicholson, the result of investigations that spring from a sense of truth or justice, and are thus immune to contingent historical social practices. Julia Robertson, for instance, criticizes the dominant professional view in the 1950s and early 1960s of the runaway as psychological deviant, arguing that this image was based on "little supporting evidence but the runaway behavior itself." She notes that even as late as 1968, in the throes of youth liberation movements, the widely held psychiatric definition of runaways was:

> Individuals (who) characteristically escape from threatening situations by running away from home for a day or more without permission. Typically they are immature and timid and often feel rejected at home, inadequate, friendless. They often steal furtively.[42]

But she does not explain why in the current period we are able to "see through" this misconception and act as advocates for runaways, uncovering the injustice of their treatment within the family and on the street. Lipschutz, on the other hand, simply accepts that historical differences in images of runaway youths must accurately reflect real differences in the material conditions of these youth. However, he does note that the image of the precocious runaway which occupies "American mythology" was valid perhaps only in the late 1960s during the "flower child" era of running away. For Lipschutz, the image of the runaway as a victim of family breakdown becomes part of the historical reportage.

If we accept that the principles underlying the juvenile justice system revolved around concepts of delinquency, then it becomes reasonable to assume that the restructuring of this system and the deinstitutionalization of status offenders signals a shift in thinking about youthful offenders and a challenge to this underlying principle. But new conceptions about youthful behavior and misbehavior do not follow automatically from the simple fact of deinstitutionalization. If this were so, it would not be necessary to create a new understanding of the behavior of homeless and runaway youths focusing on a critical appraisal of historical images of them.

Here, both the substantive and conceptual contributions of Gillis, Kett, and Platt become important. Substantively, the periodization of precocity and delinquency explains what contemporary scholars feel they must react *against* when building an image of homeless and runaway youths that emphasizes neglect and abuse. If through deinstitutionalization homeless and runaway youth can no longer be thought of as *delinquent*, youth advocates are currently struggling against perceptions of them as simply *precocious*, or worse, part of the resurgent dangerous classes.[43] Hence Rivlin and Manzo return to conflicts of the turn of the century as a kind of historical object lesson.

Youth and Modernization

By linking broader concepts of precocity and delinquency to struggles over the social reproduction of lower and middle classes, these social histories provide us with an initial frame for the shifting images of homeless and runaway youths.

VISIONS OF YOUTH IN THE CITY STREETS

> After the middle of the 19th century, Americans shaped an image of the rural past as a time when young people were firmly in their place, subordinated to the wise exercise of authority and bound tightly by affective relationships to family and community. This image of the rural past became a powerful motive force behind the construction of adult-sponsored institutions for youth in the 1890s and early 1900s. So compelling was this image that the architects of institutions for city youth returned to the countryside after 1910 and sought to provide village and farm youth surrogate experiences of the rural past. Ironically, most of the architects of adult-sponsored youth organizations were born after 1850 and possessed little understanding of the past whose qualities they sought to relate. Convinced that communal warmth and subordination had been characteristics of the past they missed all the elements of tension and conflict between age groups and ignored the footloose ways of antebellum youth.
>
> —Joseph Kett,
> *Rites of Passage. Adolescence in America 1790 to Present*, 1977.

It would be too much to claim that new social forms of youth associated with successive modernizations, and the institutions developed to sustain or contain these social forms, emerged solely or even primarily in modernizing metropolises. That would risk, as Williams notes, "accepting the metropolitan interpretation of its own processes as universal."[44] In this regard, the accounts of Kett and Gillis are quite sensitive. Kett, for instance, notes that even as late as the 1930s, the concept of adolescence was virtually unheard of in some rural areas, but in others was more vigorously promoted than in large cities,[45] albeit in reaction to the perceived evils of modernization in large cities. Kett provides the most insightful example of the simultaneous and differentiated experience of modernization in large cities and small towns *vis-à-vis* the creation of institutions for adolescents.[46] He cautions us about developing a model which presumes that institutions of adolescence "spread" from large cities, to small cities, to towns, to villages, and finally to rural areas. Some small towns synthesized older (premodern) patterns of development in these rural areas—typically associated with "youth"—with a vigorous development of adult-sponsored youth organizations more typically associated with the promotion of "adolescence." But the form itself was, nonetheless, developed in reaction to the modernizing metropolis: Kett offers as explanation that "key agents in promoting adult-sponsored youth organizations . . . sought to turn towns into fortresses of morality *in contrast to the sinful metropolises.*"[47] Ironically, the most rapid development of institutions to support adolescent activities occurred not in the "sinful metropolises," but in small towns.[48] Many of the rural traditions of youth were adapted by youthful migrants to nineteenth-century cities to meet their needs in an urban setting.

The social spaces created by child-savers—the camps, ranches, settlement houses, and so forth that they developed to carry out their programs—were also interpreted to be part of a larger cultural, ideological, and reflective response to modernization. Kett, in particular, demonstrates the way that child-saving programs, with each successive phase of modernization, tended to try to recreate structures of affinity that were seen to be threatened or lost altogether in the wake of modernization, or on the contrary, attempted in their organization and programs to embrace what were deemed to be the most forward-looking characteristics of the current phase of modernization. The structures and settings devised by child-savers to ensure the appropriate socialization of youths were as intimately bound up with ideas of modernity as were shifting conceptions of youth and adolescence. Sometimes these institutions and programs represented a nostalgic recreation of places and environments deemed threatened by modernization—in this instance rural life or specific family forms come to mind. Sometimes they attempted to adopt newly emergent cultural and institutional forms, which were themselves products of modernization—as exemplified by the reform house or the camp, at the time of their initial introduction. Often they were a hybrid of a number of different forms, simultaneously backward- and forward-looking. Camps, for instance, evoked a nostalgic reexperiencing of rural life, at the same time as they could provide youths with the most up-to-date social, leisure, and employment skills. The most extreme of these is the "space camp." For example the Job Corps at Camp Kilmore, New York, introduced within a rural setting the most advanced job-training program, which in 1966 contracted with Federal Electric to train youths for the aerospace industry.[49]

But in the eyes of these social historians, the social space created by child-savers to achieve their goals did little more than mask the larger imperatives of social control. From the evidence provided in these social histories, I think it would be fair to say that there was a strong *antiurban* impulse in the environments created for youth in much of the child-saving movement. Many programs and institutions sought locations at the edge of towns and cities.

Those that located within urban areas—and particularly in the inner city, such as the YMCAs and certain Christian programs—often did so as a defensive or offensive strategy, attempting to offer either exemplary alternatives to the existing environments, or fortressed islands. In spite of the fame of settlement houses, rarely did organizations locate in the inner city out of a strong affinity for that environment *or for the existing social structures developed among the youth there.*[50]

The strongest expression of this antiurbanism took the form of a romanticized view of *premodern* times, expressed in a predilection towards rural environments for their presumed rehabilitative influence. Sometimes romanticism of premodern rural life and the transcendental powers of environment and nature were carried to ridiculous extremes—as Kett points out in his critique of Kellog:

> He associated city life, frailty and intellectuality with sexual indulgence, and rural life with sexual restraint. Kellog generalized even beyond village life; all things natural and wild—Indians, savages, even apes—were chaste. It was as if the road to the boardroom ran through the jungle.[51]

If the biological basis of adolescence was deemed the first order of a naturalized social subject, to be unmasked in the writing of social histories on youth and modernization, then the environment was the second. Originating in an impulse that was largely anti-urban and conservative, the social spaces and programs created by child-savers are rarely interpreted as a liberatory social space of modernism.[52]

These spaces were interpreted as duplicitous, used *against* lower-class youth to hide the consequences of social control rather than created by these youth or youth advocates "to grasp the world and make sense of it." The objective of these social histories was to explicate the role of geography, and in particular the antiurban impulse in many child-saving activities, as simply masking the imperatives of class practices. Although they did not phrase it quite this way, for social historians the incessant critique of urban environments epoused by child-savers and their compulsion to recreate rural environments could be interpreted in only one way—*the city stood for explanation.*

There are parallels between the critical objectives of these social historians and the program of some Marxist geographers of the same period who saw space as a fetishism, irreconcilable with class analysis and historical materialism: "space and spatiality could only fit into Marxism as a reflective expression, a product of the more fundamental social relations of production and the aspatial (but nonetheless historical) 'laws of motion' of capital."[53] For social historians, the task was to show that the value judgments that child-savers made about unhealthy inner-city environments (as opposed to cleansing rural ones) had much more to do with class-based forms of socialization than anything intrinsic to the "environment" itself. In fact, they used their disapproval of "the city" as a metaphor for their disapproval of lower-class practices. Class inequities were, in this view, displaced to the evils of a modernizing city, and programmatic social control by the middle classes paraded under the guise of a return to the country, or the creation of more "healthful," less corrupting environments in the inner city. In these social histories, appreciation of the social space constructed by child-savers to sustain particular forms of youthful socialization fluctuates between the myopic and hypermetropic.[54] The myopic view risks environmental determinism, suggesting that environment dictates behavior. The hypermetropic view risks treating environment simply as the mask obscuring the underlying and overarching determination by class practices. In treating urban (and rural) environments largely as *context*—here Gillis is most representative, with references to urbanization simply tacked on to those of industrialization—the authors miss the critical ways that new social subjects were constructed not only in, but through, the modernizing space of the city, or as Soja would say, they miss the space-forming and space-contingent nature of social relations.[55] In this instance both urban and rural environments within which child-savers operated were not so much a mask obscuring class practices, but rather a medium through which specific practices were constituted.

HOMELESS YOUTH AND THE FOURTH MODERNIZATION

Exclure de *l'urbain* des groupes, des classes, des individus, c'est aussi les exclures de la civilisation, sinon de la société. Le *droit à la ville* légitime le refus de se laisser écarter de la réalitié urbaine par une organisation discriminatoire, ségrégative.

—Henri Lefebvre,
Espace et politique, 1968, p. 163. [56]

When Henri Lefebvre wrote this spatial manifesto in 1968, it was in the context of the demands of a range of social groups to sustain themselves in and through the spaces of the city by claiming space for what one might consider liberatory alternative projects—countering the tendency for economic and political space to "converge towards the elimination of all differences."[57] One could not envision the more desperate turn this struggle over the right to space would take twenty years later, not simply for the right to a space of difference but for the right *to exist at any cost,* as by the late 1980s the restoration of city centers produced a double result: on the one hand the ersatz celebration of difference, the apparent embrace of the marginal who struggled for place and voice in the prior two decades, but at the same time the production of a new marginality and the expulsion of masses of now homeless people in the wake of the city's transformation.

Why social historians overlooked the constitutive dynamics of space in the process of modernization and the creation of social forms of adolescence in an earlier period is, in this context, unimportant. It might be, if we accept Lefebvre's injunction, that the spatial problematic was simply less important at the turn of the century than it is today—albeit a critical factor in sustaining or transforming specific social forms, but not integral to the survival of capitalism itself—and that in the 1800s industrialization produced urbanization, whereas in the current period "industrial and economic growth . . . are shaped primarily by the social production of urbanized space."[58]

But in the light of contemporary modernization, it is hardly surprising that calls for a situated modernism, that is, a modernism which focuses on the strategies and practices of everyday life, rather than privileging aesthetic practices that have appropriated those strategies,[59] should also call for a figurative and literal space of difference.[60] Berman is most explicit in linking the two, declaring that contemporary modernism should be *in* and *of* the streets, and centered around the retrieval of a public-minded open space which offers "the capacity to interact with people radically different from ourselves."[61]

The central question is whether both literal and figurative space can be a space for real otherness, and not simply a place where deviance or "otherness" is contained, tolerated, and perhaps occasionally encountered,[62] in the case of the latter where otherness slips into a monotony of exchangeable difference. Harstock talks about the need for a space of nationalism and separatism, a nurturing space where you come together . . . to see what you and your kind can do to survive."[63] But Di Stefano cautions against the acceptance of a valorizing metaphorical space which simply reduces difference to "otherness," warning that for feminist discourse "the effort to valorize the feminine as an essentially different kind of rationality and agency . . . will occur in a space already prepared for it by the intellectual tradition it seeks to reject."[64] This last argument echoes Barthes's observation:

> If he is unable to experience the Other in himself, the bourgeois can at least imagine the place where (the other) fits in: this is what is known as liberalism, which is sort of an intellectual equilibrium based on recognized places.[65]

This question of the nature of the literal and figurative space of difference closely parallels contemporary debates on postmodernism and the different positions represented within this reaction formation. Two positions are readily distinguishable—"a postmodernism which seeks to deconstruct modernism and resist the status quo and a postmodernism which repudiates the former to celebrate the latter: a postmodernism of resistance and a postmodernism of reaction."[66] To return to the literal space of difference one might see this as a choice between a fetishized urban spectacle (see Debord and Harvey), and the riotous unpredictable spectacle which it repressed—of civil-rights movements, street riots, inner-city uprisings, Berman's shout in the streets, Lefebvre's *droit à la ville*. But, for Grossberg, this binary of *resistance* and *reaction*, which he locates specifically in terms of critical characterizations of "authentic" and "coopted" works in popular culture, is unconvincing and overly simplistic. It fails to locate the significance of social and cultural practices in the lives of ordinary people. This is because the binary "depends upon the elitist relationship that the critic establishes to those who are struggling." Grossberg continues:

> Although such a position seems to acknowledge the reality of people's struggles, such struggles are only allowed insofar as they speak their radical negativity and refuse to offer themselves as reterritorializations. But in fact, such struggles are never truly allowed to speak, for that would require us to recognize their contradictions and the forms of positivity they claim for themselves.[67]

Grossberg only hints at what this might mean for the social space of the city, noting in passing, for example, that in Jameson's critique of the postmodern space of architecture, he is unable "to acknowledge new forms of social activities and relations that have emerged especially among youth, in the spaces of postmodern architecture that he describes."[68] But his central point is that:

> People are never merely passively subordinated, never totally manipulated, never entirely incorporated. . . . If people's lives are never merely determined by the dominant position, and if their subordination is always complex and active, understanding culture requires us to look at how practices are actively inserted at particular sites of everyday life. . . . If we accept that new practices and events have appeared on the cultural and historical terrain (the postmodern), their significance and politics are never guaranteed in advance. How they are articulated—interpreted, appropriated, located within larger configurations of social and cultural practices—will determine their meanings and effect new forms of popular political struggle. Consequently we must challenge the very terms within which the postmodernist debates have structured the terrain, refusing to accept their assumptions about these emergent cultural configurations which merely describe a taken-for-granted reality, a new common sense.[69]

These new practices in and of themselves cannot guarantee the emergence of a transformative politics. But they do provide a starting point for political action. Moreover, to ignore this complex and active nature of subordination and resistance is to risk overlooking significant differences in people's subordination and to reproduce these unconsciously within the structures of new political movements. This was the failure of the union movement, which often reproduced within its own structure the inequities of racism and sexism.

There have been various attempts both to acknowledge and to theorize these differences, mostly within feminist scholarship, in a range of intellectual projects that have recently been grouped under the umbrella of "identity politics." Most important here is the post-rationalist project to come to grips with multiple divisions of race, ethnic origins, sexual orientation, age, and regional and national identities.[70] The question for feminists working in this arena has been the extent to which the emphasis on gender as a central analytical category reflects and projects a division between white, bourgeois, or Anglo heterosexual men and women, that might for other women recede in importance in the face of other oppressive structures such as class, race, ethnicity, or age.[71] In addressing this issue, the challenge here has been to avoid a return to a deadlocked bid for primacy between analytical frameworks that champion class, race, or gender as the fundamental basis of oppression. Instead, the strategy has been to recognize the situatedness of different structures of oppression, which in different places and times may privilege one form over another. At the same time one must become attuned to the way in which these structures combine at specific sites, in a manner which is transformative rather than additive—the experience of gender, for instance, transforms that of race and class.[72] This insistence on both the combinatory and fragmented nature of social identities has, as Bondi notes, turned the politics of identity into a politics of location, where "Who am I?" becomes "Where am I?" and place takes the place of essence.[73] But as Smith and Katz argue, too often the recognition, in theory, that space and social identity are mutually constitutive, dissolves in practice: in work done in this area, too often "identities are located, positioned, elbowed into an already existing mosaic. . . . The subject moves, but space stands still, fixed, unproductive."[74] Here the authors call for an approach which opens spatial metaphors to scrutiny, which recognizes space itself (and the metaphors which denote it) as socially constituted.

I would like to return now to the statement made at the beginning of this chapter, that the story of contemporary homeless youths in Los Angeles County must be seen *as a construct of, and constructive of responses to, contemporary modernization.* If we try to nail the concrete activities of service providers and homeless youth of Los Angeles County onto the slippery slope of postmodern practices, it would be tempting to begin by demarcating this particular "postmodernism" in terms of epoch and style. After all, many scholars dealing with the social history of youth have in the past two decades argued that an epochal transition in the style of transition from childhood to adulthood was imminent, although they could not agree on its contours. And some, Kett and Keniston in particular, went so far as to label the new form a "postmodern" form of youth.[75] To continue along this line, we can argue that it is not that the social experience of adolescence has shifted—for this was always a difficult proposition for lower-class youths—but that the social expectation that all youth will, should, or can experience approximately the same transition from childhood to adulthood is being called into question. Adolescence as a hegemonic norm is currently up for grabs.

But this would do what Grossberg fears the most—it would assume "that the very 'postmodernity' of particular practices or events can be read directly off their surfaces, particularly (because) a founding insight of postmodernism is that it has become increasingly difficult to confidently assume the identity or significance of particular events."[76] Or to borrow from Pinkey, it would locate this expression of postmodernism on the inside of its self-validating ideology.

The more interesting and important question is how the social construct "homeless youths"—itself embodying a new understanding and treatment of youthful misconduct—emerged as "precipitate" out of the solution of "urban experience" (whether or not we want to identify it specifically as a postmodern practice). In tracing the genealogy of the term *youth*, and related concepts of precocity and delinquency, social histories help to provide the beginning of an answer, if only by signaling what has actually precipitated as a new social form. But to arrive at a more complete answer, it is necessary to examine the first half of the dyad "homeless youths," in solution as it were, and address the way that social forms of marginality among the homeless are constructed and contested in and through the use of urban space. The next chapter, therefore, will examine literature on the geography of homelessness.

2

MANAGING MEANING THROUGH THE
PRODUCTION OF URBAN SPACE

The dimensions of homelessness today are rooted in
changes in the ecology and economy of the city.

—Kim Hopper
*A Bed For the Night: Homeless Men in New York
City, Past and Present*, 1987.

It is important to ask, on the one hand what groups possess
the need for historically invariant symbols (of the urban
environment) and on the other what mechanisms are utilized to achieve ideological hegemony. In the former case
it is apparent that the real- estate industry, homeowners'
associations, chambers of commerce and banks are the
most active managers in symbolic generalizations.

— M. Gottdiener
Culture, Ideology, and the Sign of the City, 1986.

If there is an urban semiology it is dependent on an urban
anthropology.
—Raymond Ledrut
Speech and the Silence of the City 1986.

As Chris Philo noted in his monograph on the social geography
of outsiders (in this instance, dealing with the mentally ill):

Young and Homeless in Hollywood

The notion 'social construction' can mean many things, ranging from the view that psychological problems are actually produced by the stresses and strains of urban, industrial living to the view that mental illness is simply a label which—having no ontological reference point—is applied at the whim of society's control agents.[1]

Advocates writing about the homeless in the 1980s adopted the first of these interpretations of social construction.[2] They argued, explicitly or implicitly, that contemporary homelessness is a *social construction*, to the extent that it has been produced by economic restructuring and tears in the safety net of the modern welfare state.[3] This view was intended to counter the "naturalist" explanations of homelessness, which attributed the condition to a freewheeling spirit or desire for nonconformity.[4] Philo had a different objective in mind, however, one rooted in the desire to acknowledge the power of *both* impersonal structural forces such as "the economy" and "the state," *and* the cultural and social factors—which he identifies in terms of "community norms and professional judgments" that contribute to specific views about and labels of marginalized people. He chose a middle course between the values of labelers and structural forces.[5] The problem, simply stated, was that structural forces in and of themselves are not sufficient to explain either the differing and opposing views that are held of a marginal people, or how one view might come to predominate over another. For Philo, a key factor in steering this "middle course" lay in a perspective which included at its core:

> A view of space as a resource over which all manner of conscious and not conscious conflicts are waged, . . . as a resource that repeatedly enters into the transactions passing between society's supposedly "normal members" and (others).[6]

Focusing primarily on a body of literature dealing with the geography of mental illness, Philo leaves us with two important observations.

First, the indelibly social and spatial nature of processes by which the mentally ill are sorted into specific parts of the city is exemplary of a "socio-spatial dialectic." Here we are in the center of current debates about social theory. As Soja points out, "the created spatiality of social life had to be seen as simultaneously

34

contingent and conditioning, as both outcome and medium for the making of history."[7] In Philo's case, this means that these sorting transactions by which marginal people are produced do not simply take place *in space*: they are achieved in part *through space*.

Second, one should not attempt to erect general laws dictating how mental illness and space intersect in every place at every time, but should, rather, be aware of the contextual complexities (that is, the contingencies) which preserve difference between places.

To return to the question at hand—how the social construct "homeless youths," itself embodying a new understanding and treatment of youthful misconduct, emerged as "precipitate" out of the solution of "urban experience"—it is useful to review contemporary literature on the geography of homelessness, keeping in mind Philo's observations about social construction, for much of this literature has been rooted in an understanding that:

> space is not an empty dimension along which social groupings become structured, but has to be considered in terms of its involvement in the constitution of systems of interaction.[8]

The most comprehensive treatment of this relationship between social and spatial processes in the development of a geography of homelessness can be found in the work of Dear and Wolch, which builds on a series of collaborative and individual efforts, beginning with Dear's work in 1974 on the location of mental-health facilities, and culminating in their recent work on the evolution of the service-dependent ghetto. In *Landscapes of Despair* the authors examine the interrelationship of social and spatial dynamics that contributed to the social construction of the *service-dependent ghetto*—that inner-city area to which large numbers of service-dependent and now homeless people have gravitated. The first of these processes is the long history of policies of an evolving welfare state, the second, a process of suburbanization which actively produced the inner city. A third process is the active choice of the elderly, single parents, mentally ill, and mentally retarded, all of them typically service-dependent people, who move to the inner city, where they find a range of coping mechanisms to assist them. In Dear and Wolch's analysis these three processes have operated at different spatial scales, *in a complementary and nested fashion, a descending hierarchy of spatial dynamics, each dictating the context in which lower-level dynamics would take place.* Together, and in a descending order of importance, spatial filtering of individuals, locational decisions of institutions, and processes of urbanization worked in concert to produce service-dependent ghettos in inner cities across North America (see Figure 1). When Dear and Wolch analyze the deinstitutionalization and the concentration of homeless mentally ill in the service-dependent ghetto, they are describing a process wherein space only reaffirms the marginality of the subject in question: in a quite literal sense *these people occupy a space of difference "already prepared for them."*[9]

Much of the contemporary work on homelessness can be fitted into this framework, although most studies concentrate on one of the three processes that Dear and Wolch synthesize in their work. They include ethnogeographies of the homeless, those dealing with locational decisions of shelters and services, and urban geographies of the homeless.

FIGURE 1: CONCEPTUALIZING A GEOGRAPHY OF HOMELESSNESS
(Ruddick 1991)

DYNAMICS	BEFORE STRUCTURING	RESTRUCTURING	AFTER RESTRUCTURING
I MICROSPATIAL PRACTICES	**Spatial Filtering** Duncan (1976) Wolch (1980) Dear/Wolch (1987) Dear et. al. (1980) Schmidt (1965) Reich (1973) ▼	**DETERRITORIALIZATION** ▲ **Expulsion** Baxter/Hopper (1981) Hombs/Snyder (1982) ▲	Rowe/Wolch (1989) Wright/Vermund (1990) Dear (1987) Crystal (1984) Ruddick (1989) Ruddick (1990) Robertson et. al. (1986) Deutsche (1990b) ▼▲
II LOCATIONAL DECISION OF INSTITUTION	**Institutional Location/ Concentration** Wolch/Gabriel (1984) Dear/Wolch (1987) Dear/Taylor (1982) ▼	**Institutional Dismantling/ Fairshare** Wolch (1984) Wolch/Gabriel (1987) Dear (1987) Baer (1983)	**Institutional Reconfiguration** ▼▲
III LARGER URBAN PROCESS	**Suburbanization/ Inner City Decline** Dear/Wolch (1987) Taylor et. al. (1984) Dear/Taylor (1982) ▼ **GHETTOIZATION**	▲ **Central City Revitalization/Backlash** Sexton (1983) Dear/Wolch (1987) Wolch (1989) Deutsche (1990a) Kasinitz (1985) Mair (1986)	**Hybrid Revitalization/ Ghettoization** Creation of service hubs is a constututive feature of redevelopment (San Diego, Hollywood, South Central LA, Central City LA) ▼ **POLYNUCLEATION**

Managing Meaning

Contemporary literature on the geography of homelessness has attempted to deal with the relationship between these three scales during three different historical periods (see Figure 1). The first, dated approximately from the formation of central-city skid-row areas up to a period of central-city gentrification and dismantling of skid rows, characterizes what Dear and Wolch term the rise of the service-dependent ghetto, or a period of relatively uncontested *ghettoization* of marginal people within inner-city zones of dependence. The second, a period of rapid urban economic *restructuring* beginning around the mid-1970s, characterizes a moment of deterritorialization, where skid rows were being dismantled and where groups of new homeless, swept from place to place, began to congregate in other parts of the city. The third, a process of *polynucleation* of services, is a moment of stabilization of new service networks and marginal people in different parts of the city.

What is intended here is not so much a critique of this literature in the sense of "uncovering its failings," but rather a historical-geographical mapping of its origins, keeping in mind Philo's observations about geographical (and temporal) complexities which make it difficult to erect general laws about how marginality and space intersect at every time or every place.

APODICTIC GEOGRAPHIES:
SKID ROW AND THE GHETTOIZATION OF THE HOMELESS

> If (a) decision is based on reasoning of an apodictic character it is not a decision at all: a rationality that transcends me has already decided for me, and my only role is that of recognizing the decision and the consequences that unfold from it.
>
> —Ernesto Laclau, "Building the New Left: An Interview with Ernesto Laclau" in *Strategies. A Journal of Theory, Culture and Politics*, No.1, 1985.

While Dear and Wolch explore the sociospatial dynamics between urbanization, welfare policies, and location of asylums from the 1800s on, the central dynamics that they attribute to the formation of contemporary, service-dependent ghettos date from about 1950. Here, the latest round of urbanization and suburbanization contributed to continued inner-city decline which literally prepared a zone of dependence later filled by the homeless.[10] Following the creation of this zone of dependence, institutions for the service-dependent began to concentrate in inner-city areas, in the United States largely as the result of Great Society policies of the 1960s which redirected funds to these areas.[11] As a result, they argue, marginalized people, in moving to the inner-city, reproduced their marginality in a literal and figurative space "already prepared for them."[12]

Locational decisions about services and shelters were circumscribed within the larger imperatives of suburbanization and inner-city decline: services were located in inner-city areas where local opposition was weak and fragmented, generally on the fringe of the central business district. Dear and Taylor discovered a geography of accepting and rejecting neighborhoods—the former characterized by transient populations, relatively high population density, mixed housing stock, a small proportion of families, and lower incomes, and the latter by stable populations, low population density, predominantly single-family housing, a higher proportion of families, and high income.[13] Wolch and Gabriel noted a similar pattern of service concentration in the formation of a service-dependent ghetto in San Jose, California.[14]

Ethnogeographies of the skid-row dwellers written during this period, in keeping with this framework, focus on the way in which the homeless and other disenfranchised groups reproduce themselves by negotiating the use of urban space, and in doing so, simultaneously reproduce the marginal meaning of the space, and their own marginality.[15] It is, indeed, through the "correct" interpretation of the preassigned meaning of these spaces that the homeless survive.[16] Duncan, however, makes the relationship between marginal space and marginal status explicit. In a review of the literature detailing tramps' strategies to "make use of the landscape in order to survive," [17] Duncan concludes:

> By occupying marginal space, the tramp acts out and reconfirms his social marginality in the eyes of the host group. His strategy merely reaffirms the host's perspective and causes only minimal adjustments to be made to the host's moral order.

This is not to suggest that the tramp's existence is unproblematically reproduced through the use of these spaces, for, as Duncan comments further:

> The tramp is faced with a problem that has no real solution. In order to survive without being arrested he must

occupy marginal areas, while in order to secure the
wherewithal to survive, he must often venture into high-
risk, prime areas. . . . Prime space, however, does not
have a uniformly high social value. The tramp knowing
the relative value assigned to different spaces by the host
group minimizes his risk by using prime space which has
moderate social value.[18]

Nevertheless for both the skid-row tramp in Duncan's study
and the service-dependent ghetto of the deinstitutionalized in Dear
and Wolch's work, these areas are functional—a "coping mecha-
nism," for the deinstitutionalized; for tramps, "a place where social
control is possible." It is in this sense that the geography described
by Duncan, Dear and Wolch is apodictic—the space takes the
nature of absolute truth or necessary reality. It is through the space,
in the analysis of these authors, that the marginality of the tramp or
the homeless is reconfirmed. Nowhere in these analyses is there the
possibility that marginal people might transform the meaning of
themselves and the space to which they are confined by their use
of it. Nowhere do we get the sense that more than one symbolic
meaning of this space might exist, or be evoked in use.

APOCALYPTIC GEOGRAPHIES: DETERRITORIALIZATION OF THE HOMELESS AND THE FORCED MARCH TO NOWHERE

From the mid-1970s on, one could no longer confidently assert,
as Duncan did in his study, that "the city is composed of more or
less well-defined social areas each of which is controlled by one or
more groups who sustain the moral order there."[19] Commercial gentrification of downtown areas, dismantling of skid rows in some
cities, and expulsion of the homeless from skid rows in others
prompted a new round of studies on the geography of homelessness, most of which were apocalyptic in predictions about the
final resting place of homeless people. Two contributions are central
in this work. First, these studies began to establish a link between the
emergence of a new conception of space and a new conception
of marginality. Looking specifically at the development of "postindustrial" spaces and the necessary exclusion of homeless people
from these spaces, they forged in very specific terms what Preziosi
more generally identified as the complicity between city and self.[20]

Michel Rustin expressed a similar view in more simple language. "People's identity and sense of the world is expressed and reflected in the buildings they know, just as it is by their language or clothes."[21]

Studies conducted on shelter location after the mid-1970s maintained, in their analyses, the hierarchical relationship between urbanization, shelter location, and spatial drift so clearly identified by Wolch and Dear. "Larger" processes of urbanization dictated the range of possibilities of shelter location. But now the tide had turned in the other direction: new urbanization processes were essentially antagonistic to location of services in inner-city areas, and service-dependent people became deterritorialized and dispersed throughout the city. Where marginal people of the postwar city had gravitated to a "place already prepared for them," the newly marginalized of the restructuring city had no place at all.

Beginning with Kasinitz's study on gentrification, scholars began to explore the ways in which (to borrow from Duncan) redefinition of the social space of downtowns necessarily excluded the homeless from the processes of urban expansion and redevelopment. Kasinitz argued that gentrification of inner cities brought with it a transformation in the value of public space and street space—once the domain of the poor, now the purview of the sophisticated urban *flaneur.* Street life was no longer symptomatic of poverty, but of a kind of permanent spectacle.[22] The central theme was the celebration of a social diversity, but a safe diversity (see Wilson, 1975),[23] which generally excluded people who make the middle classes feel uncomfortable. The recognition of the loss of public space that might serve as a meeting point to confront difference sparked a debate about the nature and purpose of public spaces. One the one hand, Berman mourned the loss of "truly open" public space that might act as a venue for confrontation and diffusion of tension between the middle classes and an emerging underclass. Rustin countered with the argument that specialized, segmented spaces responded to people's different preferences and ideas about who they were.[24] Sennett suggested that the city should contain heretical spaces, where people with different backgrounds and beliefs might confront one another and create new fusions of meaning.[25] Recent critics, including Rose, Deutsche, hooks, and others have challenged the notion that a "truly public space" in fact ever existed, arguing that the modern urban experience of space, while represented as a universal experience, has actually always marginalized certain others by virtue of gender or race or other characteristics.[26] Key to these arguments was the notion that *public space was a venue within and through which the cultural and social meanings of marginality and difference were expressed, and might be confronted or even renegotiated.*

Lefebvre had already made this crucial connection between the control over public space and the structuring of social identities in his spatial manifesto of 1968.[27] Yet, until very recently, the constitutive role of space in this process has not been dealt with in much of the literature on the politics of social identities. As Soja and Hooper note, work on identity politics initially attempted to assert the primacy of new binary structures, the predominance of patriarchy over class-based relationships in certain strands of feminist work, and the predominance of oppressive structures of race and ethnicity over those of patriarchy and class. It is only recently that scholars have moved away from this deadlocked bid for primacy into a more integrated understanding of these relationships, examining race, gender, and class not as additive structures but transformative ones, each shaping the experience of the other. This shift towards contingency has surfaced the inherently spatial character of the constitution of identity. As Fuss notes, once one begins to see identity as contingent, fractured, decentered, the "metaphor of position" has turned the question of "who I am" quite literally into the question of "where I stand," a politics of identity into a politics of location.[28] Yet even in this new spatial turn, concepts of position and place function at the level of geographical metaphor. Rarely are the full implications of the constitutive role of space drawn out in these analyses.[29] The most evocative of these can be found in the work of bell hooks, who challenges the reader to claim marginality, and to "enter the space of difference" as a political strategy.

The implications of these analyses are rarely extended to newly marginalized "others" such as the homeless. In literature on homelessness, the constitutive role of space in shaping and marginalizing the homeless has been analyzed more fully, but the possibility of using space to contest marginalization has, until recently, been unexamined. The central dynamic contributing to this transformation of public space and redefinition of marginality was first identified by Mair as a new round of urbanization encapsulated in the programmatic development of "postindustrial spaces." Mair, in a study based on the dismantling of services to the homeless in a skid row of Columbus, Ohio, argued that the status value that a new class of professional managers attached to a newly developing "postindustrial space" downtown required the removal of the homeless, who in a sense stigmatized the space.[30] Sexton documented a similar process in the dismantling of Phoenix's skid row to make way for downtown redevelopment.[31] This connection between the development of postindustrial city space and the stigmatization of the homeless was also noted by Deutsche, who observed that:

> New York's transformation is . . . . an effort to reconcile social contradiction by refortifying a spatial hierarchy. . . . New York's present restructuring perpetuates the production of a distinctive historical space: an economic and political space both of which "converge". . . . towards the elimination of all differences . . . . Homogenization operates forcibly by means of the literal expulsion of social groups from the city. [32]

Dear and Wolch documented a similar connection between gentrification and expulsion of the service-dependent from both downtown San Jose and the skid row in Los Angeles, although they did not link this to new conceptions of marginality and difference.[33] All of these analyses carried with them apocalyptic visions of a deterritorialized homeless people on a forced march to nowhere. Only Hopper suggested that the continuing presence of the homeless in the postindustrial city space might, in fact, cut both ways: it was not simply that the social value of the newly gentrified space reinforced their stigma, but also that their presence might undercut the ideology of growth, leisure, and wealth attached to the postindustrial city itself.[34]

The studies associated with this period documented a downward spiral of marginalization, epitomized in the work by Hombs and Snyder, titled fittingly enough, *Homelessness in America: A Forced March to Nowhere.*[35] Literature dealing with the location of services under this apocalyptic vision took the logical response that if the services and shelters to the homeless could find acceptance nowhere, then the only way to deal with the political situation fairly was to locate them everywhere. Proposals for "fair-share" distribution of services, and for community-based service models which replicated the positive features of skid row in other parts of the city were proposed by Dear, Wolch, and Baer.[36] Mair suggested that there might be ways to transform the abstract sympathy that people feel for the homeless by politicizing the issue, but offered no concrete strategy. He did acknowledge, however, that expulsion of homeless people from postindustrial city space has been an uneven process, manifest in some areas and not in others.[37] The question then became: What dynamics contributed to keeping the homeless and their services in place?

POLYNUCLEATION OF THE HOMELESS AND THEIR SERVICE NETWORKS

While visions of a restructured postindustrial city predicted the homeless would endure an unending forced march to nowhere, this, in fact, has not happened. Different homeless people negotiate their marginality in places, in a variety of ways, above and beyond their "spoiled" identity as homeless. Crystal, for example, identified a "gender gap" in assumptions about homeless people, noting that (unlike homeless men) homeless women tended to retain contacts with their children. Robertson's comparison of homeless people in downtown Los Angeles and the Westside revealed higher levels of education, lower levels of mental illness, high percentages of young and white homeless on the Westside, and less educated, older, more often black or Hispanic, and more often mentally ill homeless people in the downtown area. On the one hand, it could be argued that this finding simply supports Dear's thesis that there is a "pecking order" of deviance. On the other hand it suggests that the homeless negotiate their identity above and beyond the label of homeless—as men, women, children of many different backgrounds. Studies comparing homeless men and women and homeless people of different ethnic backgrounds showed wide variations in survival strategies, in social networks, and in uses of space.[38] As Grossberg argues:

> (People's) relations to particular practices are . . . complex and contradictory. They may win something in the struggle against sexism, and lose something in the struggle against economic exploitation . . . if their subordination is always complex and active, understanding culture requires us to look at how practices are actively inserted at particular sites of everyday life and at how particular articulations empower and disempower them.[39]

Marginality and stigma are not mantles automatically assumed by the homeless the moment they occupy a particular space, but are, rather, actively if unwillingly produced over a long period of time. Rowe and Wolch illustrate this in the gradual limiting of expectations and redefinition of "self-as-homeless" which develops as an act of sheer survival. They note:

> The deprivations which accompany homelessness lead many homeless individuals to place greater emphasis on satisfaction of short-term needs and objectives . . . the recursive relationship between daily path and life path is thus altered as immediate priorities supersede the life path. The experimental basis for self-identity becomes static and the definition of "self-as-homeless" becomes deeply ingrained, as the means and will to escape chronic homelessness deteriorate simultaneously and synergistically.[40]

At the same time, they admit that, in spite of a deterioration of will and means to escape homelessness, the homeless engage in a complex and active struggle against becoming marginal. Homeless women, for instance, often enter into lover/spouse relationships, to avoid attack, to gain emotional support and identity, to enhance mobility, but "their threatening locale, absence of traditional social networks and vulnerability to physical attack often lead them to tolerate the negative aspects of lover/spouse relationships."[41]

By avoiding rooming houses and living in encampments, the homeless not only established valuable social networks, but were able to have a more stable and better quality of life where they could direct resources to meet personal needs rather than spending all of their money on rent. Here, Rowe and Wolch made the extraordinary observation that the homeless in encampments are in fact less marginalized and more empowered than many of their housed counterparts in rooming houses on skid row. But the authors note that this process as well is a contradictory one:

> After the failure of traditional social networks to provide adequate support and thus prevent the onset of homelessness, the homeless social network proved so critical to material and emotional welfare that the adoption of an identity as "homeless community member," "panhandler," or as a service provider's "favorite" was readily embraced. While the acceptance of these new identities serves a positive function in meeting daily needs and maintaining self-esteem within the geographic and social context of homelessness, it works against developing both the means and the will to execute long-term projects aimed at reentering mainstream society.[42]

44

Managing Meaning

Their study nevertheless leads them to conclude that the creation of "safe neutral spaces" for the homeless to congregate, in the form of protected vest-pocket parks and drop-in centers, may be valuable in assisting the formation of social networks, itself "essential to solving one of their most critical problems: the inability to organize."

But is it only marginality that is reproduced here? Wright and Vermund argue no. The homeless are able to survive not simply through the correct interpretation of marginal urban space and acceptance (passive or otherwise) of their own marginality. Rather, they also use urban space to produce "small dignities" with which they struggle to redefine their social position or to force concessions from those who have power over them. Wright and Vermund, who draw their argument from an analysis of a homeless encampment in Garden Grove, California, argue that the tactical use these homeless people made of the space in the park and its environs contributed to their empowerment and their access to resources.[43] While the physical resources of this group were indeed diminished compared to their earlier housed existence, and they considered day-to-day needs more pressing than long-term goals, these homeless people never simply accepted their marginality."Contesting strategies of authority both in institutional public areas and open public areas produced a significant increase in those receiving benefits and a curtailment of repressive police practices."[44] In other words, they began to turn the tide against the increasing predominance of daily-path needs over life-path.

There are other examples of attempts of the homeless to resist marginalization, most notably through art exhibitions, the formation of homeless writers' and artists' groups, and the redesign of physical shelter such as Wodiczko's Homeless Vehicle Project. Projects such as the Homeless Vehicle Project have drawn to scholars' attention the possibility for new and creative forms of resistance, at both the symbolic and the practical level. As Deutsche notes, the design of the mobile shelter:

> Projects onto this monument, the social contradictions of the city. When Wodiczko restores to visibility the absences structuring intentional and unintentional monuments, he forces them to acknowledge what they never intended: the impossibility of their stability.[45]

SPACES OF DIFFERENCE: THEORIZING THE DEVELOPMENT
OF NEW SERVICE NETWORKS FOR THE HOMELESS

Challenging a stigmatized identity such as homelessness is, of course, not sufficient to ensure that homeless people will be able to stay in place, much less that a stable network of shelters and services might be developed to support them. The development of a postindustrial space within Columbus's downtown and the success of business people in maintaining a particular image in the area by excluding shelters and services is part of a process of managing development symbols of the urban environment. But as Mair noted, "the tendency to evict the homeless from postindustrial city space . . . has been empirically manifested unevenly."[46] To pretend otherwise would be to take the myth of postindustrialism for a universal. The contained space of the postindustrial city is in fact the isoglosses of a myth. The isoglosses are the lines which limit "the social region from which the myth originates and comes to stand for a larger society."[47] For example, it is only within the bounded region of the space of the postindustrial city that one can believe in a world of perpetual leisure, without labor or poverty. This is not because labor and poverty do not exist within this space—the homeless are a testimony to that, as are a variety of low-wage workers who service the space (janitors, sales people and so on). But their activity is rendered all but invisible by the dominant meaning of the space.

How, then, have the homeless and their services managed to remain in place in some areas where a "postindustrial city space" is developed? To address this question, keeping in mind the relationship between space and identity, it is necessary to turn to the literature on city building which addresses the way in which contradictory and conflicting interests can rally around a process of redevelopment. Within this literature, the creation of growth coalitions is intricately and intimately bound up in a process of image production—both of the coalitions themselves and the new city spaces they propose.

As Gottdiener argues:

> It is important to ask, on the one hand what groups possess the need for historically invariant symbols (of the urban environment) and on the other what mechanisms are utilized to achieve ideological hegemony. In the former case it is apparent that the real-estate industry, homeowners' associations, chambers of commerce and

banks are the most active managers in symbolic generalizations. Through the actions of these groups the representational typifications of use-values merging from daily life
are converted into ones which are more useful for the
exchange-value of property and business investment. [48]

Kasinitz, Mair and others allude to aspects of this process in the
production of postindustrial city space. Mair focuses on the activities
of the business coalition in controlling the meaning of downtown
Columbus by driving out shelters; Kasinitz discusses the transformed
meaning of the street—once the domain of the poor, now transformed into the theater of the professional managerial class.

But, Gottdiener continues,

This is by no means an automatic process of sign conversion. It is contentious and contingent, depending as it
does upon the ability of special interests to control the
symbolic interpretations of processual outcomes in everyday life. Signs of boosterism which portray a unified image
of the community must be superimposed upon in a more
fundamental socio-semiotic process involving a politics of
signs among contending groups within the city.[49]

How is this synthesis of signs achieved? Literature on the formation of local growth coalitions provides several insights. First of all,
local politics matters. The form and extent of redistributive policy
and programs do not follow automatically from conceptions of the
business community about the common good,[50] nor are they automatically restricted or inhibited by exogenous factors, such as competition between cities to attract commercial and industrial redevelopment,[51] or a climate of fiscal austerity emanating from cutbacks at federal and state levels of government.[52] Political activity
at the local level, in the form of coalition-building, organization of
communities around specific issues, or pressure from local institutions, does have an impact on the shape, content, and extent of
redistributive policy.

Secondly, these studies reveal that coalitions, and particularly
growth coalitions, do not always reflect a uniform self-evident community of interests, but are often the result of the unification of
seemingly diverse and sometimes conflicting groups as a result of
the brokerage of local politicians,[53] or even the activities of "place
entrepreneurs"—that is, local actors in government and administration who actively create new forms of policy and programs to unify
diverse interests around a common goal.[54]

Finally, they argue that the emergence of "relatively autonomous" policy, that is policy which is relatively independent of the preference of dominant economic interests,[55] can arise under a very specific set of exogenous or endogenous circumstances. Exogenous factors include a locational advantage which makes a particular area an attractive investment site, permitting the local government to make redistributive demands on developers,[56] or national and subnational fiscal aid, permitting a greater revenue pool from which to allocate monies to local programs.[57] "Relatively autonomous policy," however, can also arise as a result of endogenous conditions, specifically coherence and coordination among community-based groups and public-sector institutions.[58] In order to understand variations in policy between different communities, it is important to identify *latent* and *territorial* interests of local groups within each community, as well as the form and extent of their political organization and cohesion. These interests include neighborhood groups as well as local elected and administrative officials.[59] While this literature tells us much about the contradictory and conflictual process of coalition-building, it does not give many clues about the process of image-building which necessarily accompanies it and represents it. Yet, as Gottdiener argues, the sign of boosterism is often connected to a specific growth coalition—"the surface calm of the city image belies its constitution as the condensation of struggle between various organized groups' expressions about alternate use and design."[60]

Returning to the issue of the homeless and their relationship to postindustrial city space, we can hypothesize that the homeless and the shelters that service them might become part of a postindustrial city space under circumstances where they were first able to challenge their stigmatization by developing strategies which challenged their image simply as homeless people, or, conversely, which alter the "meaning" of their presence in the place.

Literature on the formation of urban growth coalitions reviewed above suggests that sustained support for the homeless and their services which is able to go beyond the mere "abstract sympathy" that one feels for the homeless can only be achieved if the homeless and their services identify and ally themselves with the latent and territorial interests of other actors in the redevelopment process.

While Mair establishes a convincing relationship between the status attached to postindustrial space and the stigma of the homeless in the specific cases where the homeless and their shelters have been expelled, there is nothing to suggest that this relationship is historically or geographically invariant. Indeed, as Monkonnen notes, in nineteenth-century cities, places of aid to the poor were centrally located and prominently featured buildings whose image more often contributed to boosting the city image rather than detracting from it. In this case the very presence of a poorhouse attested to the largesse of the city.

What does this suggest about the dynamics of the formation of contemporary service networks for the homeless? First of all, that the relationship between the three spatial scales suggested by Wolch and Dear is, at the moment, much more open-ended than previously conceived (see Table 2.1). As homeless people rely increasingly upon their own networks of support in the absence of services, and as constricted services rely increasingly on community networks to supplement their activities, the sociospatial strategies of the homeless themselves begin to influence the criteria for the location of services. Moreover, in areas undergoing redevelopment, where growth coalitions are not homogeneous, service providers (themselves not necessarily a homogeneous bloc) may constitute part of a local growth coalition, contributing to and legitimating the process of redevelopment, rather than being necessarily excluded from it.

CONCLUSION

If people are not simply marginalized in space but also through space, it is also through space that they attempt to challenge this process and construct for themselves different identities.

For the homeless, this symbiosis between space and self has historically directed them to skid-row areas of the city, and subsequently expelled them from these areas as the meaning of these spaces was transformed through gentrification. But this process of signification is not as unilateral as much of the literature on gentrification and displacement of the homeless has tended to suggest. The presence of the homeless in a gentrifying area or a post-industrial city space does not simply reinforce their stigma: it can undercut the tenets of the space itself, and its implicit ideology about leisure and wealth. Neither the expulsion nor the maintenance of homeless people and their services in an area is guaranteed by the redevelopment process—it is rather a political outcome, dependent upon the ability of the homeless and their service providers to identify and respond to latent and territorial interests of the local growth coalition (itself an unstable fusion of conflicting interest groups) and to present an alternative (that is, nonspoiled) identity of themselves that is somehow congruent with the emerging image of the place.

3

HETEROTOPIAS OF THE HOMELESS: STRATEGIES AND TACTICS OF PLACE-MAKING IN LOS ANGELES

The perfect metaphor for (the current landscape of human services) is provided by the homeless who nightly populate the
beaches of Santa Monica and Venice, California. They sleep
next to the ocean at the continent's edge, a little distance from
a tide that could sweep them away. This portrait of the landscape of despair presages the collapse of the human-service
system and abandonment of those in need. The lucky and
resourceful who manage to survive hang on by their fingernails
at the edge of society.

—Michael Dear and Jennifer Wolch,
*Landscapes of Despair: From Deinstitutionalization to
Homelessness,* 1987.

"Skid-Row:. . . It Won't Go Away." Despite the current political
rhetoric . . . Skid Rows are present in one form or another in every
major urban area in the world, and have existed for generations.

—Clancy Imislund, Managing Director of the
Midnight Mission in Los Angeles, *Los Angeles Times,*
December 13, 1989.

Young and Homeless in Hollywood

> Rather than remaining within the field of discourse that upholds its privilege by inverting its discourse (speaking of catastrophe and no longer of progress) one can try another path: one can analyze the microbe-like singular and plural practices which an urbanistic system was supposed to administer or suppress but which have outlived its decay.
>
> —Michel De Certeau, "Practices of Space" in *On Signs*, ed. Marshall Blonsky 1985.

In some ways these three statements represent a dialectical trinity, none completely true without the others. What is at issue here is not the differing geographies of homelessness—the immovability of a skid-row service network versus the impermanence of a camp on Venice Beach—but rather the antipodal mythologies[1] of homelessness: the first tenuous, the second tenacious.

The first insists on the victimization of the homeless, driven from skid-row to the continent's edge.[2] It is representative of one contemporary image of homelessness, fixated on the fundamentally precarious existence of homeless people—both in terms of their limited access to resources which would enable them to become housed, and in terms of the shifting geography of their daily lives.

The second insists on the inevitability of homelessness as a human condition and the complicity of the homeless in that condition—the fate of the men and (now admittedly) women[3] who "were never able to live in a structure called society" and the consequent persistence of skid-rows and their service providers. Since the nineteenth century, skid-rows have demonstrated an extraordinarily stable geography. Around the precarious existence of the homeless during this period a complex service economy has been erected, which, in the mind of service providers like Clancy Imislund of the skid-row in Los Angeles, promises to remain. This argument speaks to a second popular image of homelessness—one which blames the victim,[4] but in this case calls for a compassionate response—the expansion of an array of services which may be the victim's only hope.

These mythologies are neither strictly true nor strictly false— for, as Barthes would say, they are based on use and not on truth.[5] Their differences reflect the different political discourses from which they emanate. These discourses have arisen in a range of communities within the city of Los Angeles, both new and old refuges of the homeless—including the skid-row at Venice Beach—

but also numerous other sites in the city of Los Angeles.[6]

The mythology of the homeless as victims, about to be swept away, presages an argument by Dear and Wolch for the need to construct a landscape of caring throughout the city. Rather than recentering the homeless in skid-row, this landscape would reproduce the positive features of the skid-row service system in an array of service hubs in other communities, directed at restoring the service dependent to a life within the larger community, at the same time as the "burden of caring" is, in effect, shared throughout the city.[7]

The contrasting mythology—that of the permanence and inevitability of skid-row and the homeless that it serves—has surfaced in the context of a debate among service providers, urban planners, developers, and politicians about the logic of maintaining services in skid-row, now ripening for redevelopment and accusations that the "homeless problem" in skid-row and environs is, in fact, the result of locating shelters and services there—which has had the net effect of attracting the homeless from elsewhere. This position, which stresses the inevitability of homelessness as a human condition, moves in essence to absolve the service providers from any responsibility for their presence in the area, in face of the argument that the homeless come to skid-row only because the services are there. At the same time, it guarantees these services a long future.

By insisting on the different context in which these mythologies have arisen, I do not mean to endorse either or both, or to attribute differences strictly to historical geography. These myths are significant for the qualities they share. Their similarity, to borrow from De Certeau, is that they invert the discourse of a previous era, speaking "now of catastrophe and no longer of progress," and in doing so, downplay any role that the homeless might have themselves as agents engaged in the complex process of city-building, struggling to gain permanence in new refuges throughout the city.[8]

Of course, it might be argued that the homeless never did have any role in this process; that skid-row itself was the product of a series of economic and political crises that produced successive waves of homeless people, and a relatively stable urban geography[9] that consistently concentrated them, whether they willed it or not, first in institutions, asylums, and poorhouses, and later in marginal spaces of the inner city. But this position takes outcome for explanation.

THE SERVICE-DEPENDENT GHETTO

In fact, in exploring the forces which historically structured skid-row, Dear and Wolch insist on the active role of the service-dependent—in this case deinstitutionalized mentally ill people who "gravitated to the core areas of North American cities, which seemed to provide them the best opportunity for remaining outside the institution,"[10] opportunities that included cheap housing, support facilities, friendships, and self-help groups.[11] In *Landscapes of Despair*, they focus on three processes concentrating the service-dependent (now homeless) populations in the inner city which contributed to the rise of the *service-dependent ghetto* (the conceptual counterpart of what is popularly known as skid-row and environs), as the domain for deinstitutionalized homeless. The first of these forces was the long history of policies of an evolving welfare state, the second a process of suburbanization which simultaneously produced the inner city. The third was the active choice of the elderly, single parents, the mentally ill, mentally retarded, and physically disabled—in short, the service dependent—who found in the inner city a range of coping mechanisms to assist them.

In a critical application of Foucault,[12] Dear and Wolch argue that the surveillance and disciplinary procedures of the welfare state (born in the poorhouse and asylum and geared to "normalizing and socializing" a service-dependent population)[13] were transplanted from the institution and reproduced within the geographic confines of the service-dependent ghetto. In the process, however, these practices became distended beyond the authority of "professionals" to other agents, such as community workers, and challenged by a range of other practices, including the development of self-help networks among the service-dependent, and the weight of public scrutiny. This process of "swarming"[14] of disciplinary mechanisms—that is, the creation of a system of flexibile mechanisms of control, as one system of control is grafted onto another—was in fact unpredictable in its outcome. Foucault notes that these mechanisms are continually confronted with "agitations, revolts, spontaneous organizations, coalitions, anything that may establish horizontal conjunctions."[15] As the formation of the service-dependent ghetto demonstrated, disciplinary procedures do not spread unproblematically; rather, one set of practices might serve to confound, challenge, or underpin the basis of another.[16]

Dear and Wolch's analysis serves us well in explaining the rise of skid-row in Los Angeles. But the forces which contributed to the construction of Los Angeles's skid-row have changed drastically in the past decade. Read backwards, the formation of skid-row might appear, deceptively, as a happy coincidence between structures and agents. However, since the mid-1970s, the service dependent in Los Angeles have been forced to construct a new geography of refuge, often acting against rather than in harmony with processes of urbanization and the evolution of the welfare state. The "safety net" which provided assistance to service-dependent people in the past has ripped apart,[17] in effect producing a new homeless population out of those once protected under the New Deal, who now migrate to inner-city areas adjacent to downtown Los Angeles and to declining central cities throughout the larger metropolitan area. A relatively stable geography of cheap housing and services, once available in inner-city areas near the downtown and declining central cities throughout the greater metropolitan area, has been destroyed by new rounds of commercial and residential gentrification.[18] Faced with a decimated service system which relies on a patchwork of practices,[19] denied access to many programs because of the lack of a permanent address, or avoiding shelters altogether in a desperate attempt to maintain dignity,[20] a whole range of new homeless literally do not know their place.

In the new refuges of the homeless, even the models of control, distended as they were, now literally as well as figuratively break apart.[21] The homeless gather together and develop networks which often confound the objectives of service providers. Old modes of surveillance, service, or socialization cannot hold, and become distended. It is the police, and not the tides, that would sweep the homeless away: periodic police sweeps are needed to break up fledgling campgrounds. Ancillary outreach programs, such as the Homeless Outreach Program in skid-row, are established, designed to draw the homeless from their own social networks and recalcitrant geographies into the service system. A flotilla of vans, mobile units, and outreach workers has been organized by an array of services to search out the homeless in new or unanticipated places. Some "swarming" of disciplinary mechanisms may take place, and controls become flexibile and adapted, as a variety of institutions, from the police to service workers, attempt to expand their resources.[22] But campgrounds continue to form in unlikely and unwanted places, take root, and gain tentative permanence.

With the emergence of new homeless groups, who include families, single mothers with children, youth, and political refugees, the sites of the homeless have metastasized throughout the city. The new homeless—many situationally homeless rather than socially disaffiliated[23]—bring with them different sets of survival tactics and coping mechanisms, including intermittent employment, ties to community, friends, and lovers, and preferences for a range of different sites within the city, better suited to their survival than skid-row.

A more appropriate imagery of these ghettos transformed or transplanted, and of the punctuated and intermittent rhythms of social control in these new gathering places of the homeless[24] is that of *heterotopia*—'the co-existence in an impossible space' of a 'large number of fragmentary possible worlds.'[25]

This particular notion of heterotopia is almost buried in Foucault's elaboration of the concept, but I believe it is a critical one. Foucault offers several other possibilities for profane and sacred spaces, which often exude a static, almost timeless quality. These spaces stand either as whole, intact, and conflict-free representations of the world around them, such as the holy garden of the Persians—or they appear to offer an imaginary or symbolic solution to real conflicts in the everyday spaces of the societies within which they exist, such as heterotopias of deviation. But it is not clear how these spaces come into being or why they might change. Foucault does offer us some clues in the discussion of changes within the cemetery, from its location in the heart of the city to one at the city's edge. Here, fears about transmission of disease and questions about the existence of the soul led to the relocation of the cemetery and predominance of individualized graves. When one believed unequivocally in the existence of the soul, the problem of bodily remains seemed unimportant. As this belief was called into question, the preservation of the body began to take on more significance. Nevertheless, even in this brief discussion, it is not clear how these meanings were contested in and through the cemetery-heterotopia, or in a wider sense why heterotopias of crises were largely replaced by heterotopias of deviation. In examining the occupation of profane spaces by homeless people, this final under-emphasized commentary on heterotopias "in which coexist in an impossible space, a large number of fragmentary possible worlds," one might begin to see how these possible worlds begin to jostle one another for meaning in a bid to represent the space as a whole.[26] Much like his cursory—almost throwaway—comments on the transformative potential of "swarming of the disciplines," this version of heterotopia offers us some possibility of conflict over meaning and transformation of the function of these spaces.

Heterotopias of the Homeless

Moreover, one might speculate that it is in the process of transforming what were previously heterotopias of deviation (the prisons and asylums of the homeless), by emptying them into a carceral ghetto, that the meanings contained within them become disrupted, literally and figuratively displaced.

These heterotopias have included Ocean Front Walk and Rose Avenue in Venice, Santa Monica, Hollywood (the Boulevard, the "Troll Camp" under the Sunset Boulevard overpass of the Hollywood Freeway), and West Hollywood (Plummer Park, Oki Dog), Van Nuys and even twelve acres of public-utilities lands near Fairmont Park, Riverside, where the "Riverbottom" people have secreted themselves in the dense underbrush.[27] It is the fragmented nature of these spaces and their odd and unlikely juxtapositions that distinguish them from the service-dependent ghetto of earlier decades.

Ethnographic studies reveal the creativity in the range of place-making tactics [28] that the homeless deploy to survive. Recent studies of daily life paths also reveal the use of support networks by the homeless—shared strategies, where one person will guard meager possessions and place, while the other tries to secure and income through day labor, panhandling, and the like.[29]

These survival tactics extend beyond the collective use of limited resources. We are all familiar with stories of homeless women who pretend insanity to avoid attack, of people pretending to be traveling, watching movies, or waiting for a bus in order to find a sheltered place to sleep or sit. Here, invisibility is a means of access: "those who pass unnoticed in public places suffer less abuse and harassment."[30] These tactics express the *negotiation* of the assigned meaning of space for purposes other than those intended. This process cannot be conceptualized in the structure/agency dyad, for it refers to the *concealed* practices of agents which only apparently reproduce specific structures. These strategies can be seen as a kind of *perruque* applied to the sphere of reproduction rather than production. De Certeau introduces this concept—literally "the wig"—to express the range of covert actions undertaken by clerical workers at their offices to give the appearance of working while actually taking care of their own needs (balancing check books, making doctor's appointments) or even running their own businesses.[31]

BEYOND STRUCTURE AND AGENCY:
BETWEEN STRATEGY AND TACTICS

A central figure analyzing the negotiation of social behavior in space is Erving Goffman.[32] Goffman introduced the concept of front and back regions in the argument that social behaviors and presentation of self were spatially negotiated. Front regions denoted those spaces where people constructed a public and socially acceptable view of themselves; back regions were the spaces where they felt able to reveal their "true" selves, hidden from public scrutiny and in the company of peers.[33] The classic example provided by Goffman is the polite and attentive behavior of the waiter under the watchful eye of his clientele, contrasted with "how he really felt about the clientele" in the privacy of the restaurant's kitchen. Goffman's analysis, however, is based on a normative psychology which does not admit to status or class differences in the negotiation of acceptable social behaviors, and does not provide us with an explanation of how norms change. In spite of this, the concept is useful, for it emphasizes the uses of space in negotiating specific behaviors, and has had fruitful adaptation to studies of the homeless. For instance, in his analysis of the sociospatial relationship between police and vagrants, Rubenstein argues that:

> the policeman develops notions about what is the "normal" character of behavior in different parts of the city . . . behavior tolerated in one place is disallowed in another because it violates his notion of what is right in what place"[34]

In the same vein, Duncan argues that the homeless must learn the "prime and marginal" value of spaces, as well as the "spatiotemporal pockets" of moral law, rather than market law.[35] Examples of the former include alleys, dumps, and railroad yards, not worth patrolling by policemen. Examples of the latter include the two-block radius around churches (on Sunday morning), when panhandling is particularly good.[36]

The strength of these analyses is that they bring to light conscious and strategic uses of space employed by the homeless in their daily survival. The limits lie in the fact that they give no clue as to how the meaning of spaces change, nor as to the role that the homeless might play in that change. Here, in his distinction between strategies and tactics, I believe De Certeau provides us with the beginnings of a way out.

> A strategy (is) the calculation of power relationships that becomes possible as soon as a subject with will and power . . . can be isolated. . . . A tactic is a calculated action determined by the absence of proper locus. The space of tactic is the space of other. Thus it must play on and within a terrain imposed on it. . . . It takes advantage of opportunities and depends on them, without any base where it could stockpile its winnings.[37]

> Strategies pin their hopes on the resistance that the establishment of place offers to the erosion of time; tactics on the clever utilization of time.[38]

Service providers are often confounded by the difficulties in "pinning down" the populations they are trying to serve: among homeless youth, for instance, "lifelong" friendships can form and dissolve within a span of days. Nothing is routine. Sleep can be found on a park bench one night, an underpass in Hollywood the next, while hitchhiking in a passing car the third. In one view this characteristic forms part of an explanation of the causes of homelessness—stemming from a psychological inability to muster resources, to follow things through. Seen another way, however, it is a survival tactic of the disenfranchised. Tactics can properly be seen as one way that the homeless make fleeting, transitory uses of spaces that have been strategically organized by other actors— that is, those who have title to space and to property.

From this perspective the precarious/permanent dichotomy dissolves. It is exactly through the precarious and transitory use of spaces that the homeless gain a relative permanence in particular places. Read through the eyes of De Certeau, the precariousness of their existence has produced their tenacity, or more particularly their day-to-day employment of *tactics* that confound the *strategies* of production and control of spaces.

In the *long durée* tactics disappear from view without a trace. But they figure crucially in the organization and mutation of strategies—in this application, the development of a new geography and structure of services to the homeless. This tactical use of space is more than a simple "warrening from within" in furtive, momentary appropriations of resources.[39] A refinement of De Certeau's concept of strategy and tactics must allow that the homeless, simply by their presence in a particular place, change its symbolic meaning.[40]

In Washington, D.C., for instance, Hopper notes that efforts to boost the region's economic recovery were confounded by the presence of the homeless. "It was difficult to strike up a fanfare for a common recovery when people were sleeping on grates a few blocks away."[41]

Mair develops this argument further in an analysis of struggles to expel the homeless from downtown Columbus. Here he notes that the presence of the homeless in downtown Columbus, as a stigmatized socially deviant group that challenges the value systems of status-oriented professionals (the intended users of gentrified spaces in the downtown), threatened redevelopment. In the "postindustrial" space of the city, these new social actors, who are at once its product and in a sense its producers, come face to face. Mair outlines a matrix of values that define a basis for antagonistic interactions between the two groups. These include, on behalf of the professional-managerial strata, (i) the need for external symbolism as a medium for self-realization, and (ii) (by necessity) the defiance of social norms on the part of the homeless—such as begging, drinking in public, or existing in nonnuclear families. The mere presence of the homeless in spaces intended for other social classes undercuts the intended symbolism of these spaces.

Mair calls for the need to mobilize a "general and abstract sympathy for the homeless" which faces, nevertheless, "massive obstacles in the ideological and economic logic of the post-industrial city."[42] This, however, is only half the story.

Mair focuses on the factors that reinforce a stigmatized image of the homeless as deviant, as abnormal, as Other. But in ignoring the images that the homeless develop of themselves, he risks accepting a stigmatized vision as their reality—a conclusion that is uncomfortably close to that perpetuated by the strategists of the "postindustrial" city. This position ignores the response that comes *back* from the street, and the multiple and singular acts of resistance by homeless people and their advocates to confront and transform both these images of themselves as deviant, and the spaces that they occupy. It denies the possibility that these acts of resistance have, in small ways, begun to transform views of homeless people and provide an alternative image of the possible social and spatial configurations of this "postindustrial space."

Put this way, the *tactical* use of space at the very least challenges, if not confounds, *strategic* attempts to organize and control the symbolic meaning of this space and its intended users.[43] As the images of places play an expanded role in attracting investment, both the production and control of images associated with places become increasingly important—the presence of the homeless in all places becomes politically problematic.[44]

The impact of these singular acts is at the moment difficult to measure. De Certeau gives us few clues as to how tactics might interpolate strategies. Tactics "elude discipline without being outside the field in which it is exercised," but in addition:

> far from being regulated or eliminated by panoptic administration, (they) have reinforced themselves in a proliferating illegitimacy, developed and insinuated themselves into these networks of surveillance, and combined in accord with unreadable but stable tactics to the point of constituting everyday regulations and surreptitious creativities that are merely concealed by the frantic mechanisms and discourses of the observational organization.[45]

What I would like to call attention to, then, are the numerous particular and concrete tactics employed by the homeless simply to stay in place, and I would like to speculate on the ways that these tactics might have contributed to the transformation of strategies to redevelop these spaces. The central point is that far from being dupes—impassive in their stigmatization, impervious to new images of actors and places being produced in what Mair calls the postindustrial city—the homeless constantly and consciously negotiate these meanings, attempting to transform their relationship to those around them. Following De Certeau, I too "would like to follow out a few of those multiform, resistant, tricky and stubborn procedures"[46] which, I believe, contribute to the formation and transformation of service enclaves in skid-row, Hollywood, and elsewhere in Los Angeles.

SKID ROW, POST-1983: THE END OF LIBERALISM

> If he is unable to experience the Other in himself, the bourgeois *can at least imagine the place where (the Other) fits in:* this is what is known as liberalism, which is *a sort of intellectual equilibrium based on recognized places* (emphasis mine).
>
> —(Roland Barthes, *Mythologies,* 1968.)

Los Angeles's skid-row currently comprises a seventy-block area to the east of Los Angeles's Central Business District, which by the early 1980s included approximately ten thousand units in Single-Room-Occupancy (SRO) hotels.[47] Originally emerging in the late nineteenth century as a "mobile centralized labor pool," skid-row all but disappeared by the early 1970s. A combination of political and economic factors, including deinstitutionalization of the mentally ill between 1963 and 1980, attacks on social-service programs under the Reagan Administration, and job loss through economic restructuring have swelled and diversified populations in the skid-row area.[48]

If there is a starting point from which to date the political response of the homeless in skid-row and their conscious and collective entry into the discourse of place-making in the downtown, it would have to be 1984. By the mid-1980s, in addition to its SRO population, Los Angeles's skid-row was estimated to have the largest population of homeless people in the nation. Within the confines of skid-row, some one thousand street dwellers survived in over a dozen encampments.[49] Throughout the rest of the central business district, homeless people squatted in every conceivable pocket of marginal space, including the space under the parking ramps of the major entryway to the Bonaventure Hotel. (This symbolic panopticon evidently gazes outward with such resoluteness that it does not witness what transpires at its feet.)[50]

Whatever the equilibrium of place that existed at the time in the minds of liberal intellectuals, it was disturbed when the downtown became a staging ground for a series of strategic uses of the space, some related to the larger dynamics of city boosterism such as the 1984 Olympics or the Pope's visit in 1987, some more specifically focused on restructuring and redeveloping the skid-row area. The latter include the development of a specific plan for the area in its less stigmatized incarnation as Central City East, the movement of state and local offices to Spring and Fourth, and the approval to move the seventy-year-old Los Angeles Mission off a nearby street and "deeper into skid-row." These acts would surely be undercut by the presence of the homeless in the area: the city began a latter-day version of 1950s-style "urban removal," requiring this time the simple removal of cardboard boxes rather than the razing of houses. Whether this more precarious population of homeless in the downtown will prove, by sheer necessity, more resilient than their housed counterparts of the 1950s remains to be seen. The homeless are familiar with the tactical, transitory appropriation of spaces in the area, and quite simply have nowhere else to go. (Even the long and circuitous Trek for Justice of the homeless through Beverly Hills to the beaches in 1987 has brought a substantial number full circle back to skid-row.) As transient as they may seem, the homeless of skid-row have been engaged in an unending series of skirmishes that have now lasted half a decade.

The first incident was not a battle chosen by the homeless—a sweep of homeless campgrounds, intended to drive them out of the downtown and out of Los Angeles in order to clean up the downtown for the 1984 Olympics. But ten homeless people removed by the sweeps responded with a lawsuit that won temporary reprieve:

> a restraint on police from detaining or questioning people
> (unless criminal activity was suspected) (or) from seizing
> property unless related to criminal activity or "truly aban-
> doned" anywhere in the skid-row area bounded by 3rd,
> 7th, Spring and Central.[51]

In theory this gave homeless people a circumscribed and tactical control of this space, provided specific conditions were adhered to, that is, no suspicion of criminal activity. But this does not imply that the homeless were able to transcend, by this limited protection, the dialectical unevenness between a strategic reorganization of skid-row and their tactical inhabitation of it. Rather, the struggle was refracted into other arenas. Pushed to the fore was a debate on the potential criminality of the homeless (particularly in campgrounds), which at once raised and exorcised in the minds of the public widespread latent fears about the homeless as "dangerous classes." The media began to publicize different campgrounds. As homeless people were moved first from the secrecy of back alleys as skid-row businesses began to fence off their private property and into public view on the street, the internal organization and philosophy of different campgrounds and rationale for locating in specific areas were dissected for public discussion, providing a more complex image of the homeless—a mix of mutual aid and mutual predation.[52] At one end of the spectrum there was Love Camp—a cooperatively run camp on Towne Avenue which pooled resources to rent portable toilets, shared chores such as cooking, cleaning, and firewood search, and ran a newsletter outlining to other homeless the ways to establish and run "homeless block associations." At the other end of the spectrum, across from Jacks Market, was a pool of failed robber barons, who extorted money out of anyone trying to pass their encampment. Self-help agencies talked of a sense of community and trust emanating from the camps; police referred to them as divisional hot spots, breeding grounds for crime and the narcotics trade.[53]

The second act, the formation of "Tent City" on state land across from City Hall in December 1984,[54] was a compelling demonstration of the tactical skill of the homeless as exploiters of a spatial and temporal semiotic. Heretofore excluded from or ignored in political discourse of the city, by this act the homeless forced entry *simply by their presence* across from City Hall. They did so, moreover, at a time when they could most count on that "abstract sympathy" of which Mair speaks—who could deny the plight of the homeless so close to Christmas?[55] Finally, they basked in the protective aura of City Hall not only as homeless but also as "citizens," forcing a common identification with the public, defying treatment as "Other." This tactic, incidentally, had repeated success later in Santa Monica, when, in October 1987, "the City of Santa Monica waived a ban on camping in city parks to allow groups to remain in Pacific Palisades—as long as the stay was temporary."[56]

In a candlelight vigil a group of about forty homeless men and women gathered and sang antiwar songs, quoted Martin Luther King and the Bible, chanted "Justice for the Homeless," and held lighted candles and matches aloft in unison to symbolize their plight. Why was this privilege granted to a group of homeless people who gathered at the site, normally considered a renowned and problematic campground for the homeless? The Mayor of Santa Monica explained: "It was clear to us that this was a political protest. This is a liberal community...we do not discourage nonviolent political protests."[57]

In the former instance, the homeless succeeded at least temporarily in transforming the public image of them, simply by the space they occupied. In the latter instance, they transformed both the meaning of the space and of themselves by the way they chose to occupy it.

The homeless are both painfully aware of and unwilling to accept their stigmatization, and ready to confront new, gentrified users of their turf. On Fourth and Main, where office and government buildings encroach on skid-row, just one block away from the Midnight Mission, clusters of homeless daily confront a parade of status-minded, (relatively) well-dressed professional and clerical workers. Fashion commentary has become a running part of street repartee, a way of acknowledging, challenging, and reversing stigma. "Lady—your suit went out of style five years ago. I know because I designed it," or "Wild Thang"—this ironic comment, delivered with all the intonation that Tone-Loc musters in the MTV video, from an old black man seeing a tired, mouse-gray office worker dragging her briefcase to the bus. These are the comments back from the street that at once *invert and challenge* the relationship between commentator and subject, as well as the meanings of place that they so tenuously occupy.

In a more recent attempt to counter images of skid-row as blighted (and therefore justifiably gentrifiable), two formerly homeless couples performed their wedding ceremonies on the street directly adjacent to a park which was a well-known hangout of the homeless. If the deviance of the homeless could be exposed to the horrified eye of the public, so too could their normalcy.

These are but a couple of examples in a long series of tactical moves through which homeless people have succeeded in inserting themselves into a political discourse, and homelessness has become recognized at least by some as a political issue. These acts themselves do not of course guarantee success, either in transforming the image of the homeless in the minds of the public or guaranteeing them a political voice. Stigma has remarkable resiliency, and these acts can be discredited simply by denying their perpetrators the status of "real homeless." But the point is that the homeless *do act*, and in their tactical reproduction of daily life are perhaps not much different from the office workers in the stories above their heads that De Certeau so fondly describes. As one homeless man put it: "We are people just like anyone else, with hopes and desires, just like they have. And the right of us to exist as human beings under these conditions is a necessity, not a crime."[58]

4

BACK TO THE FUTURE: DEINSTITUTIONALIZATION IN A RECOMBINANT SYSTEM OF JUVENILE CARE

The image is the reality. And . . . I think that's what we have to spend a lot of time on, the image of this problem . . . For a lot of decision makers (in Sacramento) part of their formative years (were) when runaways became really a national issue . . . (when) these kids (were) all portrayed as white, middle class, even affluent kids. And you look at them going through a temporary crisis of adolescence, but you know they are going to make it. They're going to have the resources to pull it together after this period of being on the streets is over . . . none of them are mentioned as potential victims of abuse . . . as victims of exploitation on the streets.

—Jack Rothman with Thomas David, Runaway and Homeless Youth in Los Angeles, 1986; pp. 20–21.

Both in East Los Angeles and South Central kids are running away . . . (but) the definition of status offenders . . . is mostly relevant to a middle-class, white population . . . within the South Central community when kids run away they remain within the community. They may be lost, but they're lost within the neighborhood. The

Young and Homeless in Hollywood

(sic) very different definition than some of the stuff that we're talk-
ing about from kids running away to Hollywood . . . When kids in
those communities surface they surface as 602's (juvenile delinquents) not 601's. (status offenders). These kids don't tend to show
up as the status offender; they are going to be arrested.

— Anonymous, *Runaway and Homeless
Youth in Los Angeles*, 1986; p. 120.

In the mid-1970s, the deinstitutionalization of juvenile *status offenders* from the traditional system of juvenile care reflected and responded to a broad change in attitudes towards concepts of juvenile delinquency and modes of treatment of juvenile offenders. Status offenders, as opposed to juvenile delinquents, were youths whose acts were deemed illegal by virtue of their age (such as smoking, drinking, or skipping school). The modern juvenile-care system was founded at the turn of the century on the precept that all adolescents, if left to themselves, were potentially delinquent, but that all delinquents were inherently reformable. By the 1970s, however, this premise began to be seriously questioned, raising the possibility of a return to earlier concepts of youth and youthful behavior, revolving around a more polarized view of harmless pre-cocity versus the hardened criminality of the "dangerous classes"— in short, a return to premodern views of youth.

It is within this context that a sympathetic view of runaway and homeless youths emerged. But this view was built and not born. Service providers had to build this image by negotiating a pathway between two extremes. Homeless youths could neither be viewed as youths "going through a temporary crisis of adolescence" who nevertheless had "the resources necessary to pull themselves together"—suggestive of premodern views of precocious youths— nor could they be simply left to themselves and be allowed to surface as juvenile criminals, in an atmosphere that was increasingly punitive rather than rehabilitative—suggestive of views of juvenile criminals as members of the "dangerous classes." In subsequent chapters I will show how youth workers and service providers in Hollywood struggled successfully to build a sympathetic, place-based image of homeless and runaway youths, and how they are attempting to extend this image outwards from Hollywood to include, among others, youths who are not minors, and youths who are not strictly homeless but who grow up in an atmosphere of neglect. In this chapter, it is necessary to begin by describing the

Back to the Future

contemporary terrain of images of *juvenile delinquency* and *criminality* that service providers must contend with, and the range of institutional responses that characterize the current system of juvenile care.

There are three salient features to this newly developing system of juvenile care, which I will deal with in turn in this chapter. These are: the breakdown in consensus about concepts of juvenile delinquency and its appropriate treatment; the influence of pervasive urbanization on modes of treatment; and the growth of a "soft state" which developed partly in response to criticisms about the juvenile penal system.

First, this new system signals a breakdown of broad consensus in the juvenile system which emerged at the turn of the century, and the concepts of *adolescence* and *delinquency*[1] which sustained it. Focusing strictly on institutional shifts, it is clear that the emergent system reflects a bifurcated approach, diverging in its views and modes of treatment of status offenders and criminal offenders.[2] But this divergence in views towards status and criminal offenders is, in a sense, a move "back to the future," with a complex fusion of characteristics and assumptions of the *modern* juvenile justice system, and *premodern* views and treatments of youthful misbehavior.

At one pole, we find the return of the idea that criminal activities of youth now constitute a fundamental threat to society.[3] Of course, it might be argued that the increasingly "get-tough" approach to juvenile criminal offenders is a response to a new quality of violence and predation in youth gangs. But this shift has also occurred in the context of rising expectations and diminishing opportunities for inner-city youth, and has been accompanied by a severe reduction in programs originally intended to divert inner–city youth from criminal activity and provide them with job skills or recreational opportunities. Moreover, while lower-class behaviors of youth were simply tolerated in premodern times, and in the modern era were presumed to lead to delinquency, they are increasingly treated as evidence of potential criminality.[4] At the other pole, the courts and penal system have essentially divested themselves of responsibility for status offenders. Here, as well, there has not been a complete return to premodern conceptions of youth, where youthful precocity was tolerated or even encouraged. Status offenders have been redirected to a "soft state," mandated to serve but not detain.

The second significant feature of the new juvenile system of care is the change in treatment of youthful offenders. This change was more than a simple response to shifting conceptions of criminality and delinquency. In the past twenty years treatment and detention centers have had to contend with rapid and widespread urbanization which has radically altered the context within which they operate. In the traditional system of juvenile care, which includes the California Youth Authority (CYA) and county institutions, the predominant form of placement was in large-scale, remotely located training schools, ranches, and camps. This continues to be the case for juvenile criminal offenders, as the CYA expands its detention centers in the remaining rural areas of California. But services for status offenders and alternative placements for criminal offenders are increasingly located in urban environments. These institutions *have had to renegotiate the sign system of their environment*, producing new images of treatment and detention. Moreover, many of the once-peripheral rural ranches and camps have been engulfed by rapid urbanization, forcing changes in both their mode of operation and the criteria for placement of youths within them.

A number of alternatives are being proposed as a response to urbanization. These include a new periphery of "wilderness camps" for the hard core—organized around the disciplinary regime of boot camps and sustained by the purifying ether of "raw nature." Within the urban core, the "family" (in the form of foster homes, group homes, or temporary shelters) is supplementing the institution as an organizational principle, simultaneously serving the economic and philosophical impulses of the deinstitutionalization movement, and providing a legitimizing, less stigmatized face for surrounding communities.

The third significant feature of the new juvenile system is the rise of the "soft state." The "soft state" grew as a response to the criticisms of the juvenile system, but has had mixed success in addressing the problems identified by its critics. It has not so much transcended the conflicts inherent in that system, as reproduced them within its own structures. These conflicts include mixing of different kinds of offenders, inappropriate detention of youth, institutions that are considered too large to develop affective relationships between youth and counselors, lack of proximity to the families of these youth, and lack of integration into existing communities. But the relative "success" or "failure" of this emergent system for homeless and runaway youth must be evaluated with care. To focus solely on *diachronic changes* in the juvenile system vis-à-vis deinstitutionalization is to lose sight of the context within which these changes occurred. The service network for homeless and runaway youth in Los Angeles County must be assessed both in terms of the original objectives of the move to deinstitutionalize status offenders and in the context of the range of alternative models of treatment currently available within the state.

DEINSTITUTIONALIZATION
AND THE CHALLENGES TO PARENS PATRIAE

The history and characteristics of the California juvenile system have roughly paralleled those in other states, with the formal creation of a juvenile court in 1909, and the definition of delinquent youth who should come under its purview.[5] At the turn of the century, two private reformatories for youth existed in the state—Fred C. Nelles School for Boys, established in 1889 in Whittier (with separate facilities for girls, later to become Ventura School in 1916), and Preston School, a boys' reformatory established in 1890, in Ione, forty miles east of Sacramento. Like other states in the nation, California's juvenile detention practices suffered from a high degree of balkanization, which until 1929 included a variety of institutional forms, from boarding homes (twenty-two counties), to specially designed detention homes (sixteen counties), to hospitals (nine counties), to subsidized homes (six counties). In the mid-1930s, attempts were made to institute a more uniform system of probation and to standardize juvenile-court practices, culminating in the development of the California Youth Authority (CYA) in 1941. Following two suicides and a number of escapes from Whittier State School, the CYA assumed responsibility for the private reformatories and, in theory at least, the establishment of standards for detention and for probation in all counties.

The actual practices of California's juvenile institutions have come under repeated criticism throughout their history. But for many child-savers, the idea of detention was simply a tool to allow for effective treatment to occur. Their attitude reflected the principle of parens patriae, expressed in California's Section 502 W&I Code:

> 502 . . . . to secure for each minor under the jurisdiction of the juvenile court such care and guidance, preferably in his own home, as will serve the spiritual, emotional,

mental, and physical welfare of the minor and the best
interests of the state; to preserve and strengthen the
minor's family ties whenever possible, removing him from
the custody of his parents only when his welfare or safety
and protection of the public cannot be adequately safe-
guarded without removal, to secure for his
custody, care and discipline *as nearly as possible equivalent to that which should have been given by his
parents.*[6]

By the early 1970s, California was detaining proportionately
three times as many juveniles as the national average.[7] A large
percentage of these admissions were status offenders, although
their actual length of stay in the system was generally shorter than for
juvenile criminal offenders. In 1974, the year the federal goverment
deinstitutionalized status offenders, 45,864 of California's wards
admitted to juvenile halls—about 30.5% of its total admissions—were
status offenders.[8] By 1979, the state of California had secure facilities
for about 5,000 young people, including forty-five juvenile halls for
secure detention, and seventy-four camps, ranches, or schools for
the custody of juveniles with a combined capacity of 8,000 beds.[9]

The impetus for deinstitutionalization came from two sources.
On the one hand, there was concern over an appropriate system
of care—which would be both constitutional and effective—for
youths who had committed no real crimes, but only status offenses
(acts such as smoking, frequenting billiard halls, and running away
that were offenses only because they were committed by a
minor).[10] In the wake of youth movements of the 1960s, liberal
juvenile workers were in particular concerned over "mixing" status
offenders in the juvenile halls and county camps with a more criminal
element, as well as the constitutionality of treatment of youths within the juvenile court system.

The liberal faction envisioned an alternative placement
system for status offenders within group homes and the like, in the
community. From the mid-1960s, they began, in effect, to challenge
parens patriae, and won changes in the juvenile-court procedure,
introducing features which made it more like the adult court system.
Their intent was to prohibit juvenile court judges from ignoring
"procedural niceties in order to do what they thought best for
the child"—in effect, they challenged the social orientation of the
juvenile court system, whereby treatment of the delinquent
proceeded at the expense of constitutional rights that were
accorded criminals in adult courts.[11] In subsequent challenges,

Back to the Future

Supreme Court decisions incorporated constitutional rights of due process and proof beyond a reasonable doubt into the juvenile court procedures.[12]

If California had enjoyed a reputation for enlightened policies, and an image as a "standard-bearer" in its juvenile-care system in the early 1960s, by the early 1970s this reputation was all but shattered. A critical climate towards the existing system of juvenile care had begun to take hold from the early 1970s, including presentations by citizens' groups advocating deinstitutionalization, challenges to status offender laws by public-interest lawyers, and the sentiment of probation officers working with a newly developed diversion program for "601s."[13] Detention practices came under widespread and highly publicized criticism following the publishing of *Hidden Closets*[14] by Deputy Director George Saleeby of California's State Probation Department. The report argued that the state's juvenile halls were "needlessly bulging with children as a result of consistent overuse and abuse of detention." The report galvanized concerns about the merits of stigmatizing status offenders and exposing them to a climate which might support criminality.

GETTING TOUGH

On the side of the more conservative element in the juvenile system, moreover, there was a desire to reduce costs and overcrowding in the prison system, as well as a move to take a tougher stance on juvenile criminals. Beginning in the 1950s, youth crimes became increasingly crimes against property and crimes of violence, attributable, in part, to the transformation of street gang culture and the gradual dissolution of incorporative political structures:

> Post–World War II transformation of street gangs ended a pattern of graduation from street-corner gangs to social and athletic clubs and the underside of politics. By the 1950s new types of gangs emerged which were more predatory and less protective.[15]

By the 1970s, youth were committing more and more spectacularly violent crimes:[16]

> Four days after the 1975 (California) Legislature adjourned, Lynette "Squeaky" Fromme, an avowed member of the

73

Charles Manson clan, held a pistol two feet away from
President Gerald Ford at the State Capitol in Sacramento.
Two weeks later Sara Jane Moore fired at the President
in San Francisco. In the same month Patty Hearst was
arrested. . . .[17]

In this atmosphere of spectacularly violent crime during the
1970s, there was a *double shift* to a more hard-line approach for
youth who had committed criminal offenses—part of a general
"get tough" approach in the criminal justice system—and deinstitutionalization of youth who were simply status offenders, as well as
a more delimited specification of what a status offense was.
This involved restoring jurisdiction over truants, but removing court
jurisdiction on those deemed in "danger of leading an idle, dissolute,
lewd or moral life."[18] There is some evidence, both nationally
and in California, to support the "bifurcation" thesis which
Steinhart suggests in his historical recounting of the forces that led to
deinstitutionalization of the juvenile status offenders in California.[19]
In California, this took the form of a series of proposals specifying
both tougher treatment of criminal youth and a softer approach to
status offenders, packaged together in a State Assembly Bill
(AB 3121) which passed on August 16, 1976.

The "get-tough" tendency within juvenile care has continued,
and by the 1980s was reflected at virtually all levels of the system.
After deinstitutionalization, the distinction between juvenile and
adult court was made increasingly blurry, but by the end of the
1980s, the juvenile court resembled the adult court more because
of its increasingly punitive approach, rather than from the expansion
of constitutional considerations protecting the rights of minors. In
effect, youth going through the juvenile courts by the end of the
1980s were getting the worst of both systems. The statutory purpose
section of juvenile-court law emphasized protection of the public
rather than rehabilitation and, in California, included "such
punishment as may be consistent with rehabilitation."[20]
Criminalization of juvenile law included criteria making it easier to
try certain sixteen- and seventeen-year-olds as adults[21] in adult
criminal court with sentencing to a term in state prison for specific
offenses. Minors convicted of serious crimes were subject to man-
datory state prison sentences.[22]

The "get-tough" tendency was reflected not only at the
legislative level, but also at the administrative level, specifically
in the operational procedures governing parole. Between 1979 and
1989, the Youthful Offender Parole Board of California revised its

sentencing guidelines three times, increasing parole consideration dates for seventy-five percent of offenses, and within these, doubling the amount of time served before parole for 38% of offenses.[23] Minimum confinement times for youthful offenders were also routinely increased by adding disciplinary time and discretionary time to sentences, as well as requiring clinical treatment as part of time served, a specification which rendered youth who had completed their sentence ineligible for parole, because they were waiting in line to get into a Board program. From 1981 to 1982, time added to juvenile confinement for disciplinary reasons totaled 5,444 months statewide; from 1985 to 1986, time added under this procedure was up 138%, to a total of 12,959 months. Similarly, time added to minimum sentence for discretionary reasons increased 374% in the same period, from 3,526 additional months from 1981 to 1982 to 15,452 months from 1986 to 1987. Finally, unlike adult wards, juvenile wards did not get automatic time cuts in sentencing for good behavior; juvenile commitments to the CYA spent, on average, 4.3 months longer in detention than adult felons sentenced to and housed in the youth authority.[24]

Critics argued that the combined impact of these parole policies contributed to an attitude of "maxing out" among the detained youth: with little incentive to meet disciplinary standards, and with increasingly overcrowded conditions, they would simply "kick back" and decide to do all their confinement time.[25] The combined effect of Parole Board policies and the reactions of youth has increased the time served per youth in the state of California by an average of 7.9 months. By 1988, 9,000 youths between thirteen and twenty-five years were housed in facilities designed for 5,840, and which eight years ago housed only 4,500 youths.[26]

This shift towards a "get-tough" approach is also evident nationwide. Between 1978 and 1981, over half the states had legislation which transferred handling of serious and chronic juvenile offenders to adult courts, leading Krisberg to argue that a watershed had been reached in juvenile reform.[27] Statutory changes were identified in three main areas: those that facilitated prosecution of juveniles in adult courts (California and Florida); those lowering the age of judicial waiver (Tennessee, Kentucky, and South Carolina); and those excluding some offenses from juvenile-court jurisdiction altogether (Illinois, Oklahoma, and Louisiana).[28] A general increase in incarceration rates paralleled the move to try some juveniles as adults, as national rates of confinement in juvenile detention increased by fifty percent between 1977 and 1985, and rates of juvenile incarceration in training schools increased sixteen percent. By 1988, at least half of the states nationwide had instituted laws that made it easier to try children as adults, contributing to the incarceration of approximately 4,000 juveniles in state prisons annually.[29]

If rates of incarceration are any measure of failure of the preventative programs within the larger system of juvenile care, California's system has drastically failed its minority youth. In 1981, in Southern California's Region III, covering 2,500 square miles and including 7,125,700 people, 45% of the regional caseload of juvenile parolees came from Central and South Central Los Angeles, where the concentration of youth of color is highest.[30]

More recently, the Commonweal Report noted, in 1988 :

> The Youth Authority is becoming an institutional gulag for minority youth . . . while black youth comprise only 9% of the population at risk, they constitute 39% of the Youth Authority's inmates and are committed at six times the rate of whites. Hispanics, comprising 26% of the youth population (and fastest growing segment), account for 31% of the Youth Authority population and are committed at twice the rate of whites. The Youth Authority itself projects that, by the Year 2000, minorities will constitute 75% to 80% of the institutional population.[31]

In spite of the rising publicity on youth violence, violent crimes among youth, both nationally and in the state of California, have been decreasing. (see Figure 2.)

Studies critical of California's detention practices argue that only 51.5% of CYA's current wards are violent or chronic offenders. The rest have been either: misassigned (12.5%); could be diverted to community-based programs (11.5%); or have been committed for nonviolent crimes (25%).[32]

Whatever one thinks about the constitutionality, efficacy, or deservedness of the "get-tough" approach, when viewed in the context of broad changes in support structures for lower-class youths, it is undeniable that once widely held ideas about the possibility of sustained "democratized adolescence" through institutional support structures are now rapidly disintegrating.

Figure 2: California Juvenile Justice Profile 1976–1986

	1976	1986
At-Risk Population	3,797,000	3,444,000
Juvenile Arrests	352,294	235,800
Juvenile Felony Arrests	103,003	76,192
New Probation Referrals	162,150	124,838
Youth Authority Census	4,432	8,138
CYA Parole Caseload	7,594	4,345

Sources: California Youth Authority; Bureau of Criminal Justice Statistics; and the CYA's Population Management and Facilities Master Plan 1987–1992. in de Munro, p. 1.

One must look at this new hardened approach to juvenile crime in the context of cutbacks in support systems and alternatives for these youth. To begin with, these policies have been developed in an era of increasing "juvenilation" of poverty. For instance, in Los Angeles County, by 1980, over 40% of all children in the county lived below or just above the official poverty line. For that same year, in the sixty-six poorest census tracts in the county, with median family incomes under $10,000, 70% of census tracts had a median age of twenty to twenty-four years.[33] This trend towards concentration of poverty among the younger cohorts of the population appears to be on the rise: within the state of California, in 1979, 15.7% of the people in poverty were children; by 1984 this figure had risen to 23.1%.[34] Job opportunities for the young urban poor, and in particular for youth of color (overrepresented in CYA's institutions), are increasingly limited. Unemployment among black youth in Los Angeles County is, by some estimates, around 45% in spite of unbroken regional growth.[35] Youth employment schemes, once active in inner-city neighborhoods, have also come under successive attacks, beginning with the dismantling of the Neighborhood Youth Corps, and culminating in the termination of a Comprehensive Employment and Training Act.[36] Municipal programs such as the Los Angeles Summer Job Program have been cut back at the moment when youth gang activity has peaked as an issue of public concern.

California has dropped from ninth to thirty-third place in its per-capita expenditure on students, and by the late 1980s, it spent on its own students approximately a third of the monies provided for school for students in the state of New York. The increase in single-parent families and increase in families with both parents working have also led to a growth in unsupervised latchkey children, now estimated at about 250,000 to 350,000 in Los Angeles County, at a time when schools are cutting back on after-school programs.[37] Recreational opportunities for inner-city youths are also diminishing, as parks are being closed off and maintenance cut back. If, as social historians argue, the broad system of juvenile care was established to support and further the norms of middle-class families, this system is being transformed at a time when "normal" family structures are breaking down.

STATUS OFFENDERS

Steinhart attributes the bifurcation of the juvenile-justice system in California to a climate of horse-trading between liberals and conservatives in this period, with hard-liners introducing a series of "get-tough" policies in reaction to highly publicized adolescent crimes of the period, and with liberals threatening to block these policies unless a softer approach to noncriminal offenders was introduced as well.[38] At the statutory level, this included modification of the definition of a status offender. In California between 1937 and 1961, the definition of a status offender was so broad and inclusive as to consider minors who habitually visited public billiard rooms or habitually smoked cigarettes to fall under the purview of the juvenile courts. By the early 1970s, the definition had dropped specific references to smoking and billiards, but was still rather broad. In 1975, the definition of status offender was subject to further restriction, when the definition was amended by the legislature to delete reference to minors "in danger of leading an idle, dissolute, lewd or immoral life." However, runaways were still included in the definition of status offenders, and remained unaffected by the change in legislation until 1977, when status offenders were deinstitutionalized. The shift to a more hard-line approach in juvenile law prompted liberal and conservative elements in the juvenile- care system to press for a different system of treatment for noncriminal youth. In 1970, this began with hearings on the juvenile-court process within the Assembly Criminal Procedure Committee of the California Legislature. The report of the committee determined: "The single greatest thing wrong with Section 601 (covering status offenders) is that it uses criminal procedures and institutions to control non-criminal behavior."[39]

The re/decriminalization of youth, and more importantly the deinstitutionalization of status offenders as a consequence of

California State Law AB3121, (1976) had drastic implications for transient youths in California, paralleling developments in the system of mental health care: deinstitutionalization proceeded without the development of alternative facilities. In one proposed scenario, the portion of AB 3121 proposed by Assemblyman Alan Sieroty (Democrat, Beverly Hills) would have cost approximately seventy-five million dollars.[40] The bill passed with the prohibition of secure detention of status offenders, but without the costly services mandated. Statewide, juvenile hall admissions of status offenders dropped from 33,344 (25.4% of total admissions) in 1976 to 607 (0.6%) in 1977. In Los Angeles County, juvenile-hall admissions under section 601 were eliminated completely in 1977 after attaining levels of 6,118 in 1975 and 3,929 in 1976.[41]

In addition to a lack of state-level funding, local governments were effectively prohibited from shifting funds formerly used for the secure detention of status offenders to the development of nonsecure (that is, non lock-up) facilities by Proposition 13.[42] Moreover, general police contact with these youth was severely limited. There were substantial drops in arrests and referrals of status offenders over the same period, so that increasing numbers of these youth were not brought into the system at all, even with the reinstatement of limited secure placement (up to seventy-two hours) to check the minor for prior arrests, locate parents or guardians, and so on.[43]

THE DECLINE OF RURAL CAMPS AND RANCHES

> The new penology emphasized the corruptness and artificiality of the city; from progressive education it inherited a concern for naturalism, purity, and innocence. It is not surprising, therefore, that the cottage plan also entailed a movement to a rural location. The aim of penal reformers was not merely to use the countryside for teaching agricultural skills. The confrontation between depraved delinquents and unspoiled nature was intended to have a spiritual and regenerative effect. "Under a new atmosphere of kindness, sympathy, comfort, and self-respect," said Charles Loring Brace, "many of their vices drop from them like the old and verminous clothing they left behind. . . . The entire change of circumstances seems to cleanse them from many bad habits." Out in the country "they are not so liable to fall in with bad company and idleness does not lead them to its dangers."
>
> —Anthony Platt, "To Cottage and Country"
> in *The Child Savers: The Invention of Delinquency*
> 1969: 65.

Young and Homeless in Hollywood

Those country days are gone now.

—Charles Hamson, Deputy Director,
Los Angeles County Probation Department,
California, telephone interview, 1991.

If the past three decades have been marked by a rethinking of concepts and statutory definitions of juvenile delinquency, modes of treatment and institutional responses have come under scrutiny as well. The system was conceived of as a multi-tiered one which, in theory, placed the most serious offenders in California Youth Authority detention facilities (with the facilities themselves internally differentiated according to client group), and those who had committed milder offenses in county ranches and camps.[44] Juvenile halls were originally designed and conceived of as temporary holding facilities for minors who were waiting for proceedings within juvenile courts.

The California model of juvenile detention echoes turn-of-the-century thinking on the benefits of rural environments as a rehabilitative milieu, what Platt characterized as a broad turn away from congregate housing in the city, to group living in the country.[45] While the California model favors the country, it leaves the cottage behind. In spite of repeated efforts to adopt a cottage model of detention, CYA planners have bowed to economies of scale, favouring large dormitory settings for 60 to 100 youths.[46] As the facilities became increasingly overcrowded, mixing of different groups of offenders was the rule rather than the exception.[47]

At the county level, the model of institution which came to dominate in California was, without question, the large-scale rural institution or camp. State law permits counties to operate camps for up to 100 youths in most counties, and up to 125 youths in Los Angeles and Kern Counties. Most of these camps are "open"—that is, youth are not permitted to leave, but there is no secure perimeter or enclosure.[48] Although rural reform schools have existed in California since the turn of the century, the model of large-scale, rurally based ranches and camps that has come to characterize California's juvenile-detention system was actually pioneered during the Depression by Los Angeles County, which established a county camp in 1932 to cope with transient youth who migrated to the region in search of work. With the success of this program, in 1935 the state enacted legislation permitting other counties to set up forestry camps like the one in Los Angeles. In 1945 it backed up legislation with subsidies for these county-based institutions, resulting in a total of sixteen county camps by 1947 to supplement the CYA system. Increased state subsidy in the late 1950s encouraged further expansion, and by 1970, sixty-eight county camps were in operation, fixing the large-scale rural institution as the model for CYA detention. This number dropped slightly in the next decade-and-a-half, to a total of fifty-three.[49] (See Figure 3.)

Figure 3: California's Local Juvenile Treatment Institutions

Year	Number of facilities	Youth Capacity
1945	11	690
1955-56	16	975
1960-61	31	2,000
1962-63	41	2,800
1964-65	42	2,894
1966-6	50	3,082
1968-69	54	3,476
1969-70	68	3,677
1984	53	3,460

Sources: Blomberg, p. 44; Steinhart p. 46.

The combined system included a total of twelve state-run rural training schools and camps. Until deinstitutionalization in the mid-1970s, status offenders made up a sizeable percentage of camp clientele. In 1970, Paul Lerman estimated roughly half of camp wards to be status offenders; in 1974, at the time of federal deinstitutionalization, estimates were at around 30 %.[50]

The architects of California's juvenile detention camps were perhaps not quite as infused with rural romanticism as the turn-of-the-century child-savers had been—indeed forestry camps and ranches were supported by an array of very pragmatic financial and political considerations, not the least of which were the avail-ability of cheap land to build large-scale institutions, absence of residential opposition to facility locations, and consent of unions, which did not feel as threatened by the creation of a supple-mentary workforce engaged in fire fighting and conservation efforts as they might have been had Youth Authority wards been engaged in work which competed with that of their membership.[51]

But connection between nature and nurture was not entirely absent, either. Consider, for instance, descriptions provided by the U.S. Department of Health, Education and Welfare in its 1960 edition of "Camps for Delinquent Boys. A Guide to Planning," which was published in 1960, immediately prior to the largest wave of camp construction in California:

> (Camps) are likely to be located deep in the forests or along banks of lakes and streams. These combined factors, the intimate day-by-day contact with nature, the simplicity, informality and relative freedom of camp life, are benefi-cial for certain kinds of boys. Here, in unspoiled and unin-fected surroundings, they can make a fresh start in learning to work, play and live with others. . . . Camps located in wooded or hilly areas near a lake of stream can use the natural setting for many kinds of recreation. Such setting gives a camp a rustic and informal atmosphere which con-tributes to the unregimented character of its program. . . . [52]

This belief in the healing capacities of nature persisted into the 1980s, and infused California Youth Authority's 1981 description of their camps, provided in their forty-year retrospective.[53]

The California Youth Authority has maintained its model of large-scale rural institutions, with plans to add an additional 2,916 beds in expanded facilities. (See Figure 4.)

Figure 4:
California Youth Authority
Population Management and Facilities Master Plan 1987–1992

Fenner Canyon Camp	16 beds
Living Unit - Nelles	100 beds
New Camp - Paso de Robles	100 beds
Pre-camp - Preston	100 beds
Living Unit - Paso de Robles	100 beds
Public Service Unit - Ventura	100 beds
Stockton	600 beds
Bakersfield (3 x 600 beds)	1,800 beds
TOTAL PLANNED EXPANSION	2,916 beds

Source: CYA's Population Management and Facilities Master Plan, cited in de Munro, p. 11.

Back to the Future

In Los Angeles County, vestiges of rural romanticism that characterized some of the thinking of turn-of-the-century child-saving institutions are still evident. These are certainly preferable alternatives to contemporary juvenile jails, but the publicity given them in the media belies the more common reality faced by incarcerated youth, of overcrowding and increasing lengths of confinement without adequate provision of rehabilitative programs. For example, in the more remotely located rural ranches and camps, such as Camp Scudder and Camp Joe Scott, whose proximity to Saugus, near Los Padres National Forest, slows the inexorable pace of suburban expansion, the image of summer camp has become ever more central. The following description of the first California detention camp opened exclusively for girls in 1989, and developed as kind of a midway sentencing alternative between foster-home placement and California Youth Authority prisons, is a case in point:

> What is most striking about Camp Scott is the facility's relaxed atmosphere. The visitor is greeted . . . by the incongruous odor of fresh popcorn. The camp's director, Mary Dederick, doesn't refrain from hugging the girls, some of whom she calls "honey." Two of the most popular residents at Camp Scott are the pet dogs, Mikey and Missy. "Not much like a jail, is it?" Dederick laughingly asks as she scoops up a handful of popcorn. The Center resembles a summer camp more than a detention camp. Inmates enjoy a variety of social activities including a choir and monthly dances with boys from neighboring Camp Scudder.[54]

Underlying the preference for rural locations was the sustained sense that youth were better rehabilitated when removed from their original environments—an extension of the nineteenth-century idea that "deviancy was primarily the result of the corruptions pervading the community, and that organizations like the family and the church were not counterbalancing them, . . . a setting that removed the offender from all temptations and substituted a steady and regular regime would reform him."[55] Until recently, according to Charles Hamson, Deputy Director of the Los Angeles County SODA PAD, and twenty-eight-year veteran with the Los Angeles County Probation Department, this attitude permeated the Los Angeles County Probation Office:

> I did placement as a DPO in the middle sixties and we used to think that way. When I was putting a kid in camp,

for example, I'd put him at Circle Y Freedom Ranch out in Lancaster. . . . (You used to) figure you put him out at Mrs. So and So's or Circle Y Freedom Ranch and he's not going to have all those street folks to interact with, gangs and stuff, and he's out there by himself.[56]

But just as urbanization in a broad sense "produces" an appreciation of nature, new forms of urbanization transform and alter this appreciation. Widespread urbanization in many counties in California during the late 1960s and early 1970s has engulfed once rural ranches and camps, and substantially undercut the last vestiges of "rural romanticism" evident in juvenile rehabilitative settings. Charles Hamson offered these insights on the changing context of ranches and camps and its impact on both philosophies of treatment and criteria for placement of young wards:

> Those country days are gone now. Antelope Valley has so many group homes now it's an inner city. It was a rural place, and now look. Pomona, Glendora, San Dimas, Chino Valley . . . remember Chino Valley was "prison valley"? It's a bedroom community (now). So where are you going to send them? Some of the ranches are still around, Boys' Republic in Chino, Rancho San Antonio in Chatsworth, used to be kinda country, San Fernando Valley had fields—those are the two top group homes in the county. There was a place out in Woodland Hills. The Probation Department ran forestry camps. The O.C.C. camps were copied after our camps. The other places are privately run group homes. We still have the camps, we run fifteen camps, but they're not too rural anymore. Camp Afflerbaugh and Camp Page in the foothills of Pomona (where) we used to take kids out hiking and running—there are houses right up to it now. [57]

When once-rural ranches and camps have become engulfed in the pervasive exopolis,[58] "child-savers" have had to alter both their criteria for placement of delinquent youths and their organizational ethos to meld better with the surrounding environments. Hamson continues:

> Have you been out to Lancaster lately? It's a city. There is not much rural property left, so we emphasize that in our training all placements in SODA PAD are communi- ty- based no matter how rural the setting, and if a kid cannot behave himself just like where you live, don't put him there.[59]

Back to the Future

The service network for homeless and runaway youths in Hollywood, which replaces ranches and camps as a rehabilitative environment, is the return to a model of "congregate living in cities" for noncriminal offenders. But was not an automatic product of widespread urbanization. It was one of a range of responses to status offenders within California and other states. Alternatives include the virtual incarceration of these youths in wilderness camps, their private internment in psychiatric hospitals, or placement in the Conservation Corps. Each of these alternatives draws from its environment to expound a new organizational ethos. Experimentation with alternative forms of placement is not well developed in California, but the combined impact of severe overcrowding and fiscal strain on traditional institutions, coupled with renewed pressures to find diversified placements for different kinds of offenders is causing many critics of the system to look elsewhere for placement models.[60]

THE PERIPHERALIZATION
OF JUVENILE THERAPEUTIC ENVIRONMENTS

One response of child-saving institutions to contemporary suburban expansion has been a ripple of geographic peripheralization, as camps and programs push deeper into the wilderness. Though few in number, and operating mostly outside the state of California, in the neighboring states of Nevada and Arizona, privately run wilderness camps have been a destination point for both delinquent and non-delinquent youths placed there by the California Department of Social Services. The California Youth Authority has also experimented with an intensive wilderness program called S.U.N. (Survival Under Nature), a three-week survival trip in the High Sierra or the desert through which juvenile criminal offenders can gain early release credits.[61]

Here the healing capacity of the (once) rural affective community is being replaced by the potent elixir of raw nature. Childsavers from the turn of the century to the late 1960s could extol the appreciation of nature in fresh-air camps and ranches of the rural-urban hinterland—an appreciation still evident in the description of Camp Joe Scott above. Now, as a result of pervasive urbanization, programs must locate in deserts and "backcountry," and center around the conquering of nature as a rehabilitative act. One only has to sample the School and Camp Directory pages of *Sunset: The*

Magazine of Western Living to see the ethos underlying a new breed of "wilderness therapy."

The wilderness is the locus for a new breed of "outward bound" programs—now oriented towards troubled youths rather than adventurers—as depicted in the advertisements. But it has also found affinity with a new style of "muscular Christianity," as evangelical programs such as VisionQuest have turned to the wilderness as the locus for a multimillion-dollar juvenile-treatment program. The California Department of Social Services currently sends both delinquent youths and status offenders, at a cost of 36,000 dollars per youth per year, to a privately run camp in Nevada called Rite of Passage, as one alternative to placement in private group homes, county-run programs, or the California Youth Authority. California itself has no provision to license such a camp under the Department of Social Service Regulations for child-care facilities. However, in 1986, Assemblyman Larry Stirling (Republican, San Diego) was responsible for initiating a bill to permit the operation of "wilderness camps" in the state of California. The bill is backed by VisionQuest, which runs the Nevada program as well as other wilderness camps and a wagon train for about six hundred delinquent youngsters.[62]

The California Conservation Corps represents a second wilderness placement option for homeless and runaway youths, and one that is currently supported by state mandate.[63] In 1988/89, the California Conservation Corps was mandated by the State of California to give priority to homeless and runaway youths. Before this time it had done so on an informal basis, but according to Recruitment Officer Gil, had not attracted many youths to the program. The number of homeless and runaway youths in the statewide program has averaged about fifty per year in its seventeen centers throughout the state (with highest enrollment in winter months). The program offers full-time paid employment in conserving and enhancing the state's environment, and requires a high degree of discipline and responsibility due to some of the activities involved, such as fire fighting. At the same time youth attend school to complete high-school education. However there has been an extremely high attrition rate — roughly 75% of these fifty youths drop out every year. The staff attributes this to the extremely structured nature of the program, which most homeless and runaway youths are not able to cope with. [64]

Back to the Future

THE HOSPITAL ALTERNATIVE

An alternative development to wilderness programs has been to place status offenders in hospital "lock-up" wards, effectively bypassing the intent of deinstitutionalization. Privatization of psychiatric facilities for troubled minors has created a legal twilight zone which circumvents attempts to give juveniles due process in the event of hospitalization. In 1977, the State Supreme Court ruled that minors of fourteen years or older could not be confined in state hospitals without an administrative hearing at which the minor could contest the commitment. In the 1980s, the growth of private psychiatric facilities, coupled with pervasive television advertising about the need to hospitalize "troubled teens," has enabled parents to volunteer their children for treatment, even if the child protests admission, and has denied the children the right to terminate treatment. For that portion of the population who can pay for it, this practice effectively circumvents procedural rights granted under the Lanter-Petris Short Act of 1969, which prohibits commitment to a state hospital unless a person is gravely disabled, and ends indefinite commitment of the seriously mentally ill. Richard Polanco (Democrat, Los Angeles), Chairman of the State Assembly's Subcommittee on Mental Health and Development, notes that in the 1980s there was a marked increase in admissions of minors to private psychiatric facilities. In 1988, 35,000 adolescents were admitted nationwide—more than double the figure in 1980. He notes further:

> Fuelling admission of minors to acute psychiatric hospitals are generous health insurance policies that cover psychiatric hospitalization. Insurance companies usually do not reimburse for the least restrictive treatment, such as outpatient therapy. It is no wonder that private hospitals have found it lucrative to provide inpatient treatment, charging up to $800 per day, for adolescents who might otherwise be treated as well or better through outpatient therapy.[65]

FROM THE FOREST TO THE FAMILY

Wilderness camps and private hospitalization represent two alternative programs to rural camps and ranches for homeless and runaway youth. By far the predominant response, however, has been the use of existing family structures by the state as an adjunct to the traditional juvenile system of care. California is currently using family structures—foster homes and group homes—for a wide variety of placement needs, ranging from probation alternatives and temporary holding tanks to relieve pressure in juvenile hall, to long-term care. The philosophy underlying this placement form represents a 180-degree turn from that sustaining rural ranches and camps. The emphasis is no longer on the need to isolate wards from their communities, but the need to stave off problems following their reintegration into these communities by sustaining, as much as possible, community contacts through the period of detention.

In the development of a private system of care, again California leads the way. California has the largest group-home network in the nation, with a capacity for up to 14,000 children. The number of group homes in the state rose markedly after deinstitutionalization, from 744 in 1979 to a current 1,396.[66] In 1988, the alternative system as a whole far outstripped the capacities of the traditional one, with 42,111 children in foster care, and 10,309 in group homes, compared to 9,034 in California Youth Authority prisons, ranches, and camps.[67]

With increased dependence on existing family structures to supplement the traditional system of juvenile care, the curious twist in the traditional juvenile system after 1974 has been that the concept of *parens patriae* has not been so much abandoned as inverted. *Parens patriae* has been characterized as the notion that "care and treatment should be provided by the state to reform minors in trouble."[68] As such the state either complemented or supplemented the activities of the family. However, new developments signal a willingness of the state to legislate more directly into the activities of parents in their treatment of their children, and to use existing family structures wherever possible as an alternative to costly institutions and programs. At its extremes, this has taken two forms.

The first is attempts to legislate directly into "intact" families that until now were not under legal jurisdiction. For example, the "creative" use of the Street Terrorism Enforcement and Prevention Act to file charges against a mother, with penalties of up to a year in jail and a $2,500-fine for allegedly allowing her son to participate in a youth gang is a case in point. The introduction of the Street Terrorism Enforcement and Prevention Act in California in 1989 (not yet tested in court at the time of writing)—nicknamed "Baby Rico" because it was modeled on the federal government's Racketeer Influenced and Corrupt Organizations Act (RICO)—is indicative of this development. In the late 1970s, social historians were gently suggesting that scholars and youth workers had in the past made too hasty a connection between "gang membership" and delinquency. They anticipated and argued for a more tolerant interpretation of behaviors of lower-class youths. Fifteen years later, State law took a 180-degree turn, in defining gang membership among adults as a felony, with a potential sentence of up to three years in prison simply for belonging to a gang.

The second form of inversion of the concept of *parens patriae* is the massive expansion of a foster care system which has, in the pessimistic view, commodified family relationships as a cheaper alternative to institutionalization. Statewide, California leads the nation in the size of its foster care system. The foster care system for abused and neglected children in Los Angeles County, overseen by the Department of Children's Services, is, together with New York City's, one of the two largest in the United States. Since 1984, the Department of Children's Services has been authorized to directly intervene in child-parent disputes, to remove children from their parents, and to place them in foster homes. Average case loads for social workers in this program are approximately seventy per month.[69] It currently supervises about 50,000 children, with 33,000 of these in foster homes in any one time.[70] Taking custody of approximately 1,000 children per month, the county system has experienced such rapid and extreme growth as to defy adequate supervision.[71] With cases of abuse surfacing, the state has currently directed an inquiry into the program's operations, and public interest lawyers have filed a class action suit against the county. Moreover, attorneys claim that, with foster children comprising less than 1% of the state's juvenile population, but 25% of the delinquents in California Youth Authority custody, the current system is in effect "building an underclass."[72]

CONCLUSION

If we examine the emergence of a service network for homeless and runaway youths in California within the context of broader changes in the system of juvenile care, two main issues become apparent. First of all, service providers have had to contend with shifting attitudes towards juvenile delinquency and the unraveling of consensus about what delinquency was and how it should be treated, reflecting a fundamental transformation in the modern system of juvenile care. In California and other states, this took the form of an increasingly "get-tough" approach to juvenile criminals and expansion of the penal system, and a *laissez-faire* attitude towards status offenders, in some ways symptomatic of a return to a premodern attitude towards youth and youthful misconduct. This increasingly punitive attitude towards juvenile offenders was emerging, moreover, in the context of dwindling support structures for these youths, increasing "juvenilization" of poverty, and a deterioration of the "traditional" nuclear-family structures that the modern juvenile system of care was designed to promote and support. Service providers would have to build an image of homeless and runaway youths that treads the path between "precocious youths" and "the dangerous classes."

Secondly, while concepts of youthful misbehavior and modes of treatment were changing, in many counties the environment in which treatment took place was changing as well. In Los Angeles County, widespread urbanization was undercutting the last vestiges of rural romanticism that had imbued the state and county system of correctional ranches and camps for youthful offenders. The locational strategies originally adopted by the counties and the California Youth Authority—in particular choosing secluded areas for the regenerative attributes of a "return to nature"—was, for heavily urbanized regions like Los Angeles County, no longer practicable. In a climate which decried the impersonal and stigmatizing impact of large-scale institutions, and which legally prohibited incarceration of runaways, service providers would have to develop an organizational ethos which was both appealing to the youths they served and nonthreatening to the communities in which they located.

5

PUNK HOLLYWOOD:
REDRAWING THE MAPS OF MEANING

A culture includes the "maps of meaning" which make things
intelligible to its members. These "maps of meaning" are not
simply carried around in the head: They are objectivated in the
patterns of social organization and relationship through which
the individual becomes a "social individual."

—Clarke et al., *Resistance through Rituals*,
1987, p. 10.

When you told me you were doing your project on homeless
youth, I thought of Covenant House, and these kids who come
here from the Midwest. . . . I definitely thought fourteen-year-old
girls on the street. But I never thought me, 'cause we weren't
"homeless youth."

—Frank, member of punk squatting scene
1978 –1982.

The term "the homeless" is paradoxical. Scholars and service
providers use it routinely but almost immediately disavow its useful-
ness, noting that "the homeless" are an extraordinarily diverse and
heterogeneous group that defies any single categorization. This dis-
claimer is generally made to emphasize the complexity of services

needed to help homeless people. It is rarely used to acknowledge the various assertive identities that the homeless people seize for themselves to challenge their stigma as homeless.

When runaway youths were deinstitutionalized in the mid-1970s, they soon joined the ranks of "the homeless," in the absence of alternative services. But it was not as *homeless* that they defined themselves first and foremost, but as *youth*. This struggle for self-definition was expressed in a tactical inhabitation of space which has enjoyed a limited success. In Los Angeles County, the struggle resulted in a shifting regional concentration of services for homeless youth, from places specifically for "the homeless" (for instance, skid row) or appropriate suburban environments for the youth (for instance, suburban foster homes), to Hollywood, where the youth themselves preferred to congregate. The struggle for self-definition was also expressed for a limited time in the strategic control of space by youth within Hollywood in the late 1970s, when many homeless youth defined themselves in terms of an oppositional sub-culture of punk squatters. Between the mid-1970s and 1990, the loss of alternative supports within a counterculture and the gradual closing off and control of the social space of Hollywood by planners and providers of social services to homeless youths reduced the degree to which youths could sustain a self-defined social and public identity.

Nevertheless, the historical geography of homeless youths in Hollywood contradicts contemporary analyses of the formation of a service network for the homeless and the factors constructing the social identity of the homeless. This analysis interprets the socio-spatial processes that construct the identity of the homeless in a descending hierarchy of three levels. At the top is the process of urbanization defining prime and marginal space; second are the locational decisions of service providers. Subordinate to these two are the microspatial practices of homeless people themselves. For homeless youths, however, all three aspects evolved in a mutually defining, if unequal, relationship.

This chapter will examine some of the strategies and tactics used by youths to achieve this self-definition in the absence of social services for them. It begins by identifying the features that Hollywood shares in common with other places where homeless youths congregate to illustrate the extent to which homeless youths draw on a social identity as youths in order to survive. It then examines the factors contributing to the formation and dissolution of a punk squatting subculture in Hollywood. Space in general, and spaces of symbolic value in particular, played a crucial role in sustaining the subculture and the youths' ability to define their social and public identity as punks. Finally it examines the contemporary social space of Hollywood in terms of survival practices of homeless youth in the late 1980s. This section, addressing the spatial organization of the drug trade, panhandling, and prostitution in the Hollywood area, serves to illustrate the increasingly limited resources available to homeless youth outside of the services provided to them locally.

DEINSTITUTIONALIZATION OF RUNAWAY YOUTHS

The de-institutionalization of runaway youths in the mid-1970s was part of a massive expulsion of young people from the juvenile correctional system onto the streets of American cities. National figures estimate, somewhat conservatively, about one million young runaways in any given year.[1] State and county figures within California suggest about 200,000 to 400,000 runaways *in the state alone*—almost half the nationally estimated figure. In the City of Los Angeles, in the year before deinstitutionalization, the Los Angeles Police Department took approximately 3,900 runaways into custody. Six years later this number had dropped to about seven hundred (see Figure 5), suggesting there were large numbers of runaway youth in Los Angeles who had no contact with the juvenile care system. Deinstitutionalization had turned an unprecedented number of youth loose on the street, and on the streets they turned primarily to Hollywood.

Although Hollywood has always had associations with a seamy underside, since the mid-1960s this seamy underside has expanded. With the liberalization of obscenity laws relaxing restrictions on what could be shown in movie houses, avant-garde theaters in Hollywood, popular in the 1950s art scene, switched to pornographic films. This provoked a flood of "adult-entertainment" activities with a proliferation of topless bars, massage parlors, and live sex shows, concentrated along Western and Santa Monica Boulevards. By the late 1960s, the sex trade was firmly entrenched in Hollywood, with street prostitution especially focused along Sunset Boulevard. The burgeoning of the adult entertainment industry clashed and coincided with the growth of youth subcultures in the area. Bars and nightclubs along the Sunset Strip, then an odd-shaped section of county-owned land adjoining the City of Los Angeles, filled the void produced by an exodus of nightclub acts to Las Vegas, and began to cater to a generation of youth who, unlike their countercultural counterparts of the 1950s, had purchasing power. Hollywood Boulevard became oriented to the youth trade, with record shops, "head" shops, book exchanges, and so on.[2] From 1969 to 1975, the crime rate in Hollywood increased at double the rate of increase for the city, rising by 7.6% over the six-year period.[3] It was in this volatile geography that juvenile prostitution first consolidated in the Hollywood area.

The relative dominance of countercultural support networks and the exploitative possibilities of juvenile prostitution and drug dealing have shifted over three decades in Hollywood. Although juvenile prostitution and drug dealing were always a feature of the underground,[4] before the mid-1980s, sexual experimentation and drug use appeared to dominate as a form of youth leisure culture. Youths could avail themselves of an extended network within various countercultures as an alternative to drug dealing and prostitution. Since the mid-1980s, prostitution and drug dealing have become increasingly a feature of survival, even among youths who do not self-identify with these survival strategies, that is, those who deal drugs for cash when homeless and who engage only intermittently in trading sex for food, shelter, or cash, an activity which youth workers call "survival sex," rather than prostitution, as these youths do not view themselves as prostitutes.[5]

As revealed below, Hollywood is part of a larger runaway circuit and shares many characteristics with other destinations on that circuit. Nevertheless, the picture emerging over the past three decades in Hollywood is one of increasingly restricted options for homeless and runaway youths. It was in the bleakest period, the mid-1970s, that the punk squatting scene emerged. The dynamics of its formation have much more to do with broader developments in youth subcultures than with the particularities of survival options for runaway youths in Hollywood. But in an atmosphere of rising exploitation of juveniles, and in the hiatus between deinstitutionalization and the development of a service network, it represented a crucial alternative for survival on the streets. As will be examined below, the punk squatting scene differed from other subcultural "solutions" youths have developed in Hollywood, because it seized the very marginality of these youths as an assertive aspect of their identity.

Punk Hollywood

FIGURE 5:
INDICATORS OF NUMBERS OF HOMELESS AND RUNAWAY YOUTHS
LOS ANGELES COUNTY 1976–1989

YEAR	ESTIMATE	SOURCE OF ESTIMATE
1976	3,942	LAPD runaways in custody
1977	2,105	LAPD runaways in custody
1982	705	LAPD runaways in custody (City of Los Angeles)
1981	10,000	United Way Planning Council (County of Los Angeles)
1985	10-20,000	Rothman and David Survey middle range estimate of 28 service providers (County of Los Angeles)
1985	5,000	Hollywood LAPD estimate (Jurisdiction of Hollywood)
1985	3,600	Annual Referrals to Chief Administrative Office (County of Los Angeles)
1986-89	16,950	Shelter agencies in Los Angeles County
1986-89	8,357	sheltered
	8,593	turned away
1989	4,035	handled or turned away by High Risk Youth Service Network

HOLLYWOOD AS PART OF THE RUNAWAY CIRCUIT

There were weeks when they would just migrate out to the beach. Then a bunch would pack up, ten, fifteen would go off to Grand Canyon for a week, then go to Seattle, San Francisco a couple of weeks. . . To a great extent they traveled in groups . . . that's the thing about Travelers Aid—they're meeting the Greyhound buses. That's only going to get the first kid running away the first time. The rest typically hitchhike. . . I think there's a whole network of that, exchanging sex for rides in trucks.

—Dale Weaver, Director of Teen Canteen,
personal interview, 15 April 1991.

95

Young and Homeless in Hollywood

I've had fun.
—Jeff, twenty-three-year-old homeless youth.

The number of homeless and runaway youths nationwide who are part of a runaway circuit is relatively small. Most studies note that about 70% of runaways using services in cities across the United States tend to come from within the immediate geographic area.[6] Hollywood is no exception. In the late 1980s, only about 15% of the 8,600 homeless and runaway youth using services in Los Angeles County came from out of state, and about 25% came from within the City of Los Angeles and an additional 35% from within the County of Los Angeles.[7]

Nevertheless, interviews with youths who "travel the circuit" reveal that Hollywood shares with other communities in the United States several of the characteristics that attract homeless youth.[8] In this sense, Hollywood is far from unique, and the allure of the name alone is not the only reason that youths are drawn there.

The presence of the entertainment industry and desires for stardom are often cited by service providers as reasons for Hollywood's role as a magnet for runaways. But other reasons include a high volume of tourists, a carnival atmosphere, and the presence of a large population of stable youths. Disneyland, Daytona Beach during Spring Break, the campus of the University of California at Berkeley, and the beaches of Southern California have also been recognized as destinations for runaways.[9] There are several practical reasons for the attractiveness of these places. With other youths around in great numbers, one can blend in more effectively than in other areas and make use of infrastructure necessary for basic survival. Where there are high volumes of tourists, one can not only visit the tourist attraction, but also have a high turnover of clients for panhandling. One youth interviewed said he had run to the Berkeley area several times because: "You can take advantage of the facilities that are provided for the college kids—not that the kids will help you or anything, but you can use the showers in the dorms, hang out . . . blend in, and get cheap food."[10]

Another said "I went to Daytona Beach when they had spring break. . . . You didn't have to worry about buying anything 'cause somebody always had it. And there never seemed like there was a party that really stopped, it just went to another place."[11]

"Having fun," as Jeff put it in his interview, is one factor attracting homeless youth to different parts of the country. Before information surfaced about the abuse and neglect of runaway youth both in their families and while on the road, this observation was often used to discredit them, suggesting that they were simply irresponsible. However, roughly 60% of youth out on the street are running from abusive families.[12]

But "having fun" also speaks to the refusal of homeless youth to accept a stigmatized definition of their homelessness,[13] and in the history of service location has had important geographic implications.

In Los Angeles County, for instance, in the years immediately following the deinstitutionalization of status offenders, many service providers assumed that youth would be drawn to an area simply by the presence of services. In short, they categorized the youth in terms of their negative identity as homeless, rather than in terms of their positive identity as youth. In fact, Travelers Aid, the Salvation Army, and the Catholic Archdiocese all initially set up services in skid row on the assumption that homeless youths would follow the same patterns as homeless adults, who were congregating in that area.[14] Contemporary runaways tend to avoid the areas frequented by homeless adults, but historically this was not the case. During the Depression of the 1930s, homeless youths, also called "boy and girl hobos," tended to concentrate in the same parts of the city as their adult counterparts, albeit often in separate, protective gangs. In Los Angeles County during the Depression, the major concern among service providers was to find a way to separate youths and adults.[15]

The development of distinctive youth subcultures in the post–World War II era, compared to the 1930s, may be one reason that youth tend to gravitate to their own parts of the city. Avoidance of violence at the hands of adult homeless people may be another. The skid-row area reported 500 crimes per 1,000 persons per year for 1981 to 1985, compared to 250 per thousand citywide.[16] Among the youth I interviewed, over one-fourth volunteered safety as a reason for staying in Hollywood, in preference to areas such as skid row, citing fear of violence or death as a reason for not going there:

> It's too easy to get shot or stabbed. There's too many people down there who like to take your money and they can do it too. . . . As for the homeless people, its safer here (in Hollywood). I guess it's a different type of people . . . younger generation, too. There's a lot of older people that stay downtown and gangs and stuff, too.[17]

It should not be concluded that Hollywood is particularly safe. Crime rates in the area are only slightly lower than in skid row, running around 470 per 1,000 per year in 1984.[18] One youth revealed that he avoided sleeping in parks or other areas in Hollywood frequented by adult homeless even during the day, and when on the run and unable to find safe shelter, he had several times adopted a strategy of hitchhiking between San Jose and Los Angeles (a trip of about six or seven hours), with the sole purpose of sleeping en route.[19] Hollywood street youths have developed a number of strategies to protect themselves, including cutting out holes in interior walls of abandoned houses or squats to secure secondary exits in case of attack, a practice first adopted by squatting punks.[20] Half of the street youth in a sample of ninety-seven interviewed in 1987 reported having been in gangs as a means of protection, and almost half of those in gangs only joined them while homeless. Three-quarters of these youths carried weapons for protection, and over one-third had been the victims of violent crime.[21]

In spite of the circumstances they run from and the dangers they confront, homeless youths struggle to claim a nonstigmatized identity for themselves, simply by attending to the concerns of most "normal" adolescents, even in the most abnormal of circumstances. Dale Weaver of Teen Canteen recounted:

> There's an enormous amount of grooming going on. . . . I'll never forget this girl we threw out. If they screwed up (in our program), we'd just throw them out for the day, no big deal. . . . She was furious. She was stomping around (and) finally she said, "I need my stuff, you can't put me out for the night without my stuff." So she stomped and went over to her bag (where youths store their belongings at the center), and took out a hairbrush and hairspray and stomped out. And that's what she needed to survive through the night. . . . That's kind of where they're at.[22]

PUNK HOLLYWOOD

> The spatiality and temporality of locales are contextually intertwined and inexorably connected to relations of power from outset to outcome.
>
> —Edward Soja, *Postmodern Geographies*, 1989, 150.

Punk Hollywood

> The real problem, of course, was that we were absolutely unoffi-
> cial and we were not tolerated and as a result you were forced to
> look for alternate kinds of spaces or marginal spaces or spaces
> that became marginal after a time where no one is going to
> bother you . . . we didn't ask for much, we asked to be left alone.
>
> —Frank, Punk Squatter in Hollywood
> 1977–1981.

With the deinstitutionalization of status offenders in California in 1977, many homeless youth gravitating to the Hollywood area became part of a large and fairly stable subculture of punk squat-ters.[23] Punk squatters living in the area between 1976 and 1982 num-bered well over two hundred at their peak. They resisted (sometimes with violence) any attempts to incorporate them into fledgling ser-vices for homeless youths that were being introduced into the area at the time. During this period, punk squatters defined the dominant spectacular youth subculture in the area. But they were neither the only, nor the first, street culture for homeless and runaway youths. Nor can one assume that a dearth of formal support struc-tures "produced" this squatting subculture for homeless and run-away youths in Hollywood. Youth subcultures, particularly in the form of youth gangs, also flourish within the California Youth Authority institutions, in spite of (and some would argue because of) the prison system. In Hollywood, there is evidence of distinctive alter-native subcultures for runaways from the 1950s on, including the Beat Generation and hippies. By the 1970s, additional alternative networks included religious sects such as the Jesus Freaks, the Children of God, the Hare Krishnas, and the Divine Light Mission, as well as an underground newspaper which "allowed kids who worked there to sleep in its office."[24]

The punk squatting subculture in Hollywood should not be seen to stand for all subcultural responses that runaway and homeless youths have developed to deal with their situation. But it does serve to remind us that these youths are not solely victims, but, like other city dwellers, are also creative subjects in the environments within which they live. The sustenance of a distinct identity by punks, and their self-identification *as punks*, rather than as runaways or homeless youths, was intimately bound up in the perpetuation of their squatting subculture, itself dependent on access to and con-trol over particular material and symbolic spaces within the Hollywood area.[25]

Scholars of both spectacular youth subcultures and deviant subcultures have long been aware of the relationship between self and space. Thrasher, for instance, writing in the 1920s, notes that the YMCA attempted, at times, to supplant youth gang subcultures by constructing its facilities on the same plot of land where the youth gangs had their clubhouses.[26] More recently, it was noted that:

> Subcultures . . . are not simply ideological "constructs". . . . They, too, win space for the young: cultural space in the neighborhood and institutions, real time for leisure and recreation, actual room on the street or streetcorner.[27]

A distinct sense of self is manifest in the creation and maintenance of distinct spaces. But space is usually thought of primarily as a metaphor or a manifestation of a distinct subculture, rather than a factor in the production of this subculture.

For the punk squatters in Hollywood, the complicity of "space" and "self" had a number of implications. First, their ability to define and control space was central to their self-definition as punks rather than as homeless youths in need of services—a factor that youth workers had to contend with in attracting them to services. But it was not simply "space" as an undifferentiated container of activity (albeit under their control) which contributed to their identity. Not just any space would do. The account of the rise and decline of punk squatting culture in Hollywood suggests that the symbolic meaning of space is *at least as important* to a subculture as its physical existence. The symbolic importance of space in contributing to and reinforcing the self-image of punks was expressed in their use of the Hollywood area as a whole, both in terms of the spaces they shunned, and the spaces they shared.

Punks actively sought out and appropriated spaces that would reflect, express, and resonate with other aspects of group life. These spaces were *homologous* with the subculture as a whole, consistent with the style of the subculture, intrinsically or in their adapted forms, homologous with the focal concerns, activities, group structure, and collective self-image of the subculture. Homology refers to the symbolic fit between lifestyles and values of a subculture. While popular myth represents this lifestyle as chaotic, and subcultures as lawless forms, subcultures are, in fact, extremely ordered. "Each part is organically related to the other parts, and *it is through the fit between them that the subcultural member makes sense of the world.*"[28]

Scholars of subculture do not extend the application of this concept, homology, to the use of space itself, but rather have treated spaces simply as the place where subculture "takes place." However, the decline of the punk squatting subculture in Hollywood suggests that both the lack of access to *controllable space*, and loss of access to *homologous spaces* contributed to the transformation and decline of this culture. At its peak, the subculture made use of spaces that reinforced notions of the appropriation of the forbidden, the use of objects in a way that emphasized the sartorial, the heretical, or the profane—which were without question the distinctive markers of punk subcultural style. Such was the use of the Hollywood cemetery as a central "living room'" or the squatting of various manor houses reputed for murders or sex orgies. The cordoning off of the cemetery and repeated raids on manor houses by local police forced these youths into the streets and back alleys to compete with other marginal groups for marginal space, and denied them access to important images of self-definition expressed in the symbolic associations with their chosen spaces. *Changes in the nature of space used by these youths both expressed and contributed to a change in the self-perception of squatting youth in Hollywood*.

The punk scene in Hollywood was a subculture and a musical scene. It did not emanate from a street and squatting subculture; rather, its dynamics and philosophy of formation *led it* to a street and squatting subculture. This is not to say that many squatters in the scene did not share some of the characteristics that we might today use to identify homeless youths. As Frank recalls:

> There was a whole bunch of us (the tail end of the "first wave") who were obviously spoiled little upper-middle-class kids from families with too much power, who decided they were going to go off and try something else. . . . 'Cause I mean, let's face it, we could have all gone home (if we wanted). I had more support than most. . . . Most of the people I knew, they didn't have a good situation at home, but if necessary they could go back in an absolute emergency—they had some sort of rudimentary support.

> (But) the fact is with most of them, there are different kinds of abuse, too. . . . some kids were really running from being beaten or sexually molested or having alcoholic parents, and then there were some who were running because their parents were being too restrictive, because their parents wanted them to dress this way or go to that

school. . . . Actually, Tony was a good case of a lot of these kids. His Dad had left and his Mom was alcoholic and really abusive. . . . So I mean he'd go home some-times, and it wasn't really as much of a problem any more, cause he was big enough that he could beat the crap out of her if she went on a bender with him. But he generally didn't want to be there. But he'd go there sometimes to eat. It's hard to sit there and feel bad for yourself when you're in that kind of situation, and there's someone else who's got scars up and down their back from their Mom burning them with a cigarette when she was drunk. . . . There were a lot of women—female chil-dren are at least as abused if not more abused than males and to a large extent that's what made for this scene.[29]

Punk squatters shared more than this background of family abuse with contemporary homeless youth; many of the squatters were adolescents. Punk itself was an adolescent subculture. Many of the bands were formed by teenagers, and clubs which had age restrictions (twenty-one years and over) often suffered a lack of attendance.[30] Not surprisingly, punk squatters were young as well:

My friend Tom and I, we went on the scene together. We were thirteen at the time. Yeah, the youth thing is not all that surprising. A lot of people got into it much earlier than we did. There were a couple of eight-year-olds, who were "full on" in the scene. . . . In some cases their parents supported it.[31]

In the late 1970s, the punk subculture had a substantial core of participants who were part of the squatting scene. Although rela-tively small compared to the numbers of runaway youths who passed through Hollywood each year—by police estimates some-where around 3,900—as a relatively stable street culture, punk squatters were quite a sizeable group. There were about fifty to sev-enty punks squatting in each of the two manors, Doheny and Errol Flynn, and fifteen to twenty more each in three or four condemned apartments around the Hollywood area. After a gig (the perfor-mance of a punk band in a club), squatters and nonsquatters hung out together and numbers could run up to 200.[32] By the early 1980s, squatting punks were largely driven to the streets, now in protective gangs, but their numbers were still fairly significant: Hollywood Street Survivors, a gang formed expressly as a self-protection society for punks living on the street, had somewhere between 100 and 200 members in Hollywood. And by the mid-1980s, the devolution from "punk squatter" to "homeless youth" was almost complete: the demolition of the Garden Court Apartments in 1984 revealed a "frightening wreck" inhabited by "vagrants and punk squatters."[33] There was still a certain resistant kernel of punks and skinheads. But they now occupied a literal and figurative periphery in Hollywood, with services to chronic runaways and chronic homeless youth providing the dominant alternative for initiates—as one youth worker put it "wannabes who didn't understand the consequences of their actions."[34]

This is not to suggest that punk culture did not have its own internal dynamics of formation, diffusion, dissolution, and death, nor that the "punk squatter scene" was transformed *tout court* into a "homeless youth scene." Not all punks were homeless or runaway youths and not all homeless runaway youths would consider themselves punks.

Of the 3,900 runaways that were estimated to come through Hollywood each year in the late 1970s, punk squatters (be they stable or "commuters") were never more than 400 strong. In the late 1970s, punk squatters kept very strict boundaries between themselves and "nonpunks." Outsiders were, in a sense, "mentored in" to the squatting scene only after someone within it knew them long enough to consider them trustworthy and credible.[35] "Poseurs" (that is, pretenders) were not well tolerated. In 1977, Lee and "Shreader" attribute this simply to an "inbred and cliquish" attitude within the scene, noting that:

> There was a lot of talk about who was a "poseur" and who wasn't. Commitment and sincerity were essential, and one had to have punk credibility to join the clan. . . . Many kids who were anxious to get into this new music felt rejected by the "Hollywood 50" (the core of punks in Hollywood) . . . having escaped suburbia, having been outcasts, they now had their own group from which they could sneer and deliver visual jolts to the unimaginative, dumb suburban world.[36]

The distinction between "fans" and "bands" was not clearly drawn either in gigs or squats: "The Punk scene was so much more than the bands—even the fans had their own instant star personas."[37] Part of the punk scene's ethic was that anyone could form a band and that all bands were equal, that there would be none of the star trips that one associated with the corporate music industry. The bands that formed were often part of the squatting scene as well, both in abandoned buildings and in rented ones that became "overrun" with occupants. Punk bands often lived in communal houses, including Dangerhouse in East Hollywood, and the Canterbury, an apartment building reputed to be the site of an unsolved murder dubbed the "Black Dahlia" case.[38]

The death of the punk scene and the incorporation of many homeless youths identified with spectacular subcultures into the service network for "homeless and runaway youth" are reflective of a shift from one dominant constitutive field that was available to these youth in the late 1970s to another in the 1980s. A central factor contributing to this shift was the destruction or reappropriation of marginal space in the Hollywood area. One of the reasons that Hollywood was able to sustain itself for a long time as a node[39] for the punk scene was the availability of "free space."

There were three critical types of spaces supporting the punk subculture in Hollywood, which by Frank's ironic inference, could be likened to the cultural spaces of the new middle class:

> In terms of the space, you really had three types. You had where you were crashing essentially, you had where you were going to gigs, and you had where you were hanging out after the gigs. So it's easy to think of it in terms of— Ooh—before you go to the show, you enter the "master bedroom" and dress appropriately and then you "sit in the theater and enjoy the show," and afterwards you'd go out, "perhaps promenade on the town and have an espresso."[40]

There were places for gigs (clubs and bars); places to crash (abandoned manors and condemned buildings); and places to hang out after a gig (marginal social spaces like the Hollywood Cemetery, or certain accepted joints that were quasi-marginal, such as Danny's Oki Dogs and Astro Burgers, which tolerated punk clientele but were also the target of frequent police raids) (see Figure 6). These were not simply used as *marginal spaces* but at marginal times as well—a significant contrast to the use of Hollywood time-space by homeless youths in Hollywood by the mid- to late 1980s. For the squatting punks, a typical day would begin at two or two-thirty in the afternoon. The day revolved around hanging out and getting ready for a gig, which typically began at ten or eleven P.M. The gig was usually followed by a major social congregation, in Hollywood Cemetery, or Wattles Park, which might begin as late as two the next morning.

Clubs and bars were initially concentrated in the Hollywood

area but, beginning in 1979, suburban locations began to dominate. This process of decentering the subculture outside Hollywood, which in turn began to redefine the social space of the subculture in the center, has curious parallels to other "decenterings" affecting Hollywood's decline, such as the rise to dominance of the suburban shopping mall and the regionalized theme park.[41] Moreover, it had immediate implications for the squatting punks.

> The Hollywood area was really sort of a central hub for the scene. It's a lot like (the relationship between) downtown and Los Angeles. Downtown isn't of itself that interesting, but it winds up being a place where people go anyway. Hollywood was the same way. There was a big concentration of clubs (nearby). A lot of people would come in and eventually they would end up hanging out in Hollywood.[42]

That the squatting punk subculture was able to sustain itself for so long in Hollywood was partly due to the ready availability of condemned buildings for use and, initially, clubs to play in. But the erosion of the quality of marginal space and transformation of the subculture went hand in hand. As one punk noted:

> The manors (Doheny and Errol Flynn) were a pretty early phenomenon. Originally they were groups of like-minded people putting out political tracts, but later they just got to be places where everybody could go and hang out after a gig . . . and you'd have some "commuter punks" who'd essentially use them for a late-night gig when they didn't want to drive home. . . . The rest of us had to be there. . . .We would have stayed at Errol Flynn and "Bad Manner" and always hung out at the Hollywood Cemetery, throughout the whole scene, if it wasn't being constantly closed off and pushed out. It was only that Hollywood was in such a state the whole time that there was always some other shithole to go to. . .[43]

Finding condemned apartment buildings was often preferable to staying in the manors, because the manors were illegal: the manors were rundown but weren't legally condemned and if they were too obvious the squatters would draw the police. But in the early stages, nobody cared if punks squatted a condemned building—they would hang out as long as possible until somebody came to knock the thing down. Methods of finding such buildings were sometimes very sophisticated, which speaks to the considerable

FIGURE 6: PUNK HOLLYWOOD 1977–1980

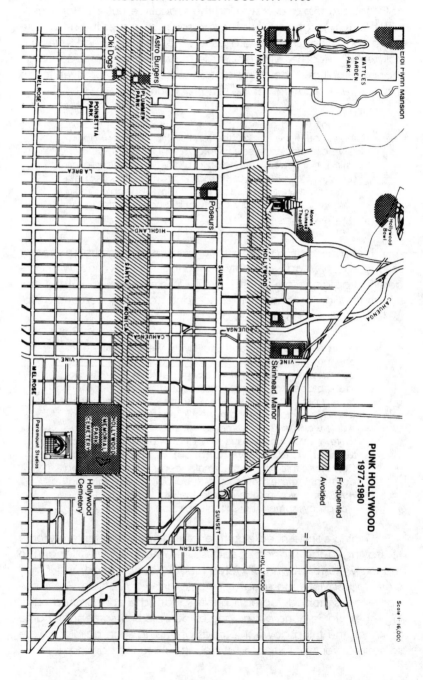

community resources that squatting punks had at their disposal.
Here is one example:

> "Mom" was wild. She was this thirty-five-year-old legal
> secretary who went through this rapidly accelerated
> "poseur" phase. . . . She would try and keep down jobs
> and would generally try to rent places, or she'd go into
> various offices and try to find out where the con-
> demned houses were, and generally take them over for
> "her children."[44]

These places were trashed both as an expression of the subculture and also at times to make them (strategically) habitable:

> You never want one door to a room unless the wall is
> weak enough that you could easily kick it through. The
> best buildings were the ones that were so heavily decom-
> posed that you could make a few holes in places with a
> hammer and you could pound your way through. . . .
> Posters and newspapers over all the windows, and usually
> the way to do it was you would break the window, and
> then you would poster or paper it over, so it would look like
> it was completely derelict, and no one was in it, but if
> someone would come in you could easily just dive right
> through it. . . . There was a lot of pure vandalism like "let's
> spray paint the walls" "let's burn part of the carpet" . . .
> but a lot of it is trying to accommodate a building to illegal
> occupation. . . . We had carpenters, we had construction
> people (in the punk scene), these people with back-
> grounds in that (to rehabilitate buildings). The issue was:
> Why the hell do that? Why the hell fix it? You're only
> gonna be in it until they throw you out. So you had no
> investment in the place, except "What kind of fun can we
> have with it and how can we get out of it once they push
> us out?"[45]

In fact, the punk squatters were a fairly stable group
compared to the current population of homeless street youths,
who, in the words of one service provider, "spend a fair amount of
time looking (each day) for a place to stay."[46] Contemporary
homeless youths use many of the same strategies to "ready" a
building for squatting.

THE ELIMINATION OF MARGINAL SPACE
AND DECLINE OF PUNK SQUATTING

> We're talking about the erosion of free space. You know, not just open space in the sense of, "Oh yeah, nice parks." We're talking about space with any kind of latitude for independent action.
>
> —Frank, former member of Hollywood punk squatting scene,1977–1980.

> In social space, which is both the material and non-material support of social relations, fragmentation is an instrument of political power.
>
> —Henri Lefebvre,*Une Pensee Devenue Monde*, 1980.

The dissolution of this fairly self-sustained and self-contained squatting culture began in 1979, and was attributable to three interrelated factors. The first factor was a generational shift: as the subculture became popular it went through a series of transformations, different generations, which might be seen as the "natural" stages of formation, dissolution, and death of the subculture. The second factor, emanating from the first, was an aspect of this generational shift: a changing attitude towards the use and abuse of marginal space. Increased destruction of marginal space led to enclosure of key marginal spaces, which denied squatting punks a valuable resource for their subculture. The third was the consequence of the loss of space. As the quality and availability of marginal space deteriorated, punks increasingly had to fight for use of marginal space on streets and in alleys, both to squat and to hang out, and formed gangs to protect themselves against other street subcultures.

According to local lore the subculture went through three generations: the first more outspokenly political, the second oriented to the musical and symbolic aspects of the subculture, and the third, dominated largely by lower-class kids, more demonstratively violent.[47] The "first wave" of Hollywood punks, beginning in 1977, could be seen as part of an intellectual avant-garde—disenchanted youth of the upper and middle classes, who spent a lot of time patrolling the boundaries of the culture.

> 1977: The poseurs were being separated from the possessed. Words like "anarchy" and "nihilism" started working their way into the vocabulary. . . . A definite Punk

core was forming. L.A. anarchists were no political activists. They weren't dealing with English economic oppression. L.A. punks were instigating a fashion anarchy and musical chaos.[48]

This first wave was concerned about the authenticity of those who adhered to the scene, which drew later criticisms of their "cliquishness."[49] But compared to the later concerns in the Hollywood scene, which focused increasingly on street survival, this cliquishness and the energy spent patrolling subcultural boundaries spoke to a considerable amount of time the first wave had at their disposal for careful recruiting to the subculture and life in the manors:

> Generally people would be brought in. You'd have people who were wandering around one way or another . . . they'd say, "Yeah this person is cool," and they'd be offered the chance to be brought in, not in terms of "OK you have to say the official pledge and then we're going to dump a bucket of urine on you" or that sort of thing, you know — they'd hang out with you more and more . . . and then you'd bring them into the circle.[50]

Frank was a member of the second wave: "Too late to be avant-garde, too early to be trendy." As he described it, the second wave shared some of the political leanings of the first, and spent some time in the manors but also began to move into squats that they named, as the manors began to be closed off and patrolled by police. The second wave had some awareness of the anarchist underpinnings of the punk subculture and were, for the most part, "mentored in" by the first wave, but they were generally more concerned with music and the style of the subculture than any larger political objective. They were not involved in publishing political tracts.[51]

The third wave, beginning in 1979, tended to be lower-class suburban youth, who were generally more bellicose and more influenced by the media image of the subculture than by its early roots.

> 1979: a separation between the South Bay working-class kids and the post-glitter Hollywood punks. The Hollywood kids didn't stand a chance. The new breed of suburban Punk was physically tougher, angrier, and more immediately REAL about their intention than the original party people.[52]

Frank described the shift this way:

> A lot of the first-wave people were pretty educated — in
> a lot of cases upper-middle-class or even upper-class
> people who'd rejected that for one reason or another.
> We did have skills. We had people who could translate —
> Spanish, Dutch, German. . . . The "first wavers" were really
> politically active—they used to publish these tracts . . . This
> was one of the big tricks you did if you were politically
> active groups, and the first wavers were. A lot of them
> would be anarchist-type tracts or Zero Work tracts, and
> then you'd sneak down to a, like, copy shop, and they
> don't really monitor those machines, so, when they
> weren't looking you'd reach over, punch the authorize
> buttons, and then just go xerox up all these copies and
> run out with a stack full of paper. . . The original punks had
> a distinctly anarchist bent and in many cases a formal
> one — they were anarchists, and they understand the dif-
> ference between Proudhon and Bakunin. The Nazi punks
> generally came in after the movement had spread its
> way out to classes other than the . . . dilettante educated
> intelligentsia, and they didn't have a lot of interest in the
> niceties of communal organization or whether throwing
> bombs is politically a good thing to do . . . They were
> more interested in the symbolism and the formalism that
> was inherent in the Nazi movement and "Oh wow, isn't it
> cool to goose step around and be part of this hierarchy?"
> Whereas we had worn swastikas as a means of saying
> fuck you, they wore them 'cause they thought it was cool
> and when they came in they really forced a change in
> the scene. You'd see black kids or Chicano kids on the
> scene wearing an SS overcoat, and suddenly, when
> these guys came in who were taking it seriously, it was no
> fun anymore.[53]

The third wave were more demonstratively destructive of
property. This feature was criticized by the first two generations of
punks on the scene, because it resulted in the elimination of important marginal spaces for punks in Hollywood.

> Hollywood Cemetery. Really important, that was like our
> living room. That was where we would go to party. What
> killed it was they put up this barbed-wire fence all around
> it, because apparently some people did go in and van-
> dalize it. *We actually discovered some of it and tried to
> put it back to rights, just because we didn't want to lose
> the space.*

Punk Hollywood

There was a problem (that) the first and second wave of punks had as the third wave came in, 'cause the third wave tended to be more media-oriented, and what they'd seen on TV. Where we would kick the hell out of somebody because they gave us shit, they would just kick the hell out of somebody to kick the hell out of somebody, 'cause that's what the media said they were supposed to do. . . .

This younger generation thought, "Yeah, that's what it's about, you trash things and you beat people up." These places that we would go as places that we could hang out and not get hassled—they were part of us, they would come too—and inevitably they would start doing stuff like—"Oh, it's cool, let's kick over the gravestones, let's break into one of these mausoleums"—it must have been end of 80–81 that somebody really fucked up some of the grave sites, and then you got these Nazi punks coming in out of nowhere going into the Jewish section and kicking over the gravestones—and after that, that was the end of that space.[54]

In 1980, the Hollywood Cemetery was barbed-wired off after it had been seriously vandalized. Following the loss of this space, punks shifted their "social center" to Wattles Park, a place which did not have the same homological resonance as the cemetery (see Figure 7).

There is some suggestion, moreover, that the third generation did not depend as heavily on the marginal spaces in Hollywood for the reproduction of its subculture, or if its members did, they made different use of them. While a few of them squatted "Skinhead Manor," around Argyle Avenue north of Hollywood Boulevard, others lived in their vans.[55]

The map of marginal spaces used by punks in Hollywood raises some fascinating questions about the way subcultures orient themselves to and draw upon space as part of the homological construction of the subculture, "the symbolic fit between values and lifestyle of a group."[56] First-generation punks recognized and drew upon the potent symbolism of marginal spaces in Hollywood, and the importance of this symbolism for the subculture offers us as powerful a reason for the initial concentration of punks in Hollywood as a simple availability of space. Marginal spaces used by first-generation punks in Hollywood were not simply the place where subculture "takes place." They were themselves the object of bricolage.[57]

Figure 7: PUNK HOLLYWOOD POST-1980

PUNK HOLLYWOOD POST 1980

Frequented
Avoided
Closed, patrolled or demolished

Doheny Mansion Patrolled 1980

Oki Dogs Closed 1990

Astro Burgers

POINSETTIA PARK

PLUMMER PARK

MELROSE

LA BREA

Hotel Hell Demolished 1984

Mann's Chinese Theatre

WATTLES GARDEN PARK

Hollywood Bowl

HIGHLAND

SUNSET

CAHUENGA

HOLLYWOOD

Demolished Early 1980

VINE

Paramount Studios

HOLLYWOOD MEMORIAL PARK CEMETERY

Hollywood Cemetery Closed 1980

MELROSE

VINE

CAHUENGA

SUNSET

WESTERN

HOLLYWOOD

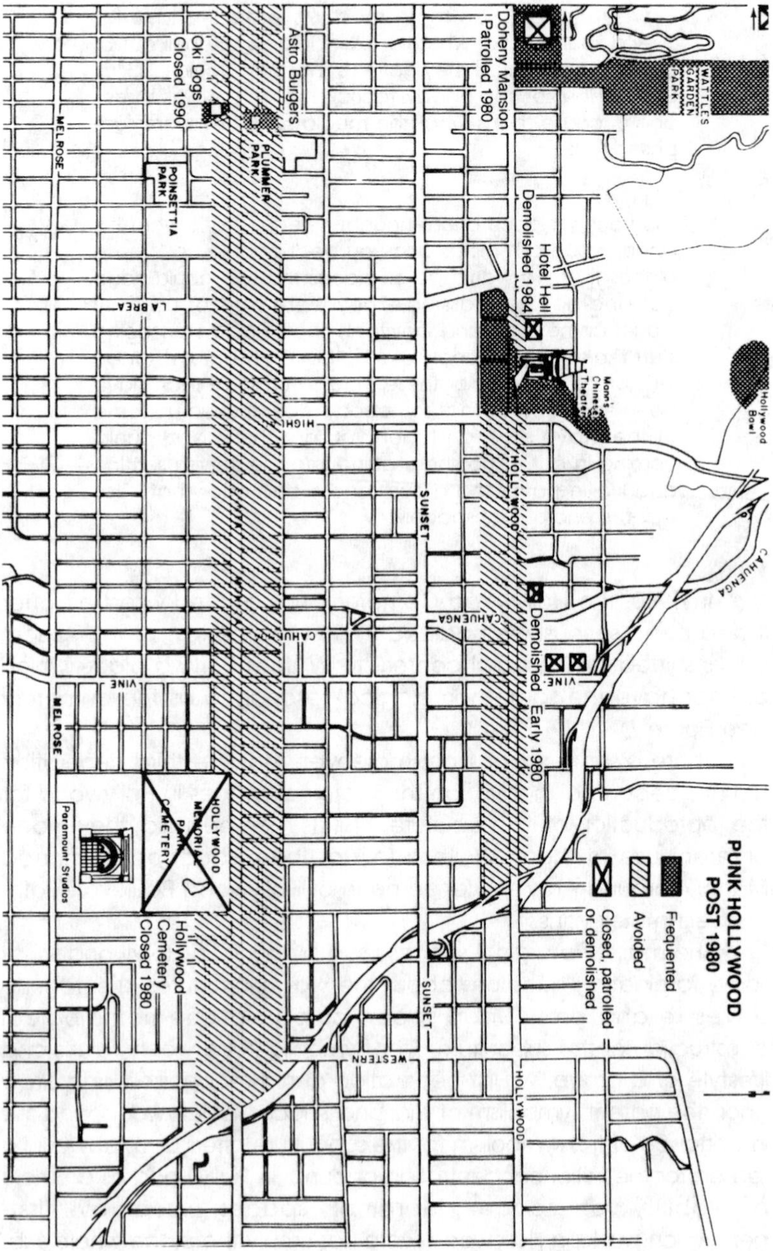

Punk Hollywood

Punks made these spaces an object of bricolage by using them in a way that changed their meaning and this change in meaning was consistent with the stylistic principles of punk subculture (see Figure 6). The message underlying punk culture was essentially that the forbidden was permitted, but the forbidden was appropriated in a way that was calculated to shock. First-generation punk subculture had distinctive signifying practices, concentrating on *"the act of transformation* performed on an object"— the act of subverting meaning rather on what is meant.[58] They were consistent with the homology of punk style.

The homology of punk style is a particularly elusive one, because one of its central principles was the subversion of meaning, or the detachment of an object from the concepts it conventionally signified. Sometimes the intent appeared to be to "empty" the object of its meaning. For example the swastika, as it was worn by first- and second-generation punks, did not signify Nazism, but was repositioned within a subcultural context which rendered it dumb, emptied it of all meaning except, perhaps, rage. Not surprisingly, for the third-wave punks, who did not share the political orientations of the first, objects such as the swastika became reunited with their conventional meanings.

The new placement of the object resonated in the homology of punk style through a precise lack of fit, or dissonance.[59] Examples of punk style that typify this lack of fit include: hole=T-shirt, spitting=applause, garbage bag=garment.[60]

The concept of homology is an important one in understanding the rise and fall of punk squatting subculture. For the squats of the first generation were also homologous, in the sense that they were not randomly chosen, void of significance for punks, or lacking in any discernible structure. Rather they were the spaces which, in their very dissonance or lack of fit, expressed a "fit" between punks' values and their view of the world. Punk squatters' use of the Hollywood Cemetery and the Doheny and Flynn mansions exemplify this: cemetery=living room, home=murder scene, home=orgy scene. Hollywood Cemetery became a living room, a party space. The manor houses of Errol Flynn and Doheny already carried their own mythologies—the former the site of much publicized and public sex scenes, the latter of a double murder.[61] Canterbury House, a large communal space for first-wave punks was rumored to be the site of the "Black Dahlia" Murder.[62]

Little is known about the extent to which this kind of spatial symbiosis is necessary to fuel and sustain a subculture, but it is noteworthy that the second and third generation of punks were driven to spaces that were simply marginal, and no longer inherently expressive of this rupture of meaning. Second- and third-generation punks used Wattles Park when the Hollywood Cemetery closed down, and they tried to confer on the park a sense of rebellion by adopting the practice of shouting "James Dean is alive!" on passing through the park's entrance gates.[63] They spent less time in the manors and more in condemned buildings, whose meanings they also attempted to transform through a process of naming—Bad Manner, Skinhead Manor, Hotel Hell—the last actually a name produced by the media.[64]

In the early years in Hollywood, punks were not usually chased out of condemned buildings (Doheny and Errol Flynn Manors excepted; here they were evicted repeatedly) but only vacated them as they were knocked down. But they were chased from the public spaces outside clubs and bars where they hung around before and after the gigs. As one punk noted, "There was no consistent pressure to make us disappear, there was only pressure whenever we did appear." Punks were generally harassed by police outside clubs where they congregated after a show.

But in 1979, this changed. Police began to enter clubs to disrupt shows, beginning with a police-induced riot in the Elks Lodge in 1979.[65] By the beginning of the 1980s, increased demolition of condemned buildings and policing of the manors forced many punks to spend more time literally "on the street" and in parks and alleys when they could not find places to hang out or squat. Before this time, towards the very end of the 1970s, some loosely structured gangs had begun to form within the punk scene, but they tended to be focused on defining internal philosophical and stylistic differences.

> The first really prominent gang that I remember in Los Angeles was a group called the Hitler Youth. It didn't matter where you were from, Hollywood area was a central hub for the scene. . . . You'd get all these different kids coming in and pretty soon they'd start staying. No turf, no wars over turf, never. They didn't fight with each other— they were more like mutual protection associations and "groups-that-went-out-to-make-trouble." They didn't have demarcated territory, possibly 'cause they didn't have *a place* that they were representing, 'cause most of them came from outside.[66]

Punk Hollywood

Other gangs included LA Death Squad, the largest of the gangs, its self-ironic doppelgänger LA Wimp Squad; and Mike's Mercenaries—which went on to form the band Suicidal Tendencies. In 1980 a new gang formed, the Hollywood Street Survivors (HSS), which was more concentrated on the practical matters of self-preservation, and included somewhere between 100 and 200 members. The transformation from squatting subculture to street protection league had two critical implications. First, members were forced to devote an increasing amount of time to the very practical matters of physical survival, which led to the formation of the league. Second, focus on survival caused members, by necessity, to sever their intermittent contact with a resident commuter population. As Frank noted:

> (The Hollywood Street Survivors) were a serious mutual protection league. They'd worked out . . . a serious code of honor. As things cracked down, there was not the same availability to parks, restaurants, cemeteries, and places where you could hang out. They spent a lot more time on the streets trying to make their own places in alleys and such, and they became much more victimized. I know there were cases of, you know, junkies preying on them and people trying to hire them as prostitutes—so they were much better tuned as a survival instrument than the previous gang (Los Angeles Death Squad), and you didn't find commuters in HSS. . . . it was that they didn't share the same experiences and commuters didn't need them. (Commuters) didn't have to deal with getting hit on by pimps or having to sleep near junkies or having junkies trying to take them for money.[67]

Even three years after the formation of Hollywood Street Survivors, and when punk as a musical subculture was definitely in decline, the success of such protective associations in a punk street subculture was still evident. Lois Lee, founder of Children of the Night, an organization to help adolescent prostitutes, noted that the remaining punks represented an obstruction to pimps trying to recruit young runaways into prostitution: "Many of the kids hanging out here are not prostitutes. They are runaways or kids alone. They seek refuge among the punkers. The pimps don't like that. They can't sell kids with Mohawks, pink or green hair."[68]

Nevertheless, the loss of "prime" marginal space, in the form of squats, forced some changes in punk survival strategies as well. The type of survival strategies that homeless youth have adopted today were generally shunned by punks, especially in the earlier years. Survival sex,[69] practiced by at least half of homeless youths in Hollywood today, and prostitution were definitely frowned upon.

> We weren't hustling for a living. In the manor houses, particularly, you didn't want to bring in an outsider; it was a dumb thing to do. You wouldn't want someone you didn't know. Prostitution was really frowned on—regardless of whether you're talking gay or straight prostitution. There were maybe people I knew, one or two people, who were doing that, but no, you'd live off whatever you could get your hands on. And maybe once, only once, I actually heard of someone even doing something like rolling a drunk to get some money.

> We just generally ignored money. It was more a matter of taking material goods that we needed as opposed to taking money to get material goods.[70]

In these instances the heightened visibility and distinction of a "punk style," which might arguably make shoplifters easier to identify, was in fact used as a mask. But to change the mask required access to private spaces such as manors or squats. A typical shoplift went like this:

> You'd go in with whatever haircut you had—you know "the purple Mohawk"—and you'd grab all the food, macaroni, cheese and noodles . . . Top Raman is the best, they're easy to steal and easy to cook . . . and the first thing you'd do is go into one of the manor houses and you'd shave off your hair or you'd change the cut, and you'd bleach it and dye it a different color.[71]

Panhandling was not part of the early punk scene in the mid- to late 1970s, at least in the form that is currently visible in Hollywood:

> Generally we'd panhandle each other, in front of a gig . . . it was "wherever you're getting it, why don't you share it with me?" . . . Usually you wouldn't pay to get in, unless you could bum the money to do it. You'd look

Punk Hollywood

> for punks who'd driven up in cars, or, the best, punks
> whose Mom had dropped them off . . . (laughter) . . . and
> try to hit them up for money.[72]

But this, too, shifted between the late 1970s and the early 1980s, and was expressed in both the types of survival strategies and the kinds of social spaces used in Hollywood (see Figures 6 and 7). First- and second-generation punks never panhandled, and rarely frequented Hollywood Boulevard, a prime panhandling area for contemporary homeless youth: it expressed too readily the values of the dominant culture that they shunned. The anarchist underpinnings of punk subculture expressed themselves in the music scene: pretensions to stardom were frowned upon, everyone and no one was a star. Desires for stardom represented a wish to become successful within and on the terms of the dominant culture.

In the late 1970s, the maintenance of the boundaries which defined punk squatters as members of an "outsider culture" included shunning money and pilfering goods directly and as needed rather than begging for handouts. The appearance of Poseurs (a store that sold punk paraphernalia) was a second-generation phenomenon. The name "Poseurs" was itself a play on the fact that only "pretenders" to the punk culture would actually *buy* paraphernalia associated with it: "real" Punks made their own hair gel and dye, ripped their own T-shirts, and so on. But by 1980 both the social and spatial orientation of the subculture began to shift:

> For some people (panhandling) was part of a regular income. For other people it wasn't. And it seemed that as time went on it became more and more of a regular income. You know (in) '77 we would mainly steal what we needed. By '80 there were a lot of them who were hanging out on the corners, full-time virtually, panhandling. There were specific cases of people making money by having cultivated their look and dressing as outrageous as they could and charging tourists to take photographs. So they would go to Hollywood Boulevard. They'd hang out at Mann's Chinese. But I don't think you could say anyone made a living from it.
>
> Once Melrose took off, Melrose was a great place to panhandle proto-yuppies, you'd really have to call them that . . . 'cause this is about '81 now, just as I was "falling out" and going back to college, and you'd wait till they came by Poseurs, and you'd hit them up. . . . By the time

117

Melrose was happening (mid-1980s), I would walk down the street, you know, somebody actually shopping for materials for some university project, and occasionally I'd see someone getting hit up for money by someone hanging out at Poseurs, who'd hung out with me on the scene . . . if it was a suit with a wallet, . . . and you need some money, they're a tree.[73]

This philosophy extended to social services as well:

We didn't care. We wanted nothing to do with services. We really didn't. I mean, any kind of outreach or outreach program that was moved in our direction we would meet with absolute derision and tell people to get the fuck out. I mean whether they were religious people, missionaries, Salvation Army, Jehovah's Witnesses, the clowns with the tract up on Hollywood Boulevard (Options House), ah, any kind of social-service workers who would try to come in and take somebody back to their parents. No. I mean, you know, there was one social-service worker who got the shit beaten out of him for coming in and trying to do something like that, I mean: "Thank you, no." I mean, the whole point was we didn't want anything to do with the whole system of, you know, smiling, smirking, good for you control. We wanted nothing to do with it. So it had better not come around looking for us.

For a lot of us you're either in the game or you're out of the game. And if you chose to be out of the game then you're really out of the game. You're not going to be out of the game and go around looking for "ooh, a nice warm cot and a hot meal" from the social services. . . . It wasn't the way to do it. It may be different now.[74]

According to service providers in the area, it is definitely different now, at least for youth under eighteen. Outreach workers still talk about a certain initial resistance on behalf of street kids to accepting services.[75] And street youth are still strongly tied to a subculture. As Gabe Cruks notes:

Street kids are a culture—and once you have that culture and that cultural identity it integrates within an area, places, streets become part of that culture—it's a very deeply ingrained culture in spite of enormously increased harassment and programs—it's people, it's places, it's businesses, it's clients, it's drugs, it's being an outlaw,

> it's that shabby glitz of Hollywood and it's knowing
> somebody who knows somebody, it's playing cops
> and robbers with the police. There's a strong peer-
> support network.[76]

While one can still find examples of youth who identify strongly with a street culture, adopting street names and forming protective associations, there no longer exists a substantial "hard core" of unreachable street youth who survive through a self-organized system. Says Dale Weaver:

> There's always the feeling that we're seeing the tip of the
> iceberg, but we're seeing everybody. Marjorie Robertson
> did research . . . interviewing street kids in Hollywood, and
> not only did she have a hard time finding 100 kids, but
> every kid she interviewed either went to Teen Canteen or
> had been kicked out of Teen Canteen.[77]

Of course, there are several reasons why a resistant subculture of punks died out. Some of them simply died:

> The group I was with, that's all I can speak for. . . .We
> (didn't become) a chronic street population. . . . Look at
> me. (I went to college.) Jamie, who was my friend since I
> was twelve, thirteen, we both went on the scene togeth-
> er—he's advertising in New York and in his spare time he's
> a police officer, patrolling the gay areas against gay
> bashers. Mike, who used to formulate acid for us, he's at
> JPL (Jet Propulsion Laboratories) now, he's a rocket scien-
> tist working on missile programs. Sandy is a teacher. Gina
> is a waitress.

> A lot of them are dead. I think that's one of the things that
> was true about our scene. *You either went on to some-
> thing else or you died.* You didn't stay there, you didn't
> become a chronic homeless lush. A lot of them died. It
> was part of it—but I wasn't doing junk. It was their choice.
> It was part of the scene. We knew it.[78]

There was also the implication that those from the first and second generations left the scene as its class composition shifted and as different kinds of punk practices were introduced that they felt no longer expressed its original intent. Whatever effect the loss of marginal space had on punk subculture as a whole, it is clear that it made it increasingly difficult for punks in the Hollywood area to sustain themselves as an independent group of squatters. Loss of space contributed to the isolation of squatting punks in Hollywood from other punks in Los Angeles, as the area became less and less of a node, and punks from other areas stopped in effect "migrating to Hollywood." LA Death Squad was a regional "gang" centered in Hollywood, but it included commuter punks and Valley punks, and numbered several hundred. Its successor, Hollywood Street Survivors, was definitely a local affair, restricted to Hollywood punks and numbering 200 members at the outside. As squatting life in Hollywood became increasingly difficult, it also became less attractive to punks from other areas. Parallel with this erosion of free space was an increased need to focus on strategies for more elemental survival—as exemplified in the development of the Hollywood Street Survivors—which changed the orientation of the punk street subculture substantially.

HEAVY METAL

> Not all subcultural styles "play" with language to the same extent: some are more straightforward than others and place a higher priority on the construction and projection of a firm and coherent identity.
>
> —Dick Hebdige, *Subculture: The Meaning of Style*, 1979, p.126.

> "A lot of people say I'm getting out of Hollywood. But I set them straight. It's like the Motley Crue song says, 'Hollywood . . . there's no escape.'"
>
> —Nikki Payne, quoted in David Wharton, "Heavy Going," 1987.

As Hebdige notes, different subcultures express different degrees of rupture. For this reason alone, the rise of punk squatting among homeless and runaway youth in Hollywood cannot be seen to represent the experience of all spectacular youth subcultures in the area. The constitutive field for runaways in Hollywood was altered not only by attacks on punk squatting subculture, but also by the rise of other subcultures—which differed not only at the level of style, but also in terms of value systems, survival strategies, and homological uses of space. According to local police and service providers, one of the largest and most visible subcultures in

Punk Hollywood

Hollywood currently, that of the heavy-metal habitués, includes a lot of runaways.[79]

Like their punk predecessors, heavy-metal runaways also live in squats, and apparently survive through a range of legal and illegal practices, including panhandling, petty thievery, car theft, and so on, but there is a significant difference. The original punks avoided money: the artifacts of punk style were originally made, not bought; one stole food rather than panhandling to buy food. Punks in the early stages of the subculture insisted that "the bands were equal, that there be none of the star trips that one associated with the corporate music industry."[80] First- and second-wave punks saw themselves as an emancipatory culture, breaking down the barriers of sexism and racism. As mentioned earlier, the one store catering explicitly to punks in Hollywood registered this by calling itself "Poseurs," the early punk term for those who pretended to the subculture without really adopting its value system. Punks avoided Hollywood Boulevard, preferring their own secluded scene. By contrast, heavy-metal youth flock to the Boulevard, and "for every shop owner who complains, there is another who makes his living off Heavy-Metal."[81] Heavy-metal adherents have sought stardom and integration both into the corporate music scene and into the local economy of the boulevard. This incorporative strategy of the subculture also infuses attitudes towards local services and shelters, and the popularity of heavy metal has influenced strategies of service provision. Oasis, a Christian charity organization, features a heavy-metal gospel-rock club near Hollywood Boulevard, where young people can listen to music and eat free food.

Among service-providers and kids using services and shelter in the Hollywood area, it is accepted local wisdom, though unsubstantiated, that the two manor houses, Doheny and Errol Flynn, are now dominated by satanic cults.[82] But if a resistant, self-contained street culture exists in Hollywood, it has been driven to its very periphery and no longer defines the central space of Hollywood for street youth.

SURVIVAL IN THE 1980S AND 1990S

By the late 1980s, homeless and runaway youths were passing through Hollywood's shelter and service network at a rate of about 5,600 per year. Males and females were almost equally represented, 56.6% to 43.4%, and while Caucasians predominated (44%), there were also a high percentage of blacks (28.5%) and Hispanics (20%). The majority were between ages 16 and 17 and from within the state of California. Intake data on homeless and runaway youth in Hollywood suggests that over 40% of the shelter population had a history of family abuse or neglect, and for youth on the street and outside of services this number rose to 60%.)[83]

If homeless and runaway youths ever had access to sub-cultural networks that offered a limited protection from exploitation on the street, by the mid-1980s this had diminished considerably. Research into the family histories of these youths establishes a clear link between the nature of neglect and abuse that they suffer in their families, and the type of practices they engage in once they were out on the street. Sexually abused youths are more likely to engage in some form of prostitution; youths with a family background of drug abuse are more likely to be abusers themselves. Homeless youths in the late 1980s are, in increasing numbers, victimized in order to survive. Where punks could draw clear boundaries around acceptable and unacceptable survival strategies, today's homeless youths are increasingly engaged in a brutally flexible approach to staying alive.

Street youths interviewed in 1987 revealed that, while homeless at least 30% of street youths had engaged in some form of survival sex, about 30% had been involved in prostitution (sex for cash), 22% had traded sex for food, and 10% had traded sex for drugs. In addition, over 50% had sold drugs while homeless, and 8% had posed for pornographic photos or movies while homeless in order to survive. Roughly 48% had attempted suicide in their lifetimes, and of these, about 26% had attempted suicide in the twelve months prior to being interviewed.[84] Service providers argue that these youths have fewer resources available to them than in previous decades. They suggest "survival sex" has emerged among homeless youths who would not normally "choose" prostitution as a way to survive on the street. The implications of this development are difficult to gauge. One could argue that street youth have developed resourceful associations with one another, or have increased access to services, both of which might enable them to avoid being entrapped in a pimp-prostitute relationship, and are thus able to extricate themselves more easily. It suggests that alternative resources on the street are diminishing; more youths are passing into casual prostitution and drug dealing because of a lack of alternative countercultural networks and supports.

Punk Hollywood

It is difficult to ascertain the role that homeless and runaway youths play within the economy of the sex and drug trade in Hollywood. The intermittent involvement in survival sex and drug deals of youths seen by the service-providers suggests that their contribution to this economy is small. But this does not include those who are heavily involved in prostitution or dealing and using drugs. With the exception of Children of the Night, programs do not deal with juvenile prostitutes, and most programs cannot take youths with serious drug problems—the waiting lists for drug treatment programs for youths are prohibitively long.

The demise of the "underground" and prevalence of homeless youths have perhaps served to make more visible some of the exploitative practices youths succumb to in order to survive. One indication of diminishing resources is the transformation of squatting practices themselves. Occasionally, relatively stable squats will form for a period of months, but these are usually in abandoned buildings that are quickly condemned. Service providers note the loss of condemned buildings for squats in the Hollywood area. This is the result of an aggressive demolition program, Operation Knockdown, that was instituted in the area in the early 1980s to secure or destroy abandoned buildings, with the intent of reducing drug dealing.[85] As a result, youth are spending an increasing amount of time simply looking for a place to sleep, and sleeping in increasingly transient places such as rooftops and the basement laundromats of apartment buildings.[86] As Frank commented: "Things must be really bad if you have to sleep on a rooftop. I wouldn't want to expose myself on that grid for anything (referring to the extensive helicopter patrols and numbered roofs in the city)."[87]

In contrast to survival strategies of homeless and runaway youths in Hollywood, the geography of juvenile prostitution and drug dealing has remained remarkably resilient over the past three decades, reflecting and reinforcing prime and marginal spaces within the community. The single major change in this geography has been the exodus of drug dealing and prostitution, which had been prevalent on Hollywood Boulevard, even in the early 1980s.[88] Now the boulevard is reserved for panhandling, drawing on a high volume of tourists and fast-food joints.[89] The hierarchy of stigmatized survival practices respects to a large degree the prime and marginal spaces of Hollywood [90] (see Figure 8).

Prostitution remains concentrated along Sunset and Santa Monica Boulevards, and panhandling along Hollywood Boulevard. Space is also defined in prime and marginal categories with respect to prostitution, with the street population getting younger and lighter-skinned as one moves east along Santa Monica and Sunset Boulevards, and older and darker as one moves west. Drug dealing and prostitution also provide sources of income for young runaways in the area—police indicate that they have picked up runaways as young as eleven and twelve peddling crack for adult dealers in different parts of the community.[91] Drug dealing remains scattered throughout the community, sometimes concentrated near specific fast food-joints. While service-providers tended to downplay Hollywood's role in the local drug economy as a reason for the presence of homeless and runaway youths there, it nevertheless is a factor, although it is unclear to what extent young people are drawn to the area for cheap drugs, or become involved in drug use as a function of being in Hollywood and being homeless. As one youth put it rather obliquely:

> I've been looking for work (in Hollywood) and I just haven't found nothing yet. I go to the Job Service, look in the newspapers, and go round to the shops nearly every day. I guess I might have to go out of this area. I don't really want to 'cause I like the environment. Everybody is more or less in a party mood, and I like to party.[92]

Although most street youths appear to favor cannabis over cocaine,[93] the easy availability of cocaine in the area is also a factor drawing youths as one reported to a Teen Canteen case worker: "I came to Hollywood because I heard coke was cheap. I could buy it, sell it, and do it for cheap. I've been around drugs all my life."[94]

The redevelopment area has a high degree of street-level drug trading. Early surveys suggested that service-providers thought drug abuse was a major problem for approximately 50% of homeless and runaway youth.[95] Robertson's in depth-study of ninety-seven street youths found 38% had some form of drug abuse or dependence.[96] As the director of Children of the Night noted, street-level drug use and prostitution are often inscribed in an intertwined geography:

> Hollywood is characteristic of the street corner drug dealer. Many streets in Hollywood can be identified as locations to buy marijuana, cocaine, crystal heroin or PCP. The sale and distribution of these drugs are as

geographically defined as the street prostitutes who use them. Drugs play an important role in the working situation of the street prostitute.[97]

Service providers have gone to great lengths to de-link the activities of these youths from possible identification with the "dangerous classes," developing terminology which emphasizes the ersatz quality of the actions. Homeless youths do not form gangs; they form "gangs."[98] Gangs do, in fact, operate in Hollywood, but unlike in the rest of the city, Hollywood does not belong to any single gang but appears to have been carved up between several citywide gangs.[99]

Whatever the causes of a flexible approach to survival, both the images emphasized by service-providers and contemporary research on the causes of running away among homeless and runaway youths retain within them the modern view of youthful misbehavior, expressed in a concept of juvenile delinquency which locates the blame in the improper management of the child's upbringing, rather than in the child him- or herself. It is not only service-providers who attempt to distance these youths from their survival strategies. Significant numbers of the youths themselves do not identify with stigmatizing strategies, but practice them out of sheer necessity. Robertson's research demonstrates that significant numbers of street youths engage in stigmatizing survival strategies, such as carrying a weapon, being in a gang, or prostituting only when homeless.[100] Service providers have noted that runaway and homeless youths often engage intermittently in prostitution, and even cite instances of squats of youth who consciously divvy up survival strategies to mitigate stigma, such as squats where the males go into prostitution so the females won't have to.[101] However, Gabe Cruks, the director of the Gay and Lesbian Center, noted that it was not uncommon in Hollywood to find the juvenile equivalent of "freakhouses," where youths were kept fed, clothed, in drugs, and available for sex. Hamid describes a similar phenomenon in New York among crack-addicted women kept in prostitution.[102] "Freakhouses vary in form, composition and the kinds of exchanges that occur within. Theoretically they could be highly instrumental money-making operations or more likely a less structured arrangement which puts older men with homes or apartments in positions of relative power over the homeless."[103]

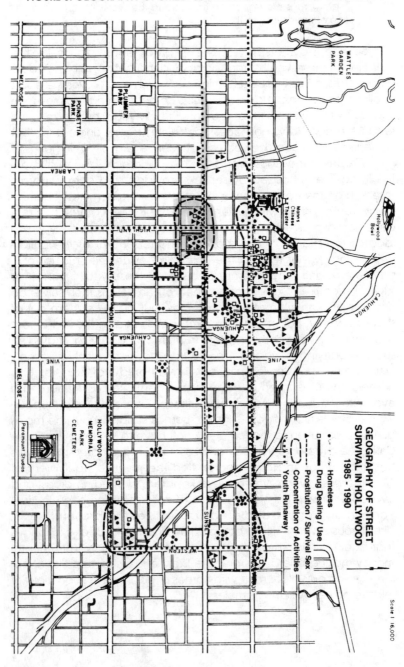

GEOGRAPHY OF STREET
SURVIVAL IN HOLLYWOOD
1985 - 1990

• • • • • Homeless
□ □ □ □ Drug Dealing / Use
▬▬▬▬ Prostitution / Survival Sex
- - - - Concentration of Activities
▲▲▲▲ Youth Runaway

Scale 1 : 6,000

Punk Hollywood

FROM A STRATEGIC TO A TACTICAL
INHABITATION OF HOLLYWOOD

The spaces available to homeless and runaway youth in Hollywood have devolved in three phases from the early 1970s on. In the first phase, youths had some limited access to and control over strategic spaces in Hollywood—a tacit support by countercultural elements, and access to places to crash, such as countercultural newspaper offices. As De Certeau notes, a strategy "postulates a place that can be delimited as its own and serve as a base from which relations with an exteriority composed of targets or threats can be managed . . . tactics play on and with a terrain imposed on it and organized by the law of a foreign power."[104] This control over strategic space continued in a limited fashion with the dominance of punk in Hollywood, and the crowding of rented apartments.[105] But tactical use of space began to predominate with the rise of manor houses as preferred squats. In addition, beginning in the 1980s, the quality and availability of tactical space began to deteriorate, as condemned buildings were demolished and punks were driven from open public spaces and forced to compete with other groups for marginal spaces in back alleys and parks. This deterioration was accompanied by a shift in the social and public definition of these youths. They were no longer viewed primarily as members of a particular subculture, but first and foremost as runaway and homeless youths who participated in various subcultures. The loss of strategic space controlled by the youths themselves was countered to some extent by the rise in shelters and services to which youths had access. Increasingly it was the shelters and services and not the youths who began to define the youths' public identity.

6

REDEFINING
RUNAWAY AND HOMELESS YOUTH

The dominant culture of a complex society is never a homogeneous structure. It is layered, reflecting different interests . . . as well
as emergent elements. Subordinate cultures will not always be in
open conflict with it. They may for long periods, coexist with it,
negotiate the spaces and gaps within it, make inroads into it,
"warrening it from within."

> —Clarke, Hall and Jefferson, "Subcultures,
> Cultures and Class," in *Rituals of Resistance*,
> 1977: 12

Covenant House talks about saving youth or children, but they are
serving 18-to-21-year-olds. Personally that annoys me, because
they're legally adults. What it get's down to is '*What's a youth*?'

> —Leslie Forbes, Director, Options House.

I think the iceberg under the tip is Hispanic kids who go out of their
way not to be visible and black kids whose family structures are so
chaotic *you could almost call them homeless even though they
are sleeping on the couches of relatives and families in their communities*—couch kids.

> —Dale Weaver, Director, Teen Canteen,
> April 15,1991.

Young and Homeless in Hollywood

Who can be considered a youth? How do we define home-lessness? In the late 1970s, following deinstitutionalization, service providers had to contend with a commonly held view of runaways as "angels" or "thieves," a polar characterization which closely mir-rored premodern conceptions of delinquent youths as either preco-cious or part of the dangerous classes. By the early 1990s, both the understanding of homeless youths and the programs that treated them had become much more inclusive: no youth was considered beyond treatment; the formally recognized age limit had extended from under eighteen to twenty-one years; services treated not only first-time runners but also "hard-core" street youths; and programs, while maintaining their identity as transitional programs, had increased the length of stay for youth from three days in the early years to as long as eighteen months. In addition, service providers were challenging perceptions of "homelessness," they began to include not only youths without shelter, but those who were, *de facto*, abandoned by their parents, growing up without supervision. Among the homeless they now include "couch kids," the "virtually homeless" who have run away to live with extended family mem-bers and who grow up in an atmosphere of neglect.[1]

Service providers have used the social space of Hollywood as an active medium to produce this new understanding. Space is not simply a mask concealing the "larger" imperatives of social control. The social space of Hollywood was redrawn for homeless and runaway youths to produce, within the community, *a different understanding of their marginality.* While unsupervised areas avail-able to these youths were progressively closed off, the services were transformed in this process as well. They evolved from simply return-ing youths to their families to simulating family structures in shelters in the local community. They also struggled to win both space and time for homeless youth in Los Angeles County.

Over the years, programs became highly differentiated in terms of the youths they would treat and the type of programs they offered. They began to negotiate the "paratactic sign system"[2] of the urban environment, both as something to contend with and something to use as a resource. This influenced the locational deci-sions of services, the image they presented to the community, and a range of the sociospatial controls they exerted on clients when outside program walls. Finally, the organizational ethos of these programs became diversified, ranging from attempts to simulate the normalcy of family life for first-time runaways to the appropria-tion of the markers of street culture as an attempt to direct chronic street youth off the streets and to some other existence—in short, in the words of one program director, to offer them "as much structure as they can stand without leaving."[3]

THE SACRED AND THE PROFANE:
FRONT AND BACK REGIONS OF SERVICE PROVISION
IN LOS ANGELES COUNTY IN THE LATE 1970S

> A region may be defined as any place that is bounded to some degree by barriers to perception . . . front regions refer to the place where the performance is given . . . the performance in the front region may be seen as an effort to give the appearance that the region maintains and embodies certain standards . . . a back region or backstage may be defined as a place relative to a given performance where the impression fostered by the performance is knowingly contradicted as a matter of course. . . . In general, of course, the back region will be the place where the performer can reliably expect that no member of the audience will intrude.

> —Erving Goffman, "Regions and Region Behavior" in *The Presentation of Self in Everyday Life,* 1959.

Goffman's elucidation of "front" and "back" regions drew on the differentiated behavior of actors between *stage* and *backstage* For Goffman, both as metaphor and example for the place-bounded nature of human behavior—in this case front and back region, a stage and backstage—represented a sutured reality which defined two separate but integral spheres of the actor's world. In other examples, front and back regions were separated into distinct spheres, where one or the other characterization dominated, and little passage back and forth ensued—the church versus the criminal's hideaway, for example. Implied, but not fully present at all times and places, was a corresponding series of oppositional dyads, between controlled and uncontrolled behavior, between moral uprightness and criminality, between social acceptability and social deviance, between the sacred and the profane. While Goffman did not use this example, a similar dyad was expressed in the relationship between "family" and "street," as viewed by turn-of-the-century social reformers, for whom

> the presence of children on the street has always been taken as *prima facie* evidence of social pathology; not as

a symptom but as a cause of poverty and corruption. . . .
The street was symbolically opposed to the home: a
profane versus a sacred world. . . . A clear association
was assumed between the private virtues of family life in
the home and the public dangers of the street.[4]

In the late 1970s, following the deinstitutionalization of runaway
youths, this dyad of family and street, front region and back region,
the sacred and the profane, reemerged in divergent philosophies
of early services to homeless and runaway youth in Los Angeles
County. It reflected antipodal philosophies about both the causes
of running away and appropriate treatment of youths. Some
services functioned almost entirely as "front regions," advocating
immediate reunification of runaways with their families, and offering
limited interim support structures. Others embodied the "back
regions" of runaway behavior. These took a countercultural stance
which tolerated or even supported the street cultures of the
runaways, and excluded the intrusion of "audiences" into their
operations—in this case, the family, the community, or even the
police. But both types of programs faced significant problems in
treating youth. Those that tended towards speedy reunification or
placement with families had high walkaway rates; those that
supported youth in their street subcultures ran the risk of simply
enabling them to remain homeless.

The growth of services for homeless and runaway youths in Los
Angeles County from the mid-1970s to the present should not be
seen as the unproblematic extension of "social control" by the state
into the community. An analysis must go beyond *identifying* the
literal "sites" of shelters and services to examining *how practices are
actively inserted at particular sites.*[5]

During the mid-1970s, service provision to homeless and
runaway youths in Los Angeles County was characterized by a high
degree of geographic dispersal and diversity of programs. They
were informal, locally based, and lacking connections to one
another. When homeless and runaway youth were deinstitutionalized in the mid-1970s, Los Angeles County had few alternative
community services for them. One extensive survey concluded:

There was a dearth of such services in the Los Angeles
area . . . this (was) rather perplexing since the popular
press has depicted the "Strip" and local beaches as
heavily populated by runaways . . . to a large extent this
picture is accurate, yet there are few agencies providing

services to these transients . . . we had greater success in recruiting runaway youth than the agencies supposedly designed to service their needs.[6]

There was, however, a "loosely defined and emerging system of juvenile diversion"[7] (places such as Travelers Aid) and the presence of a considerable underground, which was used, to the exclusion of services, by about 70% of the youth on the street.[8] But the service network that came to replace the relatively self-sustained support network for homeless youth did not develop unproblematically.

THE STREET AS BACK REGION

There is truly a balance, there's a fine line we all walk between enabling populations to be homeless versus trying to assist them not to be homeless.

—Gabe Cruks, Director, The Gay and Lesbian Center, May 30,1990.

In the mid-1970s, the County of Los Angeles had only two formally recognized programs which provided on-site emergency shelter for runaways: 1736 House in Hermosa Beach and The Gay and Lesbian Center in Hollywood. Both of these were considered "countercultural" during their early days of operation. 1736 House offered a twenty-four-hour drop-in service and was open to all youth from the area—less than one-fifth of its clientele were run-aways. It operated on a shoestring budget and provided room for up to twelve residents. The program required that staff contact the runaways' parents, but they generally attempted to "buy time (before doing so) to work with the youth." The designated length of stay was about three days, and residents rarely stayed longer than a week.[9] (See Figure 9)

FIGURE 9:
LOS ANGELES SHELTERS AND SERVICES
FOR HOMELESS AND RUNAWAY YOUTH
(Pages 134–136)

DATE	NAME OF SERVICE	TYPE OF SERVICE	AGE OF YOUTH SERVED	NUMBER OF BEDS	LENGTH OF STAY	COMMENTS
1952	YMCA Hollywood	Counsel Outreach	n/a	n/a	n/a	Housed in Evans private home
1964	YMCA Hollywood	Counsel Outreach	n/a	n/a	n/a	Outreach Formalized
1971/ 1985	Gay Community Center	Community Center	youth, adults	12	n/a	Crash, food bank
1974	1736 House	Community Center/ Emergency Shelter for Runaways Hermosa Beach	12-17 years	12	20 days	Reunification first priority
1974	Aviva Respite	Pregnant teens	12-18 years	6	—	—
1974	Helpline Youth Norwalk	Counseling and Outreach	n/a	n/a	n/a	—
1974	Salvation Army Downtown LA	Shelter-private homes	n/a	n/a	week-end	not listed 1981
1974	La Crescenta/ Canada YMCA	Shelter-private homes	n/a	n/a	n/a	not listed 1981
1974	Downey Hotline	Hotline/referral to "crash pads in private homes"	n/a	n/a	n/a	not listed 1980
1974	The Big Sisters League	Pregnant teens	16-18 years	30	9 months	—
1974	Youth Crisis Housing Task Force, Van Nuys	Counseling and foster home referral	n/a	n/a	n/a	—
1975	SODA	Pilot project	12-17 years	28	3 days	foster homes
1979	Children of the Night	Shelter adolescent prostututes	12-17 years	see SODA	see SODA	private crash 250 kids 1979/82
1980	Options House	Shelter	12-17 years	6	14 days	reunification

134

DATE	NAME OF SERVICE	TYPE OF SERVICE	AGE OF YOUTH SERVED	NUMBER OF BEDS	LENGTH OF STAY	COMMENTS
1982	1736 House	Shelter	10-17 years	6	20 days (average 3 days)	Reunification, parental consent, 30% from Watts
1981	SODA	Foster homes	12-17 years	27	3 days	—
1981	SODA	Foster homes	12-17 years	6	20 days maximum	—
1981	Stepping Stones	Emergency shelter	7-17 years	6	14 days	Low profile
1981	Angel's Flight Skid Row	Crisis Center	12-17 years	n/a	n/a	Reunification
1981	Detour Norwalk	Foster homes	12-17 years	n/a	14 days	not listed 1986
1981	Rosemary Cottage	Emergency shelter	13-18 years	6	20 days	SODA referred
1981	Centrum, Hollywood	Emergency shelter	12-30 years	100	—	Fundament-alist Christian
1982	Children of the Night	Drop in teen prostitutes	12-17 years	see SODA	see SODA	Referral beds
1983	SODA	Foster homes	12-17 years	41	3 days	25% to 35% walkaway
1983	Travelers Aid	Interception	12-17 years	n/a	n/a	Reunification
1983-1987	YMCA Homeless Youth	"Fold-up" shelter	12-17 years	20	14 days	Used as day-care/days
1984	Angel's Flight HWD	Outreach, drop-in	12-17 years	n/a	n/a	Reunification
1984	Citrus House	Transitional shelter	18-23 years	12	60 days	Emancipated minors
1984	Citrus House	Long term shelter	12-17 years	12	20 days	—
1985	1736 House	Emergency shelter	12-17 years	6 8	20 days	Youth Women with infants
1985	Aviva Center	Emergency shelter	12-17 years	6	14 days	—

DATE	NAME OF SERVICE	TYPE OF SERVICE	AGE OF YOUTH SERVED	NUMBER OF BEDS	LENGTH OF STAY	COMMENTS
1985	Options House	Emergency shelter	12-17 years	12	14 days	Reunification
1985	Kathy Boone Long Beach	Home for pregnant young women	17-27 years	11	9 months	—
1986	Aviva Respite	Shelter pregnant teens runaways	12-17 years	6	9 months	For runaways when space is available
1986	LAYN	Emergency shelter	12-23 years	20	60 days	Curfew
1986	LAYN	Outreach, drop in	12-23 years	n/a	n/a	Lunch Mon.–Sun.
1986	Casa de Los Hermanos	Refugee shelter	15-19 years	10	n/a	Boys
1986	Teen Canteen	Drop in shelter	12-17 years	2	n/a	Open Mon.–Fri. 10AM–4PM
1986	The Big Sisters League	Long-term shelter for pregnant teens/runaways	12-18 years	30	9 months	—
1986	WAY IN, Salvation Army	Outreach, drop in	12-16 years	n/a	n/a	—
1988	Children of the Night, Van Nuys	Emergency shelter	12-17 years	n/a	n/a	—
1989	Angel's Flight Hollywood Office	Outreach/drop in /referral/shelter for pregnant teens	12-17 years	2	9 months	Family reunification
1989	SODA	Non-secure detention of status offenders	12-17 years	55	3 days	Foster homes
1989	Covenant House	Emergency shelter	18-20 years	20	Individually deter-mined	Originally 100 beds
1990	Options House	Emergency shelter	12-17 years	n/a	6 months	—
1990	"Our House" Long Beach	Drop in center, food, showers, outreach	n/a	n/a	n/a	Open since April 1989
1990	Adolescent Alliance	Emergency shelter for AIDS -infected	n/a	n/a	n/a	In proposal stage

Redefining Youth

The Gay and Lesbian Center grew out of the gay liberation movement of 1969 to 1970. It began as a community center for gay people, but "evolved fairly rapidly into a frontline social service agency, addressing critical issues such as getting adequate STD (sexually transmitted disease) health care for gay men."[10] The service to homeless youth began in 1972 to 1973 as an informal, unstructured program, providing only free food, a place to sleep, and a rap group for more stable youths.[11] This was replaced in 1982 by an emergency shelter pad, set up for gay-identified homeless street youth. The shelter occupied both a literal and figurative "back region," in a house behind the community organization. The current director, who manages a newly established shelter for gay youth called Citrus House, characterized this earlier effort as a "crash pad":

> It was a good effort in terms of "Gee, we want to do the right thing." It was not a program. Basically it was sort of a crash pad. Kids got stuck back there and there was no real supervision. There was no real structure. The place itself was in very bad condition.[12]

In their early stages, several of the programs functioned as back regions within the community, if not in the wider sense of permitting street cultures to dominate their operations, then in the more limited sense of disallowing entry to an "outside audience." With a dearth of funds and lack of recognition of the problem of runaways, outreach workers have at times been forced to draw on their own limited resources, sometimes bringing youths to their own houses. Such was the case with the YMCA outreach program in the early 1950s. At the time it responded to Hollywood's role as a subcultural center for beatniks. Its youth director, Tom Evans, focused his efforts along Hollywood Boulevard, and would bring runaways back to his home, a practice now widely frowned upon by youth-service workers. When the program became formalized in 1964, a social worker and two interns were hired and this practice was discontinued.[13] In a similar case, Lois Lee ran Children of the Night out of her own home. This outreach program for child prostitutes sheltered approximately 250 children between 1979 and 1982, before more extensive funding was available.

Los Angeles Youth Network (LAYN), which serves chronic runaways, also ran into criticism in its early years because of its closed-door policy with respect to the police. Established in 1986, and concerned about the treatment its clients received from the police force, it initially withheld information from the police—a policy which brought considerable pressure to bear on the program, and threats of warrants from the police. In its earliest stages, Teen Canteen, which deals with chronic street youths, had a similar policy and was, according to its current director, "dominated by street thugs" and "controlled by the clients" that it intended to serve. Of course, one can always expect a certain amount of retrospective criticism when asking a director to characterize the "early days" of a program, or to compare current operations to those before he or she took office. However, in all cases, there were identifiable changes in the structures of these programs, especially in terms of the physical and informational access allowed or denied the police.

Both LAYN and Teen Canteen survived through a change in philosophy. LAYN, in its current form, works in close contact with the police and holds police-run, informal discussion groups in its center. For Teen Canteen, which was located directly adjacent to a bar which was the site of a prostitution and drug ring, police cooperation was essential.[14] As the former director noted :

> We needed that police back-up. We would call the police ten times for every once they called us. We needed that help. We could call the police and say, "We got a fight here and we need help," and they would be there. And they don't have to do that. They could just drag their feet.[15]

Youth were informed that Teen Canteen would act neither as catchment for the police nor as a refuge from it. Police were invited to run seminars and discussion groups. Youths with outstanding warrants or suspected in a crime would be picked up by police on the premises. Status offenders were given refuge. According to former director Dale Weaver:

> We had a working arrangement with them. It was explicit, it was out in the open, it was not written down, but it was out in the open. They (the police) wouldn't hassle kids at Teen Canteen. They would not pursue runaways—they would not respond to a mother by stomping into Teen Canteen and grabbing him and taking him way. If they were looking for a specific person who was a suspect in a specific crime, we would give them whatever information they needed. If he was here, we'd tell them and they'd come down and pick him up right away. If there were kids who were too young and vulnerable to be on the street we'd call the police, and say pick him up, and

they'd pick him up, away from Teen Canteen without any
discussion of our role in it.[16]

Teen Canteen negotiated the tensions between possible
identities as "catchment" for police or "refuge" from them by using
a spatial strategy which did not blur the boundaries between front
and back region, but instead displaced them.

For programs dealing with highly stigmatized youths there is a
circularity between lack of acknowledgment of the problem (that
is, belief that these youths were less deserving and pathological in
their behavior), lack of funding, and the need to resort to private
homes and private funding sources to treat them. This sometimes
has the effect of discrediting the programs that attempt to help
them, as questions are raised about "what really goes on" in these
unsupervised (that is, nonstate-controlled) spaces. Both Covenant
House, which targets youths between eighteen and twenty years
old, and Children of the Night, which targets child prostitutes, experienced these criticisms. The issue at stake is not the actual
practices of these programs but that they continue to operate in
back regions of unsupervised space.[17]

This has been a pivotal criticism of the operations of Bruce
Ritter, formerly of Covenant House, who was accused by one of his
clients of a sexually exploitative relationship. Says Gabe Cruks,
director of Youth Services at the Gay and Lesbian Community
Services:

> Whether he slept with the kids is not the issue—what was
> any staff person doing taking a kid home or being in a
> room with a kid? It's that whole issue of boundaries. They
> violated their boundaries, period. . . . If I have any staff
> person developing a personal friendship it's out the door.[18]

In this sense, in spite of their internal differences, there is an
underlying similarity between the autonomous punk-squatter scene
of the late 1970s and the early operations of many programs for
homeless and runaway youths. These support structures operated
to a large extent in a private or unsupervised, relatively
autonomous sphere. To this extent they were subject (in varying
degrees) to very similar charges by later critics: that they were possibly doing more to perpetuate "deviant and exploitative" lifestyles
than to transform them.

THE FAMILY AS FRONT REGION

Alternative programs operated as "back regions" to the extent that they prevented intrusions by police or the family. The remaining programs acted as "front regions," to the extent that they notified family and police immediately about the whereabouts of the runaway, and made attempts to effect a speedy reunification with the family.

Referral and hotline services constituted the bulk of remaining programs in the mid-1970s. They either connected runaways with volunteer foster homes or attempted to reunite them with their families. The foster homes were widely dispersed throughout the county, located in La Crescenta/La Canada, in the foothills of the San Gabriel Mountains, Norwalk, Downey, and at the Salvation Army in downtown Los Angeles. Much of the information about the nature and operation of these services is lost to historical record.[19] Some responded to the needs of youth and families within their own community when families reported a runaway member, others simply attempted to locate some distance away from where runaways congregated to remove them from negative influences.[20] Up until 1975, foster care appeared to be organized largely on an informal basis through community hotlines and other outreach services. Youths were often placed for trial periods in the homes of volunteers, as with the Salvation Army, which operated a program for runaways out of its downtown building[21] (see Figure 9).

The Status Offender Detention Alternative Program (SODA) began as a pilot project in 1975, operated by the Probation Department in response to the Runaway Youth Act of 1974. Youths could stay for two to three days in designated foster homes, and cool off before being returned to their families. In 1983 the program offered forty-one beds. By 1985, the program reportedly had achieved a "form of caseload equilibrium," with twenty-eight beds in fourteen licensed foster homes and an additional nine backup beds, that enabled SODA to take only appropriate placements.[22]

Whatever the merit of the foster homes approach or the benefits of a familial setting, youths could not legally be held in homes, and tended to run right back to the urban areas where they had first attempted to locate themselves.[23] By 1983, the walkaway rate from SODA homes was anywhere from 25% to 35%.[24] In 1984, of the 1,508 petitions received for placement, 220 (14.5%) were eventually filed, and 608 (40%) left on AWOL status.[25] By 1990, the walkaway rate had reached 50%.[26] Although the SODA model has persisted as

Redefining Youth

one treatment option, it became increasingly clear by the 1980s that other alternatives were necessary.

THE EMERGING SERVICE NETWORK—A SPACE IN BETWEEN

> Concrete socio-economic space appears both as the articulation of analyzed spaces, as a product, a reflection of the articulation of social relationships, and at the same time, as far as already existing space is concerned, as an objective constraint imposed on the redeployment of these social relationships. We shall say that society recreates its space on the basis of a concrete space, always already provided, established in the past.
>
> —Alain Lipietz, "The Structuration of Space: The Problem of Land and Spatial Policy,"in *Regions in Crisis*, 1980, p.289

The service network that emerged in the 1980s changed the social and spatial relationships of these youths to the metaphor of "street" and "family," to the surrounding community, and to each other. The stabilization of a service network in the Hollywood area created a new social space, an *interstitial space*, neither fully public nor fully private, neither a front nor a back region, but a recomposition of the two.

The resulting service network was a productive fusion of "front" and "back" with the tension between street culture and family life played out differently for each subculture of youths that the services dealt with.[27] By 1990, a network of services had evolved with different strategies of treatment, different locational dynamics and different sociospatial controls for first-time runaways, chronic runaways, and chronic street youths. Programs were distinguished by the age, sexual orientation, and survival strategies of the youths they served, the amount of time they had been on the street, and the frequency with which they had run from home. They also became concentrated in the Hollywood area.

"Alternative programs" and subcultural supports had represented a sphere of relative autonomy for homeless youths in the area. As they moved to Hollywood and evolved in the area, it was precisely the question of autonomy that service providers began to wrestle with. To become successfully established in the Hollywood area, programs had to develop an image in relation to the youths they served, the communities where they served, and the institutional form of intervention which they (following deinstitutionalization) implicitly critiqued. Services had to be able to attract youths without simply providing them with resources that enabled them to sustain a street culture. They had to control the youths without appearing too restrictive, lest the youth leave, or the services appear too much like institutions or juvenile halls to a nervous local community. They had to draw recalcitrant youth out of street subcultures by developing strong affective relationships which could not become an end in themselves, but rather a means to move them out of the local community. The organizational ethos which guided programs through these issues, and the images they developed both of themselves and the youths they treated, were intricately bound up with the place and space within which they operated.

Social services evolved *a complex spatial strategy in relation to the community itself.* First, they chose locations to enhance possibilities of attracting youths off the boulevards and into their programs. Locations differed among services depending on the type of youths they wanted to attract (first-time runaways, chronic runaways, hard-core street youth). Since they could no longer legally incarcerate youths in their treatment programs, friction of distance became a critical tool in attempting to modify and regulate the youths' environment. Second, these services extended the reach of their programs with street outreach, on foot or with mobile vans, sometimes as a precursor to establishing more permanent operations in a given area. Third, the programs began to choreograph the social space of runaway and homeless youths within the larger community, setting up curfews and even designating certain parts of the community "off-limits" to their clientele. These strategies were intended to modify the behaviors of the youths within the community, and to manage their image within it. By the 1990s, these spatial strategies seem almost "natural," but they were learned over the years, as services modified and built on past successes and failures.

BETWEEN THE SACRED AND THE PROFANE : CENTERING SERVICES IN HOLLYWOOD

The locational strategies of services went far beyond the simple injunction of the Homeless and Runaway Youth Act of 1974 "to be located in areas youth can easily reach."[28] Services were positioned in a strategic relationship to the front and back regions of Hollywood—the former dominated by tourists, the latter by transients and street subcultures—either to keep youths away from back regions, or as way of determining their willingness (both literally and figuratively) to leave the streets. But decentering works two ways. The reluctance of homeless youths to leave Hollywood was in the early years an important factor pulling services to the area. Teen Canteen, Angel's Flight, and the Salvation Army all moved their operations to Hollywood after operating for some years on the failed assumption that they could intercept runaways in downtown Los Angeles as they came (en route to Hollywood) from other places (see Figure 10). Decentering was not an absolute tool of social control exerted *over* the youth by the services. It expressed tension negotiated *between* services and the (metaphorical) street as alternative options for homeless youth. In general, the more attached the youth were to street subcultures, the closer the programs dealing with them tended to locate to the back regions frequented by these youths.

Decentering was used to dissuade association with street subcultures, or to "sort" the deserving from the undeserving. Centering, by contrast, was supposed to draw "hard-core" youth off the streets into services. Options House set up a storefront operation on Hollywood Boulevard in 1979, but soon moved a short distance away to a residential neighborhood, because, in the words of the current director, "we wanted to get the kids out of that environment." The program had plans to open a second facility for a longer term transitional program. This would be located on Beachwood Avenue, still further from the boulevard because according to the director, "to break the pattern you needed to move a little further from the boulevard"[29] (see Figure 10.)

Teen Canteen, a drop-in center for chronic street youth, first located on Sunset Boulevard, and then Hollywood Boulevard at Hollywood and Vine. Both streets were highly trafficked by the youth and the programs were immediately accessible to them. In 1986, Salvation Army set up The Way In, a drop-in center for first-time runners immediately adjacent to Teen Canteen at Hollywood and Vine. It eventually moved because the board decided the program was attracting youth with a "playground mentality" who simply took advantage of the services. In order to attract youths who were self-motivated enough to want to leave the streets, the program moved a few blocks east of Vine along Hollywood Boulevard, to a no-man's-land which attracted neither youths nor tourists. Said one street worker there: "If they really wanted help, they'd walk the extra block."[30]

FIGURE 10:
HOLLYWOOD AREA SHELTER AND SERVICES
FOR HOMELESS AND RUNAWAY YOUTH

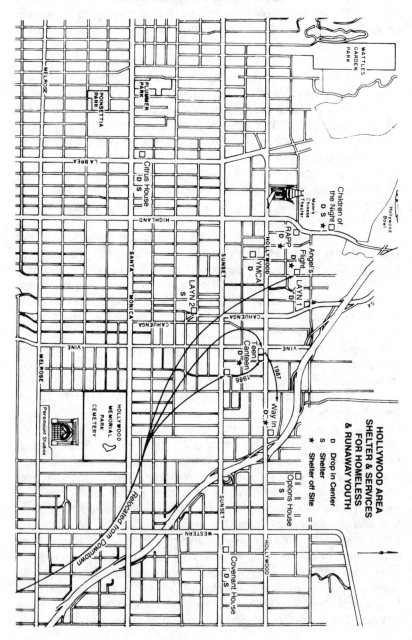

Redefining Youth

Los Angeles Youth Network, which targets chronic runaways, youths who are perhaps less committed to street life than those served by Teen Canteen, moved north of the Hollywood Boulevard to Cahuenga. Says Mindi Levins, program director:

> The biggest spatial strategy that we have in any building we pick is to be close enough to the boulevard for the kids to have access to it and far enough from the merchants that we don't have to worry about our kids disrupting anything. And they do (disrupt things).[31]

Children of the Night, which deals with child prostitutes, located some blocks north of Hollywood Boulevard on Highland Avenue, and plans to open a shelter program in Van Nuys, a considerable distance from the Hollywood area, reasoning that their clients need to be completely removed in order to be able to break all attachments with their former life.

In 1989, Covenant House opened a twenty-bed shelter on Sunset Boulevard (linked to an off-site hotel with an additional forty beds). Here philosophy and location were mutually reflective. Covenant House targets eighteen- to twenty-year-olds, youths considered to be in a categorical gray zone because they are legally adults, and therefore technically not eligible for services funding runaway youth, but who are socially and developmentally adolescents and neither suited to nor attracted to services for homeless adults.[32] When Covenant House announced in 1987 that it planned to open a 100 bed shelter in Hollywood, on or near Hollywood Boulevard, it met with substantial opposition, especially from other service providers. The ensuing conflict was mediated by local Councilman Michael Woo, who allegedly intervened on the proviso that the program be located just outside the boundaries of the Hollywood Redevelopment Project Area.[33] While Covenant House would not discuss the circumstances surrounding setting up the program, that this arrangement was made seems likely for two reasons. By locating within the boundaries of the project the program could be subject to a full environmental review before approval, a process which could jeopardize its implementation. Also, the final location on Serrano and Sunset Boulevard is in an area noted for high rates of street prostitution, just one block east of the boundary of the Hollywood Redevelopment Project Area.

WARRENING FROM WITHIN

Services had to consider not only how location, in relation to the front and back regions of Hollywood, affected the type of youth they would draw, but how the microenvironment affected their relationship to the community at large. Service providers have coexisted within the community, negotiating the spaces and gaps within it, making inroads into it, warrening it from within. The most literal example of this is the microlocational strategy of LAYN. LAYN targets neither "first-time runaways," who might be comfortably located in the "sacred" front regions of Hollywood's residential areas, nor the "hard-core street youths," whose services necessarily located in the profane spaces of Hollywood, Sunset, or Santa Monica Boulevards. LAYN served chronic runaways, youths who have repeatedly run from their homes, but unlike chronic street youth have not lived out on the street for extended periods. Chronic runaways often adopt the dress and argot of hard-core street cultures but, according to the caseworker, are "wannabes" who do not really understand the consequences of their actions. Located on Cahuenga, the facility negotiated the gaps within the social space of the community.[34] Mindi Levins observed:

> We like our location at Cahuenga by the gas station for the drop-in center. We took Cahuenga partly because it's not near the businesses but close enough to the boulevard to be visible. You need to be close to Hollywood Boulevard, you can't be ten miles away, but they (the homeless youth who come here) don't drive cars, so they don't go to the gas station. We purposely picked the location.[35]

LAYN needed to have access to the front and back regions of the boulevard, but was unwilling to locate in back regions from which the youth workers hoped to divert their clients. It was also unable to locate in the front regions of Hollywood's residential neighborhoods—in fact it had moved from such a location because of neighborhood complaints. To address this dilemma, LAYN occupied a literal space in between. It was buffered from its surroundings by a gas station, which had a (necessarily) highly transient population, and offered nothing to the drop-in center's clients.

Teen Canteen deals with "hard-core," chronic street youths. The service needed to be on Hollywood Boulevard, where the youth congregated. But it could not locate too close to prime spaces, lest it draw complaints from neighboring merchants and tenants. In the first years of its establishment, Teen Canteen rented a storefront from "Crossroads of the World," a rather kitschy tourist trap with a high tourist draw on Sunset Boulevard. The program soon had its lease revoked because the landlord complained about "the unsavory nature of their clientele."[36] A subsequent move to Hollywood and Vine presented another problem. The marginal space next to the drop-in center was a saloon, with a high volume of drug trafficking. To deal with this problem, the program developed a different set of strategies. This included covering its commercial windows with a large, wooden, open lattice, which gave a feeling of openness, yet shielded the youth inside from the scrutiny of passersby. Service providers had to keep their clients out of the saloon, a problem later "solved" when, shortly after police threatened to close down the saloon, it burned down, taking the drop-in center with it.

IMAGES OF PLACE: THE LANDSCAPE OF HOLLYWOOD

In Sacramento and elsewhere, the image is the reality. And I think that's what we have to spend a lot of time on, the image of this problem, and not only in the minds of legislators and the decision-makers but of others that might have an impact on this problem. . . . What is the image of homeless and runaway youth?

—Tom David, Supervisor Edelman's Special Conference for the County of Los Angeles: The Special Matter of Homeless and Runaway Youth. Public hearing,September 10, 1986.

Services that need to locate in back regions risk reinforcing the negative associations between the youth and the street subcultures. To gain acceptance in the community, these services not only reconfigured the social space of Hollywood, but, through images of place, attempted to renegotiate the spoiled identity of their clients. Services have often explicitly differentiated themselves from the image of the "institution," likening their organizations to a family, or to a recreation center, sometimes stretching the imagination to avoid the label of institution.

Covenant House is a case in point. In 1988, the privately funded, Christian-backed organization planned to extend its already sizeable operations (including programs in New York, Toronto, Houston, Fort Lauderdale, New Orleans, and Central America) into Hollywood. They proposed opening a 100 bed shelter on Hollywood Boulevard. Other service providers in the area argued that they would be swamped with a facility of this size, and that on such a scale Covenant House could not possibly provide the intensive personal care needed for its clientele. In short, it would risk becoming a "back region" simply providing "three hots and a cot." As a compromise, Covenant House agreed to open a twenty-bed shelter just outside the eastern boundary of the Hollywood Redevelopment Project Area, on Sunset Boulevard. In addition, they would target youth aged eighteen to twenty-one, who technically could not be served by the other state-funded programs, which could deal only with minors. A year after establishing itself in Hollywood, Covenant House opened an additional forty beds of leased hotel space, for a total of sixty beds. In its promotional literature, it attempted to forestall comparisons to traditional shelter institutions this way: "Rights of Passage offers kids a place to live for up to eighteen months in a college-dorm-style setting while giving them a chance to finish school and start careers."[37]

Another short-lived project operated a "fold-up" shelter out of a Hollywood YMCA.[38] Clients slept in a room which during the day was used by the YMCA as a children's day care center. To bridge the incongruities of locating a shelter in a day care space, and the temporary nature of appropriation of the space, it styled its "fold-up shelter" of twenty futons around a "a Japanese theme." The Japanese theme was an attempt to provide a model of normalcy and permanency for a temporary and makeshift use of the space.[39]

The two most compelling images used by services have been the invocation of family structures as a therapeutic model of treatment, and the invocation of "Hollywood" and the lure of supposed stardom as a reason for attracting youth to its streets. These represent the two polarities of a reorganized image of homeless and runaway youths, the one invoking the sanctity of the family in its treatment programs, the other recuperating the street from associations with profanity and corruption. Grounded in the dual image of Hollywood—the promise of stardom concealing the reality of degradation—service providers had a basis in which they could ground a sympathetic image of chronic street youths.

INVOKING THE SACRED—
SIMULATING FAMILY AS A THERAPEUTIC MODEL

> When we first established ourselves in a private house in a private neighborhood, all hell broke loose. There was a school three blocks away and the neighbors were afraid. We called a meeting of the Beachwood area, and explained the house rules—that we had a psychologist and twenty-four-hour staff, that the children had to cook and clean. It looked like a home, not an institution.

> —Ethel Narvid, founder of Options House, Hollywood, California, personal interview, May 30, 1991.

> This is a house and we run it like a family,

> —Leslie Forbes, Director of Options House, May 1991.

> I think of the counselors as my parents.

> —homeless youth, Los Angeles Youth Network, Hollywood, in public hearing to Little Hoover Commission, 1989.

As Ethel Narvid suggests in her account of the establishment of Options House in 1980 (the first formally recognized emergency shelter for homeless youths in Hollywood), the introduction of what was essentially a therapy program for juveniles within the urban core required an organizational ethos that not only met the imperatives of deinstitutionalization, but also provided an acceptable face for the local community. This local community included both fearful neighbors and a skeptical police force, which argued at first that the shelter would only "attract freeloaders." The "projected space" of these services had to contend with an "inherited space" defined by both a reluctant clientele and an unwilling community. For Options House, which is aimed at "first-time runners," this was achieved by stressing the "rescue mission" of the program—to provide first-time runners with a different option from the street—and by emphasizing the familial atmosphere of the organization. The emphasis on the family-type setting was a key factor in gaining community acceptance,[40] and still permeates contemporary public-relations literature on the shelter (see Figure 11).

FIGURE 11

Winter 1991

A Report From Options House

President's Report

A New Year brings resolutions of things we intend to accomplish that year. 1991 is no exception.

Nor is Options House an exception. While we continue to progress, we have not lost sight of the sobering fact that we have much ground to cover before we can make a significant dent in the problem of homeless teens who are attracted to our area. With the current recession, the potential for more teens to become homeless is very real.

We would be delighted to operate a number of homes like Options House. We've secured the funding to renovate our Beachwood Drive property. Coupled with our current Taft Avenue residence, we will double our housing capacity. With adequate funding, more houses could become a reality.

However, with many sources of public contracts and funds disappearing, we increasingly must seek ongoing support from individual donors, corporations and foundations. Unfortunately, the need for programs like Options House does not disappear just because funds may.

Please join me and my fellow Board members in making a commitment for the New Year to continue supporting Options House. With such support, we can further expand our program and fill the great void in this area of social services. A little help from a great number of friends will go a long way in helping us realize our goals.

Thank you.

Michael J. Dubelko

Director's Letter

Dear Friends of Options House,

Endings, like beginnings, inevitably inspire reflection. As 1991 arrived, my first year with the agency drew to a close. And what a year it has been! Our services are increasing to meet an ever-growing demand, the House looks terrific, our Board has expanded and grown stronger, our staff is more focused...and we raised enough funds to begin renovating our Beachwood Drive property!

During the year, family and friends have asked me, "What can you do with the kids in only two weeks?" Generally, I respond with a question: "Have you ever taken a two-week vacation? Consider how many sites you visited, restaurants you discovered, stores you patronized, experiences you had, etc." Suddenly, our two-week program seems more capable of effecting change.

(Continued on Page 3)

Redefining Youth

> Options House: Much more than a place to stay, Options House is a home. . . . We function as the breaking away point from street life to home life. . . . During their two-weeks' stay, teens experience the routines of family living—sometimes for the first time. In addition to academic tutoring, daily group therapy and individual counselling sessions, residents also share in household chores—cooking, cleaning, laundry and yardwork.[41]

The family is the organizing ethos permeating the daily routines of this and other shelters,[42] and to some extent the affective relationships between youth and youth workers. It provides a legitimate context within which to introduce structure into programs and sanctions—many homeless youths in squats organize themselves into "families," sometimes designating older members as "mom" and "dad," sometimes referring to each other as sister and brother.[43] Within the services, a family structure provides a model for daily routine, including chores such as cleaning up the shelter or drop-in center or doing dishes, and the establishment of curfews in the shelters. Here emergency shelters negotiate a fine line between the need to control the relationship of their youths to the surrounding community, and the need to fill the imperatives of deinstitutionalization by remaining "non-lock-up" programs. This is generally done by physically allowing youths freedom of movement, but imposing sanctions should curfew be violated, which can sometimes mean expulsion from a program.[44]

But the "family" is an elusive and flexible social form with many meanings. In his opening address to the Public Hearing Committee on Runaway and Homeless Youth, Haig Marikan, Vice Chairman of the Little Hoover Commission, gave a public face to this family. The hearing was convened to evaluate the success of the service network for homeless and runaway youth in the county and to decide where future funds should be allocated and whether the pilot program should become a permanent one. The face of the family, as presented by Marikan to a middle-aged advisory board, was the lost family of the 1950s—the suburban nuclear family of postwar America: "The bulk of these children never had families that resembled the Nelsons on *Ozzie and Harriet* and their childhoods were a far cry from *Leave it to Beaver*."[45]

This image acts as both the measure of failure of the actual families these youths come from and an implied promise of reconstruction, through the experience of simulated family life in emergency shelters. In these therapeutic families, shelters and service must negotiate a tightrope of contradictions, positioning themselves carefully between the simple recreation of an "actual" family, and the operation of an institution. To move too close to the model of a real family is to cross the boundaries of professional conduct. The need to manage the tension between professional and affective relationships has resulted in the creation of a separate public/private social space for these youths in the past decade (compare the "crash pads" of the 1970s), within which a strict decorum is maintained. But it has also extended "the boundary question" into a very subtle level of body politics. This was exemplified in the 1989 *Street Outreach Minutes* to outreach workers, concerned about their relationship to youths when out on the street doing AIDS-prevention outreach:

> Physical Contact on the Street: Some of the young people on the street try to hug the staff. All of the staff are uncomfortable with this because of the boundary issues that arise and because of the hygiene issues. We discussed ways to talk to the kids about what is appropriate and what isn't. Reinforced the concept that hugging is inappropriate (for reasons of professional conduct) and could be dangerous. We decided that all of us will set better limits with these young people.[46]

In emergency shelters, "the family" as a form for developing affective relationships has been a critical means of managing this tension, and of dissociating these services from the image of the (impersonal and therefore ineffective) institution. But like other organizational forms, the family is a dynamic strategy rather than a static category: homeless youths in shelters and in squats use the rhetoric and structure of ersatz families to band together and sustain relationships. Mindi Levins noted:

> Since they came into the program . . . they're all "brothers" and "sisters" or related—they make a network of whoever they hang out with—husband, wife, brother, sister. When we started kicking a bunch of them out because they weren't working on stuff (i.e. following therapy treatment), they said that they'd become like a family, we 'd broken up their family.[47]

The "family structure" is an organizational form both for homeless youth in squats and for service providers in shelters, and the lines of relationship are a source of constant renegotiation. But more important, the insistence that services are organized as ersatz families has been critical in sustaining an image of homeless and runaway youth as victims of dysfunctional families, as the experience of Options House suggests. Other programs adopted this strategy as well. In 1981, Lois Lee, founder of Children of the Night, publicized her planned facility for juvenile prostitutes as a program "to build a family for children who did not know one." The newspaper article covering the program went on to note, "Their pimps are substitute fathers that they are usually lacking at home."[48]

By implication, services and shelters for runaways reintegrate the youths into the bosom of the simulated nuclear family of the postwar era. In doing so, they link the youths to an image of adolescence and juvenile delinquency that came close to being dismantled in the wake of deinstitutionalization.[49] This image located the reasons for delinquent and criminal behavior (and hence the solutions to it) in an improperly managed upbringing.

But the experience of "family life" is a simulation. The programs must prepare the youths within a matter of weeks for family life in some imagined elsewhere. The counselors must develop affective relationships with the youth, but only in settings that are strictly monitored to prevent abuse (or allegations of abuse.)

Service providers are, of course, well aware of the difficulties of achieving such an objective in the short space of two weeks. Since Options House first introduced its storefront on the boulevard in 1979, it is clear that the common understanding of a "homeless youth" has broadened substantially in Los Angeles County. At the time, the program was designed to serve "first-time runners," neophytes under eighteen years old who were offered an option (as the program name suggests) to the alternative "choice" of life on the streets. The program was two weeks long, the time presumed sufficient to give runaway youth a taste of "normal" family life, to identify and begin to treat their problems, and to return them to their families or locate alternative living arrangements.

But for programs serving "harder-to-reach" youths, such as Children of the Night and Covenant House, which do not depend on state funding, the maximum length of stay is unspecified and decided on a case-by-case basis. State-funded services have also used tactics to extend their programs, sometimes "reentering" the same youth in a program up to three times. Options House runs a six-bed shelter targeting first-time runaways. In this program the maximum length of stay is two weeks, but the organizers will, on occasion, extend this to four weeks, and are planning to open a twelve-bed facility which would include six six-month beds. The irony of quick turnover, as the director noted, is that quick movement through a program can sometimes jeopardize the objective of reunification: "the ability to reunite kids with their families would be stronger if you had longer-term programs."[50] Citrus House will enroll clients in its independent-living program as many as three successive times in order to extend the limits of their stay. As the programs have evolved, stays have become longer and longer. LAYN now houses youth for up to two months, Covenant House will accept youth formally for up to eighteen months and informally for indefinite periods. Options House is proposing a six-month 6-bed transitional program to allow more time to work with youths and their families (see Figure 9). The programs formally appear as a "bridge" between street life and family life. But as they attempt to deal with increasingly recalcitrant clientele and dysfunctional families, this bridge has extended in length, and the destination recedes into the distance. The point is not to question the true intent of these programs, but rather to recognize the way in which they have out of necessity, negotiated the lengthening path between street and family.

RECUPERATING THE PROFANE:
FROM "STREET" TO "WALK OF FAME"

> Through its star system, Hollywood took ordinary Americans, which by and large the stars themselves were, and endowed them with qualities of transcendence. . . . This dynamic connection transformed Hollywood into an emotionally energized American place, touched by myth and magic.
>
> —Kevin Starr, Inventing the Dream 1985, p.320.

> From its beginning in St. Louis, Missouri, during the California Gold Rush days, Travelers Aid Society has been in the forefront of assisting displaced persons in need. Now a century later, a new "Gold Rush" to the glamour and excitement of Hollywood brings thousands of homeless and runaway young people to its streets. Unfortunately, what they find is the stark reality of violence, prostitution, exploitation and drug abuse.
>
> —Travelers Aid Society of Los Angeles, Promotional Literature for Teen Canteen (n.d.)

Redefining Youth

I think the idea of Hollywood is a factor (attracting homeless youth). It's America's relationship to media and stars. It may sound hokey or naive, but with a number of kids—when you really explore with them—(you discover) I came here to be a star—not to be an actor, not to be a musician—to be a star, to be discovered, to achieve recognition.

—Gabe Cruks, Director, The Gay and Lesbian Center, West Hollywood, May 30, 1990.

The first pole of a reorganized image of runaway and homeless youth centered on the family. The second pole focused on the duplicitous nature of the urban environment they ran to—specifically the dual image of Hollywood. This has been critical in developing a sympathetic public image of homeless youth, in spite of the wide range of stigmatized practices they engage in once away from home.

Since 1980, a number of services have set up acting workshops and star seminars, and used this aspect in their advertising about programs. Teen Canteen has been most graphic in this association, capitalizing on its location on Hollywood Boulevard and using the Walk of Fame in its logo and promotional literature (see Figure 12). Runaways may have left the sacred environment of the family for the profane environment of the streets, but it was not just any street. These were the streets of Hollywood, the "Walk of Fame"—a 2.3-mile stretch along Hollywood Boulevard evoking dreams of stardom. The YMCA, Teen Canteen, and Angel's Flight have all held acting workshops and seminars for youths seeking stardom. This has had the dual effect of legitimating the presence of these youths in the area, and providing a meeting point for community members and youths that was not structured around the youths' homelessness.

To evoke the desire for stardom both destigmatized the youth who ran to Hollywood and placed the burden of the problem on the community producing this image itself. Service providers produced a "nonspoiled" identity for these youth—as *precocious* youth, in the premodern sense which romanticized early attempts at independence. But this precocity is simultaneously admired and decried in a way that is intricately bound up with the place-making mythology of Hollywood.

FIGURE 12

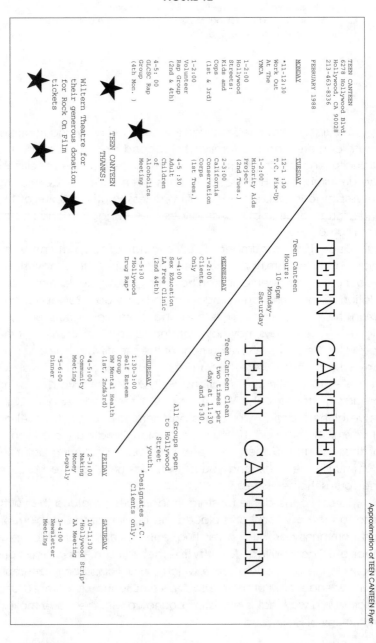

TEEN CANTEEN
6278 Hollywood Blvd.
Hollywood, CA 90028
213-463-8336

FEBRUARY 1988

TEEN CANTEEN

Teen Canteen
Hours:
10-6pm
Monday-
Saturday

Teen Canteen Clean
Up two times per
day at 11:30
and 5:30.

All Groups open
to Hollywood
Street
youth.
*Designates T.C.
Clients only.

MONDAY
*11-12:30
Work Out
At The
YMCA

1-2:00
Hollywood
Streets:
Kids and
Cops
(1st & 3rd)

1-2:00
Volunteer
Rap Group
(2nd & 4th)

4-5:00
GLCSC Rap
Group
(4th Mon.)

TUESDAY
12-1:30
T.C. Fix-Up

1-2:00
Minority Aids
Project
(2nd Tues.)

2-3:00
California
Conservation
Corps
(1st Tues.)

4-5:30
Adult
Children
of
Alcoholics
Meeting

WEDNESDAY
1-2:00
Clients
Only

3-4:00
Sex Education
LA Free Clinic
(2nd &4th)

4-5:30
*Hollywood
Drug Rap*

THURSDAY
1:30-3:00
Self Esteem
Group
HW Mental Health
(1st, 2nd&3rd)

*4-5:00
Community
Meeting

*5-6:00
Dinner

FRIDAY
2-3:00
Making
Money
Legally

SATURDAY
10-11:30
"Hollywood Strip"
AA Meeting

3-4:00
Newsletter
Meeting

TEEN CANTEEN
THANKS:

Wiltern Theatre for
their generous donation
for Rock On Film
tickets

Approximation of TEEN CANTEEN Flyer

156

Redefining Youth

Greg Carlson of Angel's Flight, reflecting on his prior attempts to obtain funding for young, homeless, Hispanic refugees in other parts of the county, explained it this way:

> Most of your drop-in centers are in Hollywood for two reasons. One, there are kids here, at least the kids are visible, and two, funding. If you're writing a grant you're going to pull on the hearts of people more if you're working with runaway and homeless youth, and they're in Hollywood— because of the big bad city. If you're working with eighteen to twenty-one-year-olds in Pacoima, it's not as exciting.[51]

In this sense Hollywood is exemplary of a peculiar inversion of the respective weight of its mental space over its political and social space. This *space of representation* of Hollywood is more than simply an *outcome* of concrete material practices. Representations themselves become a dynamic in the unfolding of specific practices.

FROM INTAKE TO OUTREACH—
THE CHANGING ROLE OF BACK REGIONS

Service providers did more than provide a new type of refuge and acceptable image for youths within their walls. During the 1980s, they developed a coordinated spatial strategy throughout the community of Hollywood, including a systematic outreach program, a code of conduct for street workers when dealing with youths in the community, and the designation of profane spaces in Hollywood—areas that youths could not frequent without fear of expulsion from their programs.

Several programs had a policy which forbade their clientele from gathering in front of the service waiting for it to open, or from panhandling within a specified radius of the service. In the case of Teen Canteen, the youth risked expulsion from the program for the day.[52] In the case of Los Angeles Youth Network, this might result in permanent expulsion from the program.[53] LAYN also prohibited its youth clients from hanging out either along Hollywood Boulevard (where they might disturb the shopkeepers), or in parts of the community known for drug trafficking and prostitution.

Young and Homeless in Hollywood

Outreach efforts existed as early as the 1950s, when Tom Evans ran an informal program out of the YMCA. Both Teen Canteen and Angel's Flight had outreach workers in Hollywood in the early 1980s as a precursor to establishing drop-in centers in the community. But outreach was an informal affair, not systematized within or between services. In 1988, the Division of Adolescent Medicine received funding to coordinate an AIDS-outreach program to street youth, and to provide formal training for outreach workers in the area. The program was established out of con-cern over the high-risk behaviors of many youths on the street, in particular their practice of survival sex (often unprotected), and their practice of sharing IV needles. For the first time, services in the area were pulled together into one coordinated system which planned outreach times and routes, discussed "street etiquette," exchanged information on where youths were hanging out and developed a public face for outreach workers, with T-shirts and business cards that gave them legitimate "presence" on the street. With this last act, they conferred upon themselves the role of "opening positions" within the community, that is to say, a public role ascribed to strangers whom one can approach in a formal or institutional position.[54] Service workers began systematically to patrol the "front regions" of Hollywood and to set up office in its "back regions" (see Figure 13).

Angel's Flight developed a widening set of outreach routes, all with initial concentration along the tourist areas of the boulevard. LAYN "set up offices" in two areas heavily frequented by homeless and runaway youths—Oki Dogs and Plummer Park.

This last act was a calculated inversion of the meaning of the space. For almost two decades, Oki Dogs had been tactically inhabited by a variety of Hollywood's street subcultures, and had gained a reputation as a hangout and connection point for dealers, prostitutes, homeless and runaway youth, punks, and a variety of other subcultures. From the beginning of the 1980s, back regions such as this one tended to be simply closed off by police or municipal action, in the constant raids on the manor houses and the barbed-wiring of the Hollywood cemetery, and the municipally sponsored demolition of squats.

These back regions had a contradictory function, which service workers began to exploit in the late 1980s. The closing of Oki Dogs and Plummer Park in 1990 was, in the eyes of outreach workers, a very controversial and detrimental act. Mindi Levins, case worker at Los Angeles Youth Network, commented on the implications of closing these areas down:

> Oki Dogs . . . was attracting street kids. This is a sleaze pit.
> Kids are congregating here, they're dealing drugs here,
> their prostitution connection's here, the younger kids are
> getting hooked up here, all true—all those bad things
> were happening. And I hated Oki Dogs 'cause to me it
> was the sleazeball place of the earth. But by closing
> Oki Dogs what do you solve? You either push it under-
> ground or you push it elsewhere. The great thing about
> Oki Dogs was you knew where the kids were. You knew
> where to reach them. By closing it you weren't stopping
> any of that going on. In fact you were blowing the
> whole network outreach workers had really infiltrated,
> (they'd) really know how to work it. This was an entrance
> point into social services. There will be a new Oki Dogs,
> there already is, in some ways, but it just scatters the
> problem. Oki Dogs was one of the best places to do out-
> reach cause you could just sit there for two hours (and
> reach everyone).[55]

While Oki Dogs functioned as a hang-out and point of contact
for homeless youths, Plummer Park was, for many, their squat:

> Plummer Park was basically where they were living, and
> that's what became a problem. It was younger kids,
> a large amount of Russian immigrants, a summer camp
> and tennis courts, so in the middle of all this, was a
> big grassy area with homeless people, their IV drug
> needles, their condoms from the social worker—nothing
> was kept a secret. There were anywhere from ten to
> thirty homeless people there on a given day. It was
> basically teenagers. . . . The age could be as young
> as thirteen years. But I did run into some as old as thirty-
> five years—and they would move back and forth
> between Oki Dogs and Plummer Park—Oki Dogs 'cause
> the food was really cheap and they could panhandle.
> The owner was sympathetic. . . . It was a good place for
> outreach workers.
>
> The biggest thing that happened from (its closing) is a lot
> of people on the street scattered. So outreach has
> become more difficult. I don't know where they've gone.
> They've moved to Poinsettia Park, up to Jamaica John's;
> a lot are walking the streets.[56]

The closing of Oki Dogs and Plummer Park was, according
to service providers, initiated by an east-end homeowners' group in a

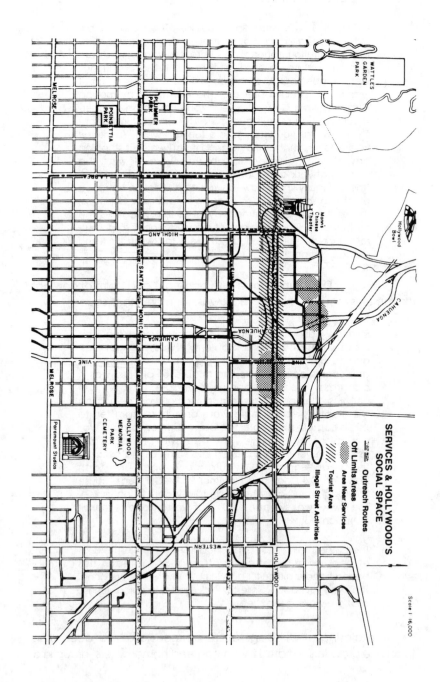

SERVICES & HOLLYWOOD'S
SOCIAL SPACE

Outreach Routes
Off Limits Areas
Area Near Services
Tourist Area
Illegal Street Activities

Scale 1 : 16,000

newly gentrifying neighborhood.[57] On their impetus, the City of West Hollywood held a public hearing to see if there was enough support to close down Oki Dogs and the food bank (opened generally for homeless people) at Plummer Park. What is important here is that the closing down of these two back regions did little, according to outreach workers, to stop activities such as prostitution and drug dealing in the area, which simply scattered throughout the area. What it did achieve was to stop these activities from defining the social meaning of the space in the surrounding neighborhood. Clearly, this action was not concerned so much with cleaning up the neighborhood *per se*. This would have been achieved more effectively if these "back regions" had been left to operate as they were, providing a point of entry for service-providers to homeless and runaway youth. Residents were much more concerned with the way these back regions had come to define the larger social space of the community. Their goal was *to change the dominant meaning of the space*, rather than change the activities that went on there.

CONCLUSION

One of the most deeply mourned victims of the contemporary modernization processes is the suburban nuclear family of the post-war era. Forget for a moment that by the late 1960s and early 1970s, women and youths were chafing at the sterile environments of suburban households, that feminists were trying to find words to describe "the problem with no name," and that part of the youthful rebellions of the 1960s was against a suburban "social factory" glutted with useless gadgets. This moment was virtually submerged by the mid 1980s, in a wave of nostalgia for the 1950s and the imagined lost worlds of *Ozzie and Harriet* and *Leave it to Beaver*. Viewed in this perspective, the emergence of "the family" as one organizational ethos for shelters and services to youths in Los Angeles County could be seen in the same critical light that social historians recently aimed at turn-of-the-century rural child-saving institutions—as a misplaced nostalgia for an era, eliding all its conflicts and difficulties.

But the emergence of restructured "families" in this service network can also be seen as a victory on behalf of service-providers and youths simply to stay in place, in the face of attempts to dislodge them. Ersatz family relationships and affective ties to local communities respond to the pressures to develop alternative forms to large-scale institutions, utilizing informal structures of family and community to fill the void left by a divesting welfare state. In addition, these "family-based" programs fit well into the housing stock and small-scale commercial structures in inner-city neighborhoods. These programs marked a departure in spatial strategies from those of earlier camps and ranches, a rethinking of criteria for "appropriate placement" vis-à-vis surrounding communities, and the development of a place-sensitive organizational ethos.

The services to youths that emerged in the Hollywood area from the mid-1970s to the 1990s used space to reflect and reinforce particular modes of treatment for these youths. In the early years, the polarized views of service providers were expressed in distinctly different relations to metaphorical front and back regions—family and street.

But space was more than "simply a representation" of different and opposing views of homeless and runaway youths; it was a medium of struggle through which these ideas were contested and transformed. The ineffectiveness of these early approaches forced a rethinking of spatial strategies, a recomposition of the relationship between front and back regions, and a recuperation of models of street and family within the Hollywood area.

Far from simply offering an "alternative" to street life, contemporary services have, in a sense, cast a net over a range of sociospatial relations within the community. The result is a new public social space with a tightly imbricated monitoring and control of the use of the surrounding communities—a larger spatial praxis.

7

HOLLYWOOD RISING

Anyone who wants to claim a share of public space in a modern city is forced to share it with some of the people of the underclass, and so to think about where he stands in relation to them. . . . Most of the great public spaces in history—Greek agoras, Italian piazzas, Parisian boulevards—would rate as failures, because all were turbulent places, and needed large police forces on hand to keep the seething forces from exploding. On the other hand, some of the world's most sterile shopping malls would rate as shining successes. . . . the real failures in public spaces are not the streets full of social, sexual and political deviants, but rather the streets with no deviants at all.

> —Marshall Berman, "Taking it To the Streets: Conflict and Community in Public Space," *Dissent*, 1986: pp. 480–482.

The Hollywood Cleanup and Restoration Council which is working to change the shabby appearance and even shabbier reputation of Hollywood Boulevard . . .staged a rally today at the famed corner of Hollywood and Vine to applaud area businessmen and merchants who have cleaned up their storefronts. . . . After the ceremonies the crowd carrying blue-and-white pickets signs that read "Hollywood Clean Up Your Act" . . . crossed paths with

Young and Homeless in Hollywood

Hollywood's street people—a man selling balloons out of a suit-
case, a toothless women begging dimes and quarters, several
barechested weightlifters in tight jeans flexing their muscles, punk
rockers with green and pink hair, a pair of fresh-faced teenagers.

The street people, who usually attract the stares,
gawked in turn at what to them was an odd assortment, well-
dressed businessmen, older women in straw hats, uniformed
California Conservation Corps workers wielding brooms and mops,
and middle-aged men in Hush Puppies and walking shorts. . . .
Three street people, dressed in dirty cutoff jeans and carrying a
sign that said "Get Out of Our Ghetto" taunted the marchers with
a mini-parade of their own.

—Carolyn McGraw, "Hollywood Cheers its
Cleanup," *Los Angeles Times*, April 3, 1983.

Where does Hollywood stand in relation to its underclass, its
homeless? By Berman's standard, with its "toothless women
begging dimes, barechested weightlifters, green-and-pink-haired
punk rockers and dirty street people," Hollywood would rate as a
shining success. Yet much of the contemporary literature on urban
development and the homeless concludes that the homeless (or
any "others," who by their very difference, undercut the symbolic
meaning and status of redeveloping urban areas) must ultimately
be removed from that space for redevelopment to "succeed."

In spite of this, homeless youths and their services were not only
not expelled from the area, they became an integral part of the
redevelopment process. By the 1990s, service-providers for homeless
youth had been able to choreograph the use of space of their
clientele within the surrounding community, negotiating the tensions
between prime and marginal, front and back spaces within the
area. The resulting praxis was not simply the outcome of a struggle
between services and clientele. Rather it was inscribed within the
larger imperatives of community redevelopment, the attempt to
boost growth in the area through the formation of a growth coalition which would unite and "broker" a range of competing and
congruent interests around a common plan of urban growth. This
process was not simply the brokering of interests but also the
production of yet another *imaginary*, but one tied to a shared vision
of a specific place, the "imagined community" of Hollywood.

Neither the emergence of a growth coalition in Hollywood in
the 1980s, nor its broad strategies for redevelopment were unique to
the area. In large cities and small towns across North America

during this period, attempts were made to revitalize declining down-towns. Inscribed within a broader economic restructuring, which was manifest in a shift from manufacturing-based to service economies in the rise of the so-called "postindustrial city," these efforts shared the common objective of reanimating the street as a focal point for consumption, a kind of permanent spectacle.[1] This marked a change in the spatial imperatives of development, in terms of the renewed focus on "the street," on street retailing as a vehicle of redevelopment and on the "social mix" of the street as a selling point in that redevelopment, a shift from regionally developed malls to street retailing. To achieve this, it was necessary to transform fundamental perceptions of the street and what it signified. As Kasinitz notes:

> during the post-war period . . . a spilling of private lives into public spaces—street life—was perceived as symptomatic of poverty, degradation and social marginality. . . . Gentrification, in contrast, promotes the positive value of the street and street life, which is to say public life. . . . The new image of the inner-city celebrates the street as a kind of permanent festival.[2]

In many cities, this renewed interest in the street was intended to promote the inner-city as a new object of consumption, a fusion of the ideals of community with those of marketplace, often accompanied, as Kasinitz notes, by the almost voyeuristic marketing of the diversity of inner-city life (compared to the sterility of the sub-urbs), and evoking idealized images of the preautomotive city. It is within this space that the horizons of acceptable diversity, the lines between difference and deviance, were being negotiated.

The particular symbolism evoked in this fusion of community and market varied from one downtown to another. These particu-lars were often predicated upon the specifics of the locale, produc-ing a range of images from Fisherman's Wharf to the Gaslight District. The success of a revitalization strategy often rested, among other things, on the presumed authenticity and locally specific nature of this communal marketplace, although, as David Harvey has commented, in this unceasing drive towards differentiation, these places all eventually begin to resemble one another.

But it would be to easy to dismiss the specific symbolism evoked in such boosterism as nothing more than an ersatz differ-ence, simply masking the larger imperatives of the market. Images produced in the process of boosterism may indeed be "ersatz," inauthentic simulacra,[3] in that they often evoke past times and places that never existed—the creation of a Greek quarter in a Portuguese neighborhood in downtown Montreal being a good example.[4] Nevertheless, the images evoked are more than epiphenomena. They are one medium through which the character of a growth coalition is shaped, a medium through which various urban actors are "dealt in" or "dealt out" of the growth process, a medium through which difference and deviance, the right to a particular public space, are contested or negotiated.

Both the places evoked and the symbols which come to represent them are *polysemous*—that is, the places themselves are capable of supporting a whole range of symbolic referents; in addition, any one symbolic referent is open to multiple interpretations and allegiances. It is the chaotic nature of the signifier that gives it the potential of evoking the dreams, desires, and wishes of competing, sometimes even conflicting interests who read in the signifier, each for themselves, its "real" meaning.

In this process of sign production as an act of boosterism, some places and signifiers are more conflict-laden, more open to interpretation than others, as conflicting groups and class interests attempt to recuperate their histories and objectives within the place and signifier. This in itself may provide insights into the contemporary trend of evoking false histories, creating simulacra which reference a nonexistent original whose "real meaning" therefore, cannot be fought about or contested by different groups who wish to be represented or reflected in the production of a particular space.

In inner-city redevelopment, the selection of a particular image is part of the larger process of sign boosterism, through which, "the representational typifications of use values emerging from daily life are converted into ones which are more useful for the exchange value of property and business investment."[5] This process, moreover, is intended to portray a unified image of the community which is "superimposed upon a more fundamental process . . . involving a politics of signs among contending groups in the city." Sign boosterism reflects the interests of specific growth coalitions, and one arena where alternative visions of a community's future are fought out is through competing signs.[6]

In Hollywood, redevelopment plans projecting an image of the community as a venue for international tourism focused on contemporary and nostalgic allusions to both the "the glamour years of Hollywood" and Hollywood as a vibrant locale for the entertainment industry. These were countered by the opponents to redevelopment with a very different set of symbols: the "real Hollywood" was "Hollywood, Our Town," evoking the image of small-town America; the area of Hollywood planned for redevelopment was "Occupied Hollywood."[7]

HOLLYWOOD

> When the West was filled, the expansion turned inward, became part of an agitated, overexcited, superheated dream life. The film studios threw up their searchlights as the frontier was finally sealed, and the romantic possibilities of the old conquest of land turned into a vertical myth, trapped within the skull.
>
> —Norman Mailer, "Superman Comes to the Supermarket" in *Smiling Through the Apocalypse*, 1969, p. 13.

The allusion to Hollywood's stars has been a recurring theme in attempts to boost its development ever since the name of the place was transformed from Hollywoodland to Hollywood. The transformation of Hollywoodland to Hollywood in literature boosting the town suggested excitement, anticipation, the "agitated, overexcited, superheated dreamlife" desired by the potential tourist, for in Hollywood one expected to see the stars, not in the theater but in their "natural habitat."

Contemporary recountings of Hollywood's history nostalgically recall the town's golden era of the 1920s, the "glamour years" when it enjoyed a reputation as a commercial center, locus of the movie industry, and tourist attraction. These elements fed off each other synergistically, as the commercial center catered to the fashions of the stars, and tourists came in the vain hope of seeing their favored star in action.[8] The presence of "stars" in the area was sustained in the 1930s by a proliferation of restaurants and clubs, and during World War II by such places as the Hollywood Canteen, where stars regularly entertained the troops. Whether or not Hollywood actually enjoyed a heyday or golden era in the beginning of the century related to its role in the movie industry, this role suffered two displacements in the following decades which both contributed to its decline and dictated, to some extent, strategic attempts for its revitalization.

Young and Homeless in Hollywood

Successive plans to regenerate Hollywood can be understood as attempts to contend with and even replicate, within the Hollywood community, the suburban and exurban models of development which were the perceived reasons for its decline.

By the 1950s, the growth of suburban life and mall culture had the double effect of reducing overall movie attendance nationwide—thus affecting the movie industry—and of shifting local attendance from Hollywood Boulevard to suburban malls. A second factor contributing to Hollywood's decline was the dislocation of film production shooting from Hollywood and Los Angeles, as studios moved to suburban locations. If tourists had ever hoped to come to Hollywood to "see the stars" on set (an objective which, as McWilliams points out, became futile as early as 1925 with the introduction of enclosed sound-proofed studios) these hopes were now ended.[9]

Perhaps the most ironic aspect of Hollywood's decline and its efforts at revitalization was the attempts to recapture the elusive and infinitely regressing sign of stardom appropriated by Walt Disney and expressed in Disneyland in increasingly hyperreal evocations. The first of these thefts by Disney began, as one scholar comments, with the "invention" of Disneyland itself: "Disney took over and elaborated the principle of Hollywood, but also inverted it. He separated out the actors immediately, and withdrew them both from the audience and from citizenry—thus offering a direct competition to Hollywood—a theater without players—i.e., Disneyland."[10]

The second and perhaps more outrageous theft was the simulation of Hollywood Boulevard, rebuilt in painstaking detail, first in Disneyland and later in DisneyWorld. The ultimate irony was that the simulated boulevard (minus the riffraff, the homeless, and the garbage) drew more tourists than its real counterpart, which was only an hour-and-a-half-hour drive away from Disneyland in Anaheim. As Umberto Eco notes: "Disneyland tells us that faked nature corresponds much more to our daydream demands. . . . Here we enjoy not only a perfect imitation, we also enjoy the conviction that the imitation has reached its apex and afterwards reality will always be inferior to it."[11]

The difficulty in strategies for Hollywood's redevelopment lay in the fact that, unlike Disneyland, in Hollywood the absence of the stars represented a problem, not an opportunity. For it is not the theater but the stars "in their natural habitat" that tourists expect to see when they come to Hollywood, the stars *outside* of their theater.

Hollywood Rising

The "star" has been the principal *sign* in virtually all attempts at Hollywood's redevelopment, but it is a sign in a chain of regressing signification. Almost since its beginning, this connection has been bolstered intermittently with permanent but once-removed evocations, such as the sidewalk of Grauman's Chinese Theater, where one can see the hand- and footprints of the stars, or momentary real-life injections, such as the attendance of the stars at a movie premiere—an extravaganza also pioneered by Grauman in the 1920s, at the Egyptian Theater—or the opening of the Hollywood Canteen as part of the war effort in the 1940s. Not parenthetically, the monuments to the stars in Grauman's cement have an evocative rather than didactic function, not so much to preserve memory or a sense of the history of the industry and its major players, but rather, in the guise of history, to satisfy the urge of the tourist to see already-known and still-famous stars. Enshrined memory of the stars is subject to the travesties of time, as insiders claim that the basement of Grauman's Chinese Theater is "literally loaded with concrete slabs of long-forgotten stars."[12]

In the 1950s, businessmen along the Hollywood Boulevard substituted the evident lack of stars with a memorial, the Walk of Fame. More recently, during Hollywood's centennial year, the boulevard itself (but, significantly, *not* the stars who inspired it) was cause for celebration in a book entitled, *The Hollywood Walk of Fame*. Commissioned to draw tourists to the boulevard, the book carries this regressing significance one step further than the Hollywood Chamber of Commerce (its funder) perhaps intended. The author writes: "Even if you are reading this book from outside Hollywood, you can still enjoy the excitement of actually walking down the Walk, and identifying these celebrities."[13]

HOLLYWOOD: THE MALL AND THE STREET

Tourist expectations for Hollywood are extraordinarily high, in fact so high that they can never realistically be met (tourists will probably never be shopping with Hollywood's famous media personalities during their visit). However, Hollywood is a long way from coming close to meeting even realistic expectations. . . . Tourists expect to be walking amongst the stars rather than being continually panhandled.

—Halcyon Ltd., Hollywood Boulevard Tenant Retail Inventory, p.54

Young and Homeless in Hollywood

Growth coalitions have had different ways of dealing with Hollywood's relationship to the stars. Between 1970 and 1990 two very different approaches emerged. The first proposed simply to import the regional mall back to Hollywood and ignore the Boulevard; the second focused on the Boulevard as the organizing principle of redevelopment. In the mid-1970s, the strategy was to disembody and detach the significance of Hollywood's role as producer of the stars from any aspect of the ongoing production process. The idea of stardom was linked to the glamour days of the 1920s and 1930s, the legendary place name of "Hollywood."[14] Any reference to Hollywood Boulevard focused exclusively on its appeal in terms of "architecturally significant buildings . . . reminders of the colorful periods of Hollywood's heyday."[15] The eccentric character of life along the boulevard was to be down-played: "There is a tremendous amount of activity along the Boulevard, although it is not always of the most upstanding variety. . . . Tourists come expecting to find some last vestiges of the old myths." The central social problem of the period was considered to be the community's high crime rate, associated with pornography, prostitution, and drug sales.[16]

Allusions to the sign of Hollywood as "Hollywood!" would be captured in museums and evoked in naming—for example, the regional mall envisioned for the east end of Hollywood Boulevard was to capitalize on the place name recognition of its location—Hollywood and Vine. But no attempt would be made to link it to the actual street; the project was to be a fairly typical enclosed region-al mall. The Hollywood Revitalization Plan basically ignored "the street," attempting to improve social and economic conditions in the area contained within the boundaries of the Hollywood Community Plan through a series of disconnected enclaved efforts at residential improvement, commercial revitalization, and so on.

The plan intended to reimport the regional mall and theme park models of development uncritically back into Hollywood. In fact, the driving force of commercial redevelopment was to be the construc-tion of an internally focused regionally oriented retail mall, to be situated at the eastern "end" of the community, the intersection of Hollywood and Vine, and expected to capitalize on the name recog-nition associated with the movie industry, and have spin-off effects on the boulevard and surrounding streets.[17] The mall was to serve a surrounding regional retail market of approximately 300,000 people.

In addition, consideration was given to the establishment of a Theater and Entertainment District along Hollywood Boulevard which would capitalize and build upon existing movie houses and tourist attractions like Grauman's Theater. The influence of theme-park planning was evident in this scheme, as the Hollywood Revitalization Plan indicated:

> Using the museum market as a basis, there might be 2,500 to 3,000 visitors in Hollywood each day in the future. . . . The implications of that number of visitors in terms of the organization of thematic material and provision of access to events are quite clear. The Universal Studios tour system and the Disneyland system are quite well known examples of how to organize and orchestrate the movement of large groups of people. . . . It is for that reason that the Theater Entertainment district in the Hollywood Core area has been conceptualized. The museum and the great movie palaces would be the focus of such a district which implies the need to have a means for assembling and guiding visitors. The patterns of activities in the District would be choreographed and directed by trained guides who in some instances might travel with groups as in Universal City, or simply be stationed in specific destinations to receive meandering visitors.[18]

As John Kaliski, Principal Architect of the Community Redevelopment Agency, and later responsible for the *Hollywood Urban Design Plan* commented: "It was going to be a fairly typical redevelopment project and to a certain extent it was justified, because the underlying zoning was exactly the same as it was in downtown Los Angeles . . . the design guidelines could have been invented for any place. . . ."[19]

By the late 1980s a very different strategy was adopted. The Hollywood Redevelopment Plan, together with the Hollywood Boulevard District Urban Design Plan, marked a return to the street as an organizing principle for redevelopment, abandoning any attempts to choreograph movement on the Boulevard in the style of Universal Studios or to construct an internally focused regional mall.

The Hollywood Redevelopment Plan related all elements of a comprehensive community plan *whose central focus was the street.* In a sense, the mall was now returned to the street: the strategy of mall development was superimposed onto Hollywood Boulevard itself. But this was a problematic strategy, because of the sheer size of the Boulevard, and the attendant difficulties in attempting to manage its diverse merchant population the way one would a shopping mall. As John Kaliski noted:

> In our plan, Halcyon basically did define the boulevard as
> a shopping mall. It has the same amount of square
> footage as a super-regional. It's just that unlike a super-
> regional, that has about one-quarter to one-half-mile to
> walk one end to the other, Hollywood has 0.7 miles from
> one end of its downtown core (to the other) . . . IBI and
> Halcyon came up with a three-node concept . . . west-
> end tourist, middle community and east-end live enter-
> tainment.[20]

Consideration was given by the president of Hollywood's Chamber of Commerce to "managing downtown Hollywood much like a property manager operates a shopping mall," a strategy which included coordinating cleaning, joint promotional efforts, coordinated business hours, and so on.[21] In addition to superimposing the grid of the mall onto the full length of the boulevard, any large-scale construction on the boulevard was subject to design specifications that opened it to the boulevard. This marked a break with earlier planning strategies which included enclosed malls which might have the effect of drawing shoppers off the boulevard. Now, all new construction would be oriented towards and enhance Hollywood Boulevard. As Principal Architect of the Community Redevelopment Agency, John Kaliski noted:

> Our public space is the streets and sidewalks, not the
> parks. In terms of quality sidewalk space, we insisted that
> buildings be oriented towards the street entrances (and)
> have a clear orientation to the sidewalk. Going back to
> Jane Jacobs, we tried to prevent any internalized space.
> We basically made it impossible to build shopping malls in
> the plan.[22]

A central feature of the plan, as Kaliski suggests, was the carnival atmosphere of Hollywood Boulevard itself, inscribed surreptitiously within the grid of the mall on the boulevard: along the boulevard "puller" stores and attractions were located at discrete intervals in a strategy which echoed the planning of internal space of a regional mall. Rather than stimulate development through the confines of an enclosed mall, or create a simulated festival in a street where none had existed before, this strategy contended with the existing carnival atmosphere of the boulevard, an ambience which it did not create and could not control, but nonetheless hoped to harness: unable to "kill the street," the plan was to accept the "complex and chaotic things" that went on in it "as unique."

Hollywood Rising

HOLLYWOOD AND HABITUS

> What acts as a magnet for homeless kids? The entire Hollywood acts as a magnet. We want to be selective. We want to say, "Well, we want this great little city, we want it to be a magnet for tourists, so they'll bring in their dollars and they'll spend lots of money. So we'll rebuild the Ramada Inn and make it look beautiful and have these nice restaurants, so we're going to consciously be a magnet," and on what level do you cut off? (The tourists are) a means of survival for the street kids. If there was not a means of survival they wouldn't be here; they'd be somewhere else."
>
> —Gabe Kruks, Director, The Gay and Lesbian Center, May 30, 1990

In other North American cities, the revitalization of the street was often tied to some preindustrial notion of the union of community and marketplace, believed to have existed in a mercantile era. In Hollywood, the era referred to was Hollywood's Golden Age, but what was marketed here was not the small shops and farmers' markets of the mercantile age, but the notion of stardom.

The implications of this peculiar commodity for the formation of a local growth coalition can be understood only by exploring the notion of stardom in more detail. Stars and the myths created about them (both on screen and in the reports of details of their presonal lives) have functioned in America as an affirmation of *habitus*. The stars of the various entertainment industries can be understood as epitomizing a particular set of orienting practices of a style of life that, among other things, embodies a particular habitus. Habitus can be considered as the classificatory scheme that is at the same time a system of ultimate values. This role of Hollywood in "producing" habitus is mythical in two senses: first, it does not necessarily "produce" habitus in the sense of inventing it, but rather *affirms* habitus, in the sense of disseminating and popularizing particular kinds of lifestyles, attitudes, and values through the television, music, and film industries, always embodied in particular individuals or types of individuals. Second, the relationship of this particular place—the town of Hollywood—to those symbols of habitus—the stars—is an imaginary one. Stars were present in Hollywood only in the early years of its history as a movie center. Nevertheless, the myth is important in structuring the nature and intent of tourist consumption in the area. To go to Hollywood is in some sense to participate in this production writ large, or for some to validate a particular habitus in the hopes of seeing one's favorite star, even to offer self as habitus in the hopes of becoming a star, to be "discovered."

Hollywood's role in the affirmation of habitus has had both a specific and a general form. It was specific in the sense that one can chart, in Hollywood's film-production and star system, the glorification of specific lifestyles and strategies, which recognized and provided "answers" or strategies (to draw from Pierre Bourdieu[23]) to the conflicts and tensions of the everyday lives of Americans. In this sense, stars model a particular *habitus* for a targeted audience. One can chart the rise and fall of a particular habitus, for example, in the early films which attempted to explain American values and way of life to an audience of new immigrant women, or in particular stars from various periods—Doris Day, Mae West, James Dean, to name a few—whose lives, as they were represented on-and-off screen, responded to a particular set of problems and issues in the lived experience of their fans.[24] To come to Hollywood in the hope of meeting a favored star was, perhaps, to partake in a set of solutions to a lived dilemma experienced by the fan.

But stardom also affirmed the notion of habitus in a general sense. In the general sense, the myths embodied in the stars and revealed in the movies, however different they are from one another, participate in the same fiction, namely, the fiction of habitus itself:

> the production of a commonsense world endowed with the objectivity secured by consensus on the meaning . . . of practices and the world. The homogeneity of habitus is what—within the limits of the group of agents possessing the schemes (of production and interpretation) implied in their production—causes practices and works to be immediately intelligible and foreseeable and hence taken-for-granted.[25]

This is true, arguably, even for the genre of contemporary movies which thrive on the unresolved disruption of meanings and practices: in this case, perhaps ironically, it is the unresolvable disruption which becomes foreseeable and intelligible to the fan.

What makes the legacy of Hollywood different from other places in the process of sign production, then? It is not the overwhelming dominance of a single industry in developing images about the place or its supposed inhabitants, although that is much of the practical activity of the entertainment industry. Nor is it the fact that Hollywood's image is geared to the promotion of a mix of shopping and tourism, for a long time considered the key engine for growth in the area. Here one could point to Faneuil Hall, or Fisherman's Wharf, or any number of festival marketplaces that have mushroomed. These latter share with Hollywood the characteristic of being identified as *liminal spaces*, that is, spaces of commodified desire.[26] As Wright notes, "Theme parks, tourist developments, natural attractions, even theme restaurants can assume the shape of liminal space." Zukin explains the development of liminal spaces through convergence of cultural producers and "cultivated" (that is, properly socialized) cultural consumers. This process is assisted by "trade fairs, department store promotions, and museum events that have become major urban attractions."[27] One can say that participation in these activities, and occupying these places is a way of expressing affiliation with a particular habitus, that is, "the cognitive structures which themselves structure the orienting practice and activities of agents."[28]

Hollywood does not stand for one particular habitus, as do the liminal spaces cited by Zukin, but rather evokes *the idea of habitus itself*. Why is this important? It means that, unlike Anytown USA, the *representational space* of Hollywood has more weight, variety, and referent than its *real space*. Hollywood has often been considered the metonymy of America, and as Mark Royden Wichell notes, "If Hollywood is in many ways an exaggerated metonymy of America, then there are as many possible responses to it as there are versions of the American experience itself."[29] It is this metonymy which introduces an uncontrollable element into Hollywood's imaginary. The central factor that distinguishes Hollywood from many other declining central city areas is that its image, the space of its representation, is larger than its real social space. Unlike a Columbus, Ohio, which needs to manufacture and disseminate a particular distinguishing image as part of its boosterism, Hollywood needs to selectively control the overabundant array of images that exist about it. Competing groups wishing to define or determine the dominant image of Hollywood have a ready-made assemblage of images to draw on and exploit to illustrate their ideals.

In the late 1980s, marginal characters (the poor, the deformed, ethnic subcultures, victims) became a point of fascination for Hollywood studios.[30] "Stardom" has all manner of subcultures as a referent, not all of which help to promote the kind of street-oriented retail that boosters might have in mind. The resulting popularity of Hollywood among diverse social groups is simultaneously a problem and a potential upon which to build its appeal. Part of the obstacle to the redevelopment of Hollywood in the 1980s lay precisely in the contemporary basis of success of the Boulevard. A potential division existed between the small businesses along the Boulevard that benefited from the "carnival atmosphere" which thrived on a low-end tourist and retail market, versus big business, which hoped to transform it.[31] The Boulevard had little appeal for the wealthier, international, tourist market or the affluent residents who lived north in the Hollywood Hills.[32] About 60% of the stores on the Boulevard were T-shirt shops, fast-food joints, and trendy discount fashion stores, including at least a dozen that catered to the youthful music subcultures such as heavy metal. The major tourist clientele were relatively young (in their twenties) low-income males.[33] With this clientele predominating, local merchants faced the same dilemma that their counterparts in regional malls did vis-à-vis youthful markets: youth represented both a potential disruption to business and "legitimate customers with money in their jeans." Local retailers complained about the presence of runaways and transients on the boulevard: in fact, their vision for the area could be characterized as a sociological agenda for change, dealing with street transiency and crime rates, rather than as an explicit development strategy.[34]

CRITICAL REGIONALISM

> Hopefully the (Hollywood Redevelopment) Plan falls within the realm of critical regionalism. . . . We're trying to acknowledge that which makes this place particular . . . there's a small core in Hollywood that is ideologically opposed to redevelopment, period . . . a libertarian core . . . on one level they've succeeded in a good way—they really got the (Community Redevelopment) Agency to be much more directed towards incremental growth . . . in my mind they're part of this critical regionalism.
>
> —John Kaliski, Principal Architect, personal interview, May 19, 1990.

The focus on the street as a motor for redevelopment highlighted the presence of runaways and transients as a growth-related problem. But it did not dictate the contours of a solution. Arguably, increased police presence with "sweeps" of the area could be one approach to dealing with the street population—as was evidenced in policing of other highly trafficked tourist areas in Los Angeles, such as Venice Beach,[35] and was used from time to time in Hollywood as well.[36] What was important, however, was the role that service providers played within the local growth regime.

As Fainstein and Fainstein note, when one examines the outcomes of development processes across cities, the alliances and divisions between groups may differ historically and geographically, but nevertheless "the same fault lines continually reappear and become urban trenches about which redevelopment skirmishes are fought."[37] In the 1970s, when development was attempted under the Hollywood Revitalization Plan, service-providers were scarcely involved in the process, and the one officially sanctioned service to homeless youths in the area was Options House.[38] Ten years later, service providers were a substantial presence within the community, including over ten agencies within the Hollywood area that provided some combination of counseling, outreach, drop-in facilities, and shelter. If one were to position Hollywood's service-providers on a map of these urban trenches in the 1980s, they occupied a shifting middle ground first championed by elements of the no-growth coalition and later by elements of a pro-growth coalition that together had stalemated in the previous decade.[39] In effect, the involvement of service-providers in the redevelopment process represented a shift in the arena within which the politics of growth was debated, from a political and public process to an administrative one, wherein the shadow state came to play an increasingly important role.[40] In an area such as Hollywood, characterized by a large immigrant population and a high percentage of tenants who were marginally (if at all) aware of the redevelopment process, it was the service-providers who came to stand for "community." The reason that service-providers were able to play this role rested, in part, on the reorientation of redevelopment strategies to the street. In addition, they represented a face of social need in the community which did not, of necessity, conflict with development objectives. During the 1970s, under the Hollywood Revitalization Plan, one of the single greatest obstacles to redevelopment was opposition to condominium conversion, which tenants fought in a bitter and protracted court case.[41] Condominium conversion and residential gentrification in general were also important aspects of the Hollywood Redevelopment Plan, as analysts felt that Hollywood Boulevard needed support from upgraded residential neighborhoods.[42] Social demands from the community, such as a moratorium on condominium conversion, would have threatened the objectives of redevelopment. The inclusion of shelters and services for homeless youths, so long as their image was properly managed, did not. As such these services threatened neither the extant territorial needs of the community nor the latent objectives of growth.

Service-providers mediated their relationship to existing business and avoided locational conflicts. In brief, they established that it was not the presence of services that drew youth to the area, but the image of Hollywood itself. Having established the boosters as responsible for Hollywood's role as a magnet for runaways, the service providers offered themselves as intermediaries, managing the relationship between recalcitrant youths, retailers, and residents.[43] If the presence of homeless youths in the area could be established, in part, as a *consequence* of local boosterism, it could logically be presented as a social need which the development process should address.

The vision for the future of the boulevard and the community at large was to be developed through the Project Area Committee (PAC), the local elected body required by state law to comment on and usher in the Hollywood Redevelopment Plan.[44] The PAC was formed in 1983 to provide community input into drafts of the Plan. While all Redevelopment Project Areas are required to have a PAC for community input and representation, the Hollywood PAC differed significantly from those in the redevelopment projects that preceded it. It quickly became the institution through which competing objectives of development were fought, as different factions within the Hollywood community struggled to control it.

The fault lines around which redevelopment would be fought were laid in the previous decade as the Revitalization Committee clashed with the local council office over the nature of the Hollywood Revitalization Plan—a struggle which eventually led, in 1980, to the disbanding of the Hollywood Revitalization Committee which had provided citizens' input into the plan (see Figure 14). The issues emerging during the late 1970s revolved around the question of historic preservation of commercial and residential buildings in the area, and the pressure for residential gentrification. The latter galvanized around the attempt of developers to convert residential apartment buildings to condominiums—a move which tenants' groups were first able to block through court action, although the court decision was later overturned.[45] The issue of social needs of the community was scarcely raised: homeless youths were attended to through a separate and sister organization, the Hollywood Human Services, which established Options House.[46] All of these issues were to resurface in a different constellation during the planning and implementation of the Hollywood Redevelopment Plan in the 1980s, and service-providers would now play a central role.

FIGURE 14: FAULT LINES OF HOLLYWOOD'S REDEVELOPMENT
(Ruddick 1991)

PLAN	MOTIF	SYNTAGM	ISSUES	DISCERNIBLE FAULT LINES
Hollywood Revitalization Plan 1977	Stardom: Hollywood "glamour days"	–Enclosed Mall –Theme Park	–Condominium conversion –Crime/drug dealing/ prostitution	–Tenants organized through Neighborhood Watch versus residential developers
Hollywood Redevelopment Plan Community Redevelopment Agency 1986	Stardom: Contemporary Hollywood as center of entertainment industry	–"The street" –Hollywood Boulevard	–Eminent domain –Historic preservation –Social needs of the community –Design, quality of tourist-related projects on Hollywood Boulevard	**Project Area Committee (P.A.C.)** –Elected –Dominated by business coalition,but incorporates issues of social needs, historic preservation **Project Area Committee (P.A.C.)** –Elected –Controlled by "anti-growth" representatives, including members of Save Hollywood Our Town, president of Merchants Association, Hollywood Home Owners and Tenants Association **Hollywood Advisory Coordination Council (H.A.C.C.)** –Appointed by Councilman Woo, City of Los Angeles –P.A.C. disbanded, some members incorporated in H.A.C.C.

The political fault lines within the Hollywood community were latent and unstable. One existed potentially between wealthier homeowners and tenants in the Hollywood Hills and poorer ones in the flatlands. The former were represented by such groups as the Whitley Heights Association, the Hollywood Heights Association, and the Melrose Hill Homeowners Association, the latter by the Hollywood Homeowners Association. Another existed between the small businesses on Hollywood Boulevard, represented by the Hollywood Merchants Association (although among individuals one could find equally volatile supporters and opponents to redevelopment), and the large business and commercial interests and large real-estate owners. (See Figure 15).

The new orientation of the plan to a collective and diverse fantasy as a resource raised a critical question: Whose fantasy would dominate in the representation on the boulevard? This issue was fought out in three distinct phases, each characterized by a different constellation of interests representing the Hollywood community. The first phase, the preplanning period for the Hollywood Redevelopment Plan from 1983 to 1986, was characterized by a dominance of business interests on the PAC. However, there was also a significant effort on behalf of the council office to broker different interests, accommodating the plan to its critics. In the second phase, immediately following the plan's approval in 1986, critics won control of the PAC. They were united not so much in a common alternative vision as in opposition to the plan as it stood, from a variety of distinct and often uncomplimentary positions. In the third phase, the PAC was disbanded and replaced by the Hollywood Advisory Coordinating Council (HACC).

When the PAC was first elected in 1983, it was dominated by members of the Hollywood Chamber of Commerce, who generally favored redevelopment,[47] but there were critics represented on the PAC as well, including Brian Moore (head of Save Hollywood, Our Town), and Doreet Rotman, president of the Hollywood Boulevard Merchants Association, and owner of the boulevard's Snow White Cafe. During the planning stage, Teen Canteen made accommodative gestures to the redevelopment of Hollywood. On the suggestion of the district office, in 1984 it obtained a Summer Youth Employment Grant to put its clients to work cleaning up Hollywood Boulevard.[48] This was a demonstrative, if symbolic act, linking runaways to the positive features of redevelopment. The youths wore T-shirts from Teen Canteen, and scrubbed the length of Hollywood Boulevard with mops and brushes. Not surprisingly, Doreet Rotman suggested that social needs should be addressed in the redevelopment process, with particular emphasis on runaways and the transient element along the boulevard. She argued that if 0.5% of tax-increment money could be set aside for the arts in redevelopment projects, then one could also do this for social services. At this point, the presence of homeless and runaway youths functioned as an important metaphor for the larger relationship of redevelopment to the social needs of the community, because they were the most obvious and visible representation of the negative consequences of boosting Hollywood. The suggestion gained support from the

FIGURE 15: HOLLYWOOD PROPERTY
OWNERS WHO WILL BENEFIT UNDER REDEVELOPMENT

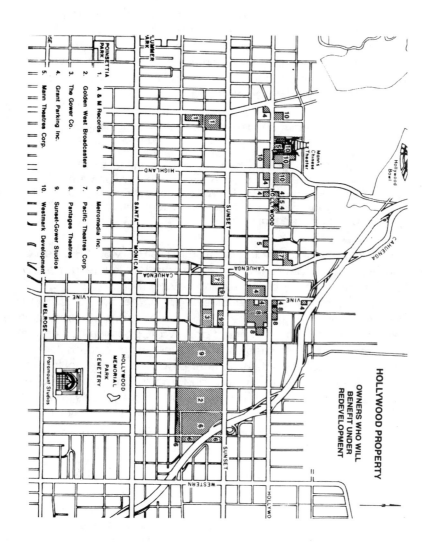

office of the councilman. On the suggestion of his planning deputy Gilda Haas, Councilman Woo proposed a much higher sum of a total of 10% of the tax increment money from redevelopment in an effort to accommodate opponents to redevelopment.[49]

While many service-providers for homeless and runaway youth were oblivious to the redevelopment process, and preoccupied by their day-to-day activities, those who were aware played an important role within the PAC, and were considered to represent the "moderate" voice within the community. Some, like Dale Weaver, made a conscious effort to forge the link between redevelopment and service provision to homeless and runaway youths:

> I was interested in redevelopment. I testified at the open hearing for the Social Needs Committee and got some kids to come. There's a lot of money involved. . . . I thought it worth my while to be involved. The tack I took was that their job (the Community Redevelopment Agency) was to make Hollywood more attractive and that gives them some responsibility for the fact that it attracts people that need help.[50]

Finally, the residential population in the Hollywood Hills, represented by several homeowners' associations, were generally displeased with the quality of existing development.[51]

In spite of the Social Needs element of the plan, a kernel of opposition won control of the PAC in the elections of September 1986, four months after the plan's approval. Opposition came from three main sources; homeowners in the hills, who were displeased about the quality of redevelopment proposed for the Boulevard; and homeowners in the flatlands and small businesses, both concerned about the Community Redevelopment Agency's potential misuse of eminent domain. The next three years were marked by a struggle between pro-growth and slow-growth advocates over control of the PAC, and law suits against CRA and specific projects on Hollywood Boulevard which effectively slowed down the redevelopment project by requiring that projected revenues from tax increments be held in trust until the case was decided.

The position of service-providers to homeless and runaway youth in this struggle was clearly on the side of moderates and against critics of the plan. In September 1986, moderates on the Hollywood Coordinating Committee (HCC) dismissed their PAC representative on the grounds that he was too uncompromising in his opposition to redevelopment. The HCC was an umbrella organization of local services and community groups. Their representative on the PAC was Brian Moore, a vocal critic and leader of Save Hollywood, Our Town (SHOT). The move to oust Moore was led by Norris Lineweaver, head of the Hollywood YMCA, which under Lineweaver had expanded its operations to provide shelter for runaways. The representative proposed to replace Moore was Dale Weaver, a known moderate and director of Teen Canteen. This move was met with an angry response from critics within the PAC, led by Doreet Rotman, who accused Lineweaver of "strong-arm tactics" in ousting Moore.

Following this action, Save Hollywood, Our Town filed a lawsuit against the PAC, claiming improprieties in its elections and procedures. The suit, which was heard two years later, effectively prevented the utilization of any tax increment funds from the project, which were put in trust until the suit was to be decided.[52] In the elections of November 1986, slow-growth forces effectively took control of the PAC. They included representatives of the Hollywood Homeowners and Tenants Association, and Bennett Kayser of Save Hollywood, Our Town. The councilman attempted to mitigate their influence on the PAC by proposing, in September, 1987, to appoint an additional six members, but this proposal was rejected by the PAC. In June, 1988, representatives of homeowners associations, the Project Area Committee, and the Hollywood Boulevard Merchants Association wrote a collective letter to the mayor complaining that extreme abuse of discretionary authority had resulted in a total breakdown in communication between the agency and Hollywood residential, business, and development communities. They demanded a means of monitoring the CRA with respect to Hollywood.[53] By mid-1989, slow-growth advocates had lost on all fronts in their attempt to halt the plan. In April, 1989, the Superior Court ruled against the PAC's claims that it must serve for the lifetime of the plan. In June of 1989, the Superior Court ruled against SHOT's lawsuit against the Hollywood Redevelopment Plan. The decision was appealed (to no avail) with funds drawn largely from small-business and property owners on Hollywood Boulevard.

The court rulings effectively rendered opponents to redevelopment irrelevant to the political process. This paved the way for the third phase of community representation in the redevelopment process. In May, Councilman Woo had gained municipal council approval to disband the PAC and appoint a Hollywood Community Advisory Council in its place. The Hollywood Community Advisory Council was formed in August, 1989. In an accommodative gesture, it invited participation from members of the old PAC. It also included several service providers active on the social needs sub-committee, and historic preservationists who were appointed to the design review committee.[54]

In 1990 the first survey of social needs of the community was completed. Based on interviews with 484 area service-providers and community representatives, it identified the top five priorities for social needs in the community, to be used as a basis for allocating tax-increment funds. Surprisingly, although a community survey ranked homeless youths and transients as top priorities, in the end these groups received a low ranking, based on the consultants' estimation that these groups had inflated rankings because of their heightened visibility, and should not be accorded as much weighting because they "weren't really part of the community."[55] The decision did not threaten the presence of services to homeless and runaway youths in the area; the network of services was already adept at gaining funding from a diversity of sources, and did not need to depend on the redevelopment process.

CONCLUSION

The change in the form of boosterism played an important role in the eventual incorporation of social needs into redevelopment planning. The shift from enclosed mall to street in the 1980s set preconditions within which the social space of Hollywood Boulevard could be examined and even marketed in the context of redevelopment. The motif of Hollywood's redevelopment was also influential. What was alluded to was not a specific period of Hollywood's role in the entertainment industry, or a particular genre of star, but the concept, the possibility of stardom itself. This fantasy of stardom had many variants which went well beyond the confines of a particular status group for whom developers might want to target tourism and commercial developments. The sign of boosterism, in addition, did not simply reflect the interests of a particular growth coalition, as exemplified in the contrasting visions of "Hollywood!" and Save Hollywood, Our Town. The sign also shaped the potential character of the growth coalition in unexpected ways. Service providers to homeless and runaway youth were able to justify their interest in the redevelopment process partly on the basis of the sign which attracted their clientele to the area. But it was not only the symbolic link to the place that implicated service providers to homeless and runaway youths; it was also the role of service in the production of a new social urban space within Hollywood, one which, at the outset, managed the tensions between Hollywood's role as a magnet for young transients and its role as a tourist and commercial center. Service-providers became the intermediaries mitigating the negative impacts of Hollywood's role as a magnet. Finally, service-providers intervened not only in the symbolic production and social management of the space, but also in the political process of place production.

CONCLUSION

The impossibility of an ultimate fixity of meaning implies that there have to be partial fixations—otherwise the very flow of differences would be impossible. Even in order to differ, to subvert meaning, there has to be *a* meaning. . . . Any discourse is constituted as an attempt to dominate the field of discursivity, to arrest the flow of differences, to construct a center. We will call the privileged discursive points of this partial fixation, *nodal points*.

> —Ernesto Laclau and Chantal Mouffe, *Hegemony and Socialist Strategy*, 1985, p. 112.

The formulation of modernist universals is in every case a productive but imperfect and in the end fallacious response to particular conditions of closure, breakdown, failure and frustration. From the necessary negations of these conditions, and from the stimulating strangeness of a new and (as it seemed) unbounded social form, the creative leap to the only available universality—of raw material, of medium, of process—was impressively and influentially made.

> —Raymond Williams, *The Politics of Modernism*, 1989, p. 47.

Young and Homeless in Hollywood

One scarcely needs to restate that we are living through a period of fundamental dissolutions, the breakdown of an old order and transition to a new one. What has interested me most about this process, however, is not the substantive form of the new order, be it new modernism, postmodernism, neofordism, post-fordism, or whatever else one might chose to call it, but rather the dynamics through which the new is constituted. How does meaning become fixed (even if only partially)? How do we leap from the "raw material of process" to "new universals"?

This book is about the dissolution of one social imaginary, the juvenile delinquent, and its eventual replacement with another imaginary, among a series of others, that of the homeless youth. The concept of juvenile delinquency can properly be called a modern concept, and the array of institutions that have, since the turn of the century, proliferated to "treat" juvenile delinquency, constitute the modern system of juvenile care. Since the mid-1970s, there has been a fundamental transformation in both the concept and the system of treatment, which both signal and respond to a shift in our understanding about what youth and various kinds of youthful misbehavior mean. A number of new and dominant images have emerged on the horizon. Two of the most immediately recognizable are the "youth gang" and "homeless youth." This is not to say that these did not exist during the modern period, but rather that the treatment of both and the interpretation of behavior of both was fused within the concept of juvenile delinquency, and addressed within an all-encompassing (if internally differentiated) system of juvenile care. Since the mid-1970s, however, these two images, (actually two social imaginaries, in the sense that they are collectively understood images) have come to represent very different understandings of youthful misbehavior and treatment. If we accept a definition of modernism that moves beyond the bounds of a narrowly defined avant-garde to the way that ordinary people make sense of the world (and certainly one of the characteristics of postmodern thinking is dissolving these boundaries), these social imaginaries can be understood as part and parcel of a new modernism.

To explore the dynamics by which these new meanings became fixed, I chose to focus on a specific locale and specific time frame—Los Angeles, California, between 1975 and 1992. Like Raymond Williams, I believe that the emergence of a new modernism is intimately bound up in the character of the metropolis. That is, new universals develop in and are disseminated from very specific and privileged locales (one of which is, in the current period,

Conclusion

Los Angeles), although I understand modernism in the much broader sense as including, even originating from, ordinary people. But Williams's observation signals a more intriguing problem, because he problematizes both the "context" and the "product" in the metamorphosing metropolis, and the particular modernism that emerges to make sense of the metropolis. As the evocative passage from Bret Easton Ellis's *Less Than Zero* suggests, and what every pink-haired Ronnette knows (without ever having read Williams or Ellis), meanings of self and space are inextricably intertwined, the "fixing" of one is simultaneously a process of fixing the other.[1] But how does meaning become fixed?

To unravel an answer, I began by investigating literature that deals with the creation (or subversion) of social forms in and through space. Four sets of literature were relevant to the topic. The first dealt with the broad transformations of social forms of youth and adolescence, and the institutions involved in their proper socialization. The second addressed the subversion of social forms in the production of youth subcultures. The third examined the role of space in producing the stigma of homelessness. The fourth dealt with the way place entrepreneurs, growth coalitions, and local regimes create and manage the image of particular places.

Each offered partial insights, but each treated the other as context. Social historians identified broad transformations from the premodern form of youth to a modern form, adolescence, which helped to contextualize contemporary transformations in forms of youth and concepts of youthful misbehavior. They were sensitive to the corresponding shifts in environments and philosophies of treatment. But they saw these environments as a mask of the larger imperatives of social control, rather than as a medium through which specific practices of control were constituted. Sociologists addressing the subversion of social forms of adolescence in youthful subcultures offered a set of coordinates one could use to position a range of responses to dominant meanings, including the concepts of bricolage, homology, slippage of meaning, and rupture, but similarly treated space as context, the place where subculture takes place. Literature on the geography of homelessness linked the process of stigmatization of the homeless to the attempt to produce and control the meanings of new spaces within the city. Here a monologue of meaning flowed from the new postindustrial spaces, marginalizing the homeless further in the process, with precious little back talk. In this literature there is no exit from this process, no way that the stigma could be challenged or resisted. And the predictions of the homeless and their shelters' being driven from the space of the modernizing city belie a more complex process of expulsion and entrenchment. Literature on the production and control of the signs of boosterism explained the sign as a condensation of struggle between organized groups, producing a real and symbolic unity reflected in and through the sign itself. But it did not consider how organized groups might shape or reshape *their own image* in that process. Yet if we look at the process of stabilization of a service network for homeless youth in Hollywood, it is clear that all of these occurred simultaneously, that they stabilized together.

Since the mid-1970s, imaginary "homeless youths" have become inscribed in and through the landscape of Los Angeles County. The image of these youths as dual victims of dysfunctional families and a modernizing city could not be derived simply from the diverse narratives that they offer of themselves. It has emerged out of a range of equally valid ontological referents which, both historically and currently have included personal histories of abuse, lack of shelter, poor employment opportunities, occasional participation in illegal and criminal activities, or identification with subcultures, any of which might point to a different set of labels and treatment. In the years immediately following deinstitutionalization of runaways from the juvenile penal system, policy makers were reluctant to make any generalizations about these youths. Individual stories and surveys were considered too particular. To a large extent the development of a sympathetic image of homeless youths was initially fought and won on the self-contained terrain of images.

This terrain had credibility precisely because of the sense of malaise that has surrounded and propelled policy development, and because of the basis of that malaise. Homeless youths had been doubly disserved by the juvenile system—not only in its inability to treat their problems, but also in its lack of categories even to recognize that runaway and homeless youths existed. Observations that homeless and runaway youths had "slipped through the cracks of the system," or were not "showing up" in conventional records maintained on juvenile delinquents triggered a profound unwillingness to make general statements about who homeless youths were. Limited surveys were just that, limited. They could not and did not pretend to speak for more than the immediate sample of youths surveyed. They were a specific truth, bound to a particular time and place: to the street of this or that city; to this or that type of shelter; to the season when the survey took place; to the age, gender, or race of interviewees; to whatever else was happening on the street

Conclusion

at the time that might influence the presence or absence of homeless youths (heat wave, police sweep, rock concert). Moreover, and perhaps more profoundly, there was the recurring sense of unease among service providers, that service providers were seeing "only the tip of the iceberg," that many youths, for reasons not fully understood, were not being attracted by existing services offered them. In this sense, the situation of runaway and homeless youths paralleled that of other homeless people. Like "the homeless," the meaning of "homeless and runaway youths" became as infinite as the places and circumstances that they found themselves in, and as varied as individual histories and personalities.

In the absence of an overarching image of homeless youth, the dynamics which contributed to the development of the social imaginary, homeless youth, interested me as much as the particular qualities of the imaginary. As Laclau and Mouffe suggest, meaning does not spring from any privileged essence, but is constructed out of a range of ever-present and almost infinite possibilities. But how did meaning become fixed?

In *Places on the Margin*, Robert Shields talks about the relationship between meaning and space in terms of a process of *social spatialization*, whereby "sites become symbols (of good, evil, or nationalistic events), and in tandem with other sites can be taken up in metaphors to express (gendered) states of mind, of affairs and different value positions (for example, "It will be his Waterloo"). For Shields, this process of social spatialization "designate(s) the ongoing social construction of the spatial at the level of the social imaginary."[2] His primary concern is with the movement from the social to the spatial, the way that landscapes are infused with particular meanings—California as "Lotus Land," Canada as "the True North Strong and Free."

My concern has been largely in the other direction, in the movement from the spatial to the social, in the way that people draw on, construct, or even *surface* sometimes dormant values associated with places in order to construct or validate meanings about themselves. I say "largely" because, as the case study shows, meanings of self and space tend to surface *together* each is a medium of the other's formation.

Shields talks about the way that people construct meanings about themselves, in "transcending and suppressing their own experience in order to identify with broader social groups."[3] But this presupposes the existence of a "broader social group" or at the very least a commonly held image of one with which people would like to identify. This may explain how individuals fix themselves to meaning, but it does not explain how meaning itself becomes fixed, or rather how individuals fix themselves *through* meaning.

How does meaning become fixed in the absence of a dominant? The language of Laclau and Mouffe, in this regard, is unselfconsciously spatial. They talk of "stopping flows" of difference, of "constructing a center." Meaning becomes fixed in and through the control of space. This includes not only a control of the use, but control of the images of that space. To disrupt a space is to disrupt the meanings that adhere to it. It is no accident that inherently spatial concepts of strategy and tactics, front and back region, prime and marginal space, decentering and centering, motif and syntagm, which I drew on in the book to explain "homeless youths" apply equally to the dynamics of building new spaces for homeless and runaway youths and to the structuring of understanding about who they are.

In the changing social imaginary of homeless and runaway youth, I have identified four substantially different spaces which accompanied four historically dominant images of these youth. These might be called the "institutional" spaces of reformable delinquents; the "wild" spaces of punk squatters; the "sacred" spaces of the family; and finally the "hybrid" spaces of the social services, which brought family and street, sacred and profane together in a new constellation. But one must do more than identify the different qualities of the spaces they inhabited. To name these spaces and the people who inhabited them tells us little about how they (people *and* spaces) were formed or transformed.

It is clear that as long as runaways were held within the juvenile penal system, any distinctive image of them was incorporated into a more general image of juvenile delinquency. During the modern era of juvenile justice, as discussed in Chapter Four, the broad and inclusive concept of juvenile delinquency was reflected and reinforced by placement of delinquents in relatively undifferentiated "nature" camps. There was some distinction made between camps according to the type of wards that they held and the severity of their crimes. But the similarities between these various rural settings, and the idea that nature could indeed have a spiritual and regenerative effect on young juvenile delinquents, expressed a symbolic fit between the setting and the contemporary concerns and beliefs about the origins of juvenile delinquency. This observation, however, does not bring us beyond a conception of space as reflector of societal processes.

Conclusion

Nor can it anticipate the way that urbanization itself triggered a change in thinking about treatment of delinquents, simply by reorganizing their social relationships in space. The concept of delinquency and ideas of appropriate treatment were themselves *disorganized* by the fact that the context for treatment had changed, or, in the words of a deputy director within the Los Angeles County Probation Department, that "those country days are gone." Pervasive urbanization meant that juveniles could no longer be sequestered in rural settings from the evils of the modernizing city. For the more recalcitrant this meant exile to the wilderness, where a new fit was found between "raw nature" and rehabilitation, or conversely the transformation of boot camps to jails.

Here space did not simply reflect society, but transformations of space reacted back upon social forms of organization, exemplifying the dynamics of a sociospatial dialectic, the ceaseless interaction between social and spatial forms (if, for a moment, we can think of them as separate).

The real story begins, however, with the crisis of the social imaginary "runaway" which occurred with the onset of deinstitutionalization. With the lack of prepared space for runaway youths, there was no fixed center to organize their meaning, no single or dominant image around which various ideas about runaways could be ordered, nothing to "stop the flow of difference." This did not lead to an insurmountable relativity and proliferation of meanings, wherein all positions were equal. First of all, the capacities available to different actors (the youth, the residents and property owners in Hollywood, the state) to appropriate and define the meanings of spaces were not equally shared, but exist in an unequal relationship.

The concept of *prime* and *marginal space*, used by Duncan in his analysis of tramps, links space and social status in a way that might be fruitful for this analysis.[4] But it suggests a landscape of *pre-given meaning* within the city, which the tramp must negotiate but cannot transform. Prime and marginal space better describes the logic of ordering of the postindustrial spaces of the city, a hierarchy of exchange values, rather than the logic of disordering that the homeless perform by existing in these spaces, by transforming their use. More important, the concept of prime and marginal space suggests a symbolic value that flows exclusively from the exchange value of the space, not a multiplicity of potential and competing symbolisms that derive from use or juxtaposition of uses.

Duncan's conception of the ordering of space and meaning,

in a sense, proceeds from the vantage point of the colonizer, one who looks at the exercise of power, but from the vantage point of the ruling group. It is the view held by Dear and Wolch in their analysis of the homeless. Like the colonizers in Memmi's analysis, they take the position (in their theory, if not in their practice) of the "colonizer who refuses." They are sympathetic to the homeless, but construct a theory of power over the homeless, not of power for the homeless.[5] They focus on the way stigma and marginality are reinforced by a particular logic of ordering space, rather than on the attempts to confront this marginality and stigma. This type of analysis performs the absolutely crucial service of demonstrating how stigma is *produced*, rather than assuming it resides within the stigmatized as an innate quality. But it does not give us clues as to how stigma might be confronted, or how new meanings might be developed for or by the homeless who challenge their stigma. Little wonder that analyses of this sort lead to apocalyptic visions of the fate of the homeless, wandering in an unfixed landscape of despair.

An alternative approach would be to focus on the diverse ways that the homeless attempt to confront marginality, recognizing that their "practical daily activity contains an understanding of the world."[6] For the homeless, and the homeless youths among them, the capacities to challenge the pregiven meaning of space are expressed in the tactical appropriation of space and the use of subversion, what De Certeau calls a *perruque* ("wig").

Subversion has little transformative potential when it represents the routine subterfuges of agents whose actions are already inscribed and submerged within particular structures. The office worker who appropriates his or her workstation for personal business is an example of this. But the tactics of the homeless have a slightly different quality. The homeless subvert the meaning of structures that were not intended for them, where they would otherwise "have no legitimate business," except by virtue of their subversive activity (for example, using movie theaters to sleep in). Like the office worker who conducts private business from his or her desk, the homeless people who sleep on the bus, who rest at the bus stop while pretending to wait for a bus, are, of course, pretending to do something in the guise of something else. But unlike the office worker, it is the pretense itself that gives the homeless person the air of legitimacy. It is *through pretense* that the homeless create heterotopias, impossible life spaces which graft the subverted meaning of one activity onto the structure of another.

Tactics, in the sense that De Certeau introduces them, are the first clue to understanding how meanings might become fixed, or at the very least temporarily subverted, in and through the use of space.[7] Tactics are, in this sense, the glowing coal that keeps a particular meaning alive until it can find a place to sustain light. For De Certeau, tactics are the differential appropriation of space and the circumvention of power over that space, according to "prime time" and "marginal time." Or as I once saw graffitied on a wall in East Berlin—*Für Euch die Macht. Für uns die Nacht* (For you the power. For us the night).

If there was a common characteristic running through the sites that homeless youths in Los Angeles County occupied by tactical appropriation, it was their quality as sites of leisure: the beaches, Hollywood, Sunset Strip, or Disneyland, for example. Their return to these sites in spite of attempts to relocate them elsewhere was the manifest insistence that they be considered first and foremost as youths, rather than as "homeless" (to be served by the skid-row missions of downtown Los Angeles), or as "delinquents from normal families" (to be relocated in more appropriate suburban family environments). Similarly, if we look at the larger process of polynucleation of services for the homeless throughout Los Angeles, this suggests that this new pattern of service locations (outside skid row) was a response to the tactical inhabitation of space by the homeless. But is this enough? What does it matter to the meaning of homelessness if shelters and services are scattered through the city rather than concentrated in skid row?

However, it is not from these multiple and infinite subversions that "difference" is maintained, at least not to the public eye: through tactics the homeless can survive only by appearing to be something else entirely. It is only through these subversions that the homeless can survive at all.

To return to homeless youth, under what conditions did they move the faint glimmer of their social identify from a glowing coal to light, from the daily Sisyphean effort of social reproduction demanded by tactics to a more routinized, generalized acceptance of them *on their terms*, with tactical accommodations and reinforcement by newly created structures? How did they "stockpile their winnings?" The concept of tactics alone cannot help us at this point. And if we do not move beyond it, it presents us with a danger far greater than that of simply describing how power is exerted over marginalized peoples. To speak exclusively of tactical forms of resistance is to risk normalizing, even romanticizing, the condition of the marginalized people, humanizing the face of poverty in a way that demands no further action.

Young and Homeless in Hollywood

Here I think the concept of tactics bears further refinement in order to explain the various ways that space (and meaning) can be seized. The tactics described thus far are the *tactics of invisibility*. In one sense homeless youths "stockpiled their winnings" through the tactics of invisibility by returning repeatedly to Hollywood as "youths," and holding out long enough to force services to move to Hollywood. But this was only a limited victory.

The second kind of tactics might be called the *tactics of rupture*. Here, once again, the meaning of the space is manipulated or diverted, but with an important difference. The space is manipulated in such a way as not to simply *conceal* the identity of the marginalized, but to seize or *affirm* that identity. For the Riverbottom people in Riverside County, both concealment and rupture were part of their spatial praxis. In its most extreme form, these tactics of rupture manifest themselves as "Punk Hollywood," extreme because in and through the control of a material and symbolic space within Hollywood, youth, who would otherwise be considered runaways or homeless were able to create and sustain a different image of themselves. The concept of rupture is already well developed in literature on youth subcultures, but it overlooks the crucial role of space and control over space in affirming a new identity. Here we must draw on other concepts of space and self.

Goffman's concept of *front regions* and *back regions* offers greater possibilities. There is, in the concept, an implicit order and privileging of front over back regions, as orderly, civil, sacred, and so on. Goffman does not look at how the meanings of front and back regions might be transformed by individuals, much less by groups, but he leaves us with a kernel of self-reflective resistance. He suggests that, in the passage between front and back regions, back regions become the space in which one can reflect on the presentation of self to the public in the front region, that this presentation is in fact a calculated act on behalf of the individual rather than an unthinking response to the demands of one social space over another. Moreover (although he does not recognize this), Goffman provides us with examples where the privileging of front over back region is highly unstable, where one could easily imagine the inhabitants of the back region either rejecting or even embracing their status. Such is the case in his counterposition of church and criminal's hideaway.

To return to the case study, Punk Hollywood expresses a social space where the ordering of front and back regions were clearly inverted. Punks made a tactical appropriation of this space, these back regions within Hollywood. But they did so in a way which changed the value of the space. These spaces did not confirm for them their own marginality, but became their privileged front region. Punk squatters thus claimed the "essence" of marginality in social and spatial terms. Through the tactical inhabitation of particular spaces, punks created a rupture of meaning. Rupture is the process by which an order of equivalences is reversed. The very attributes valued by "society at large" are shunned by those who are denied those attributes. Rupture is the act of choosing the position of outlaw. Rupture does not so much attempt to "magically resolve experience of contradictions" as represent the experience of contradiction itself.[8] Here, moreover, it is more than the simple material availability of space that is important. The space must have a symbolic meaning that resonates, that is homologous with the particular identity of the group. The meaning of punk squatting subculture was destroyed as much by denying them the potent symbolism of particular spaces, the sealing off of these "spaces of rupture"—Hollywood Cemetery, the Errol Flynn and Doheny Manors, and finally Oki Dogs—as denying them any space at all within Hollywood.

But even this is not enough. One cannot simply "enter the space of difference," one has to make difference overflow the space it occupies, insinuate itself into other spaces. The destruction of punk squatting space and the decline and transformation of the subculture as it was pushed literally into the streets precluded this possibility. But the tactical inhabitation of Hollywood by homeless youths ultimately forced a *suturing* of meaning, between metaphorical street and family, between a sacred and profane existence. The new understanding of homeless youths that emerged from this tension is not just a simple cooptation of oppositional subcultures, which would imply that the subculture was simply incorporated into a preexisting understanding of homeless youths. Service-providers were forced to change their understanding and mode of treatment of youths in this act of suturing the positive identities that the youths chose for themselves and the images they had of runaways in a new space within Hollywood.

In this process of suturing, service-providers made the meaning of homeless youths homological with the emerging, ultimately dominant, symbol of redevelopment. Service-providers linked the presence of youths in Hollywood to the very act of boosterism, to the lure of "stardom" perpetuated by the entertainment industry and by local growth coalitions. This image of homeless youth was the metaphor through which the linking of "social needs" and "redevelopment," normally separate spheres, made sense. The coalition that emerged in the creation of a redevelopment plan for Hollywood was at once the medium and outcome through which new social identities of the community and the place were constituted and stabilized.

To talk about this process of production of space and self is also to describe different kinds of spaces from which different kinds of meaning might emerge. There are a variety of hegemonic nodal points from which meaning flows, with no predetermined center.[9] Among these nodal points, one might identify three formal types of space within a landscape of meaning. Each of these is inscribed within a particular political economy of production of space. The first is the space of the citadel. This is a space of *exclusion*, a "marked" space, like the postindustrial city space that expels or submerges all other meanings except those of the privileged classes to which they cater. This is the space described in most geographies of homelessness. Its character could be described as *monological*,[10] or *apodictic*, for it destroys any alternative meaning of an object under investigation: the juvenile penal system could also be considered a space of exclusion, or monological space, because it submerges all contestatory meanings into an overarching image of juvenile delinquents and appropriate treatment modes.

The second space is the space of the ghetto. This is a space of rupture, or potential rupture, the "forgotten," devalued space occupied by those who are excluded, who may accept the "non-marked" status imposed on them, or who may seize their own forms of subjectivity in and through the claiming of that space. Within the "ghetto" of Hollywood it was punk squatters who chose spaces and tactics of rupture. This was the space of Punk Hollywood.

The third space, however, lies between the citadel and ghetto, where a kind of hybrid of new meanings are produced. This is a space of *suture*, where meanings are fused together to produce something new. This was the space of service-providers, which fused the meaning of street and family, sacred and profane. Spaces of suture arise where production of place must occur through hegemonic alliance, and not sheer dominance. Here, place-making is a social and political act which does not automatically follow from "naked economics." The space of Hollywood in the 1980s is a space where meaning must be sutured. Had Hollywood's revitalization been successful in the 1970s, with its distinct enclaves of mall and office space, Hollywood might very

Conclusion

well have become an apodictic space, destroying alternative meanings. That this particular meaning of homeless youths originated in Hollywood is no accident, it is the place where the meaning "made sense." It made sense because the juxtaposition of "homeless youth" and "Hollywood" played into larger societal fears about the dissolving middle-class family and the evils of the modernizing city. But it is only in this place that such an image could emerge. As one service-provider noted, money was not forthcoming for Central American homeless youth in Pacoima.

` The relationship between these spaces—apodictic, ruptured, and sutured—is not, in itself, fixed. As I finished the research for this book, service-providers were attempting to extend the sutured meaning of homeless youth beyond its limited acceptance in places like Hollywood to areas like South Central Los Angeles, where images of youth as the "dangerous classes" are becoming fixed. This might be considered an example of the isoglosses, the second wave of implantation of the myth of homeless youths:

> Every myth can have its history and geography; each is in fact a sign of the other: a myth ripens because it spreads. . . . it is perfectly possible to draw what linguists call the isoglosses of a myth, the lines which limit the social region where it is spoken. As this region is shifting it would be better to speak of waves of implantation of the myth.[11]

This project is both very timely and very difficult. It is an attempt to challenge the chain of equivalences which is currently being forged between criminalization and racialization of certain youths, forming an image of the dangerous classes that now underlies contemporary discussions of the treatment of "youth gangs." Here youth advocates have a more challenging task ahead of them than they did in repairing the image of homeless youth from a punitive approach to a rehabilitative one.

Youth-advocates have done much to reweave the tattered safety net for homeless youth in America over the past twenty years. However, much work remains to be done. In building a support network for homeless and runaways, youth-service providers struggled with a "constitutive outside" attempting to *subvert* rather than *confront* gendered and racialized images of homeless youth. Funders must also secure funding and support in appealing to our nostalgia for the white middle-class family, and in a sense build this image from within, with the knowledge that half their clientele are young women and almost half are young men and women of color.

This endeavor is only partially sucessful. Young women who run away and who turn to prostitution for survival remain literally and figuratively "outside the project," helped by only one service which relies entirely on private funding to meet its objectives. One has to ask why no parallel government-funded project has been established.

Moreover, if we look at the Los Angeles riots of 1992 and the lack of federal aid which followed this outburst—relative to the river of federal funds following the Watts riots—it becomes clear that the contemporary restructuring of the welfare state, like that of the penal system, is more than ever before firmly entrenched along racialized divisions. And the structures and systems which oppress and divide youth are becoming organized more tenaciously and perniciously around socially constructed differences of race than perhaps any other form.

To follow youth advocates in California and move beyond the delimited provision of services for youth in Hollywood, we must begin to understand—for youth of color—how the concentration of services in Hollywood reconfirms rather than challenges what Barner Hesse terms "the regionalization of white and Black identity."[12]

This is a more difficult undertaking. The socially constructed and spatially constituted differences around race, and the structures which support and perpetuate the racialization of certain others have a much longer and deeper history, a greater economic, political, and social investment and an existence more intransigent in time and space than those which, in the mid-1970s, criminalized homeless youths as outcast from "the modern family." This challenges us to acknowledge that some differences are indeed more significant than others, and that these differences require much wider and more concerted efforts and more sustained political action to deconstruct. This does not mean that we should abandon the project of deconstructiing differences in favor of accepting some idea of essential forms of oppression. This, in effect, would be a return to the holy, unchanging trinity of race, gender, and class. Nor is it enough to demonstrate, in theory, the potential fluidity of socially constructed differences by resorting to anecdote or delimited examples of when and where gender, race, or class has in fact "not mattered." Rather, it is crucial to analyze the material practices which have served to make some differences more trenchant than others, to dissect how these differences have become constructed and discursively embodied in space and over time in a whole range of spheres. These practices are difficult to

Conclusion

confront, for they are the very same ones which privilege most of us. As a white, female member of the new middle-class it is easier for me to identify differences that have been disrupted by my own class practices (such as the fluidity of contemporary gender role among my class) than those that are supported by my class practices (such as the persistent racialized divisions in and outside of academe). But if we are to take this project seriously, we as scholars must begin to identify and to unravel the "deeper filaments and more tenacious tendrils of power," that privilege us over and separate us from our brothers and sisters.

NOTES

INTRODUCTION

1. John Berger, *The Look of Things* (New York: Viking, 1974), p. 40

2. Nirvana, "Smells Like Teen Spirit," 1991.

3. Ernesto Laclau and Chantal Mouffe, *Hegemony and Socialist Strategy: Towards a Radical Democratic Politics* (London: Verso, 1985), p. 25

CHAPTER 1

1. Marshall Berman, *All that Is Solid Melts Into Air: The Experience of Modernity*, (New York: Penguin, 1982), p. 15.

2. Jane Addams, Founder of Hull House, Chicago, in *The Spirit of Youth and the City Streets*, (Chicago: University of Illinois Press, 1972), p. 15.

3. I use the term *youth* as a general term to refer to the transition from childhood to adulthood. *Youth* refers specifically to a premodern form of this transition, compared to *adolescence* which was considered the more tightly age-graded modern form. I use *youth* not to reference the premodern form, but rather to signal that the term *adolescence* is no longer a hegemonic norm, and expectations for this transition now vary widely.

4. Chicago and Los Angeles have been widely accepted as two paradigmatic sites of urban and societal transformation. See Edward Soja,

Notes to Chapter 1

Postmodern Geographies: The Reassertion of Space in Critical Social Theory (London: Verso, 1989); and also William Sharpe and Leonard Wallock, "From 'Great Town' to 'Nonplace Urban Realm': Reading the Modern City," *Visions of the Modern City: Essays in History, Art and Literature*, eds. William Sharpe and Leonard Wallock (Baltimore: The Johns Hopkins University Press, 1987), pp. 1–50.

5. By modernization I mean "a continuous process of societal restructuring that is periodically accelerated to produce a significant recomposition of space-time-being in their concrete forms, a change in the nature and experience of modernity that arises primarily from the historical and geographical dynamics of modes of production." Soja, p. 27.

6. Tony Pinkey, Introduction to Raymond Williams, *The Politics of Modernism*, (New York: Verso, 1989) , p. 11.

7. See Marshall Berman, *All that Is Solid Melts into Air*, p. 5. See Larry Grossberg, "Putting the Pop Back into Postmodernism," *Universal Abandon? The Politics of Postmodernism*, ed. Andrew Ross (Minneapolis: University of Minnesota Press, 1988), pp. 167–190.

8. See Marshall Berman, "The Signs in the Street: A Response to Perry Anderson," *New Left Review* 44 (1984), pp. 114–123.

9. See Lawrence Grossberg, "Putting the Pop back into Postmodernism," *Universal Abandon? The Politics of Postmodernism*, ed. Andrew Ross (Minneapolis: University of Minnesota Press, 1988), pp. 167–190.

10. Roland Barthes, *Mythologies* (New York: Hill and Wang, 1972) pp. 109–158. Selected and translated from the French by Annette Lavers.

11. Walter Benjamin, "Paris, the Capital of the 19th Century," *Reflections: Essays, Aphorisms, Autobiographical Writings*, Peter Demetz, ed. (New York and London: Harcourt, Brace, Jovanovich, 1978), pp.146-162

12. Henri Lefebvre, *The Production of Space*, translated by Donald Nicholson -Smith (Oxford, Cambridge: Blackwell, 1991), *passim*.

13. Marshall Blonsky, *On Signs* (Baltimore, Maryland: The Johns Hopkins University Press, 1955), p. xxx

14. Jacques Lacan, "Signs, Symbol, Imagining" in Blonsky *op. cit.*, pp. 203–210.

15. John Shotter, *The Cultural Politics of Everyday Life* (Toronto:University of Toronto Press, Toronto), pp. 198–200.

16. Benedict Anderson, *Imagined Communities* (London: Verso 1983, 1989), pp. 14–15.

17. I am indebted to Rob Shields for a discussion which helped me to clarify the position of the concept of the social imaginary in relation to others. Any errors in interpretation remain my own.

18. See Raymond Williams, *The Politics of Modernism. Against the New Conformists*, ed. and Introduced by Tony Pinkey (London: Verso, 1989), p. 47.

19. John R. Gillis, *Youth and History* (London: Academic Press, 1964).

Notes to Chapter 1

20. Williams, p. 4.

21. See Talcott Parsons, "Age and Sex in the Social Structure," *Essays in Sociology* (Glencoe, IL: The Free Press, 1949).

22. Of course some attempted to prolong this view: See Frank Musgrove, *Youth and the Social Order* (Bloomington, IN: University of Indiana Press,1965); Frank Musgrove, "The Problems of Youth and the Social Structure," *Youth and Society* no. 11 (1969), pp. 38–58; J.S. Coleman, *The Adolescent Society* (New York: Free Press, 1961); M. Abrams, *The Teenage Consumer* (London: Routledge and Kegan Paul, 1959).

23. John R. Gillis, *Youth and History: Transition and Change in European Age Relations 1770–Present* (New York: New York Academic Press, 1991), pp. 214–215; see also D.H.J. Morgan, *Social Theory and the Family* (London: Routledge and Kegan Paul, 1975), pp. 39–48. For a similar but more sympathetic critique of Parsons's work see Hyman Rodman, "Talcott Parsons's View of the Changing American Family," *Marriage, Family and Society*, ed. Hyman Rodman (New York: Random House, 1967), pp. 262–286.

24. A range of critical British sociologists took an oblique swipe at this formulation by exposing the class bias of concepts of adolescence, delinquency, and deviance. See John Clarke, Stuart Hall, Tony Jefferson, and Brian Roberts, "Subcultures, Culture and Class: A Theoretical Overview," *Resistance Through Rituals: Youth Subcultures in Post-war Britain*, eds. Stuart Hall and Tony Jefferson (London: Hutchinson & Co., 1976), pp. 9–74; Graham Murdock and Robin McCron, "Youth and Class: A Career of Confusion," *Working Class Youth Culture*, eds. Geoff Mungham and Geoff Pearson (London: Routledge and Kegan Paul, 1976), pp. 10–26; Mike Brake, *The Sociology of Youth Culture and Youth Subcultures. Sex and Drugs and Rock 'n' Roll?* (London: Routledge and Kegan Paul, 1980), especially pp. 41–45.

25. See K. Keniston, *The Uncommitted Youth: Alienated Youth in Society* (New York: Dell, 1965). See also John R.Gillis, *Youth and History*, p. 209.

26. Anthony Platt considered child savers to include youth workers involved in both public and private institutions and the penal system. See Anthony E. Platt, *The Child Savers: The Invention of Delinquency* (Chicago: University of Chicago Press, 1969).

27. Joseph Kett, *Rites of Passage* (New York: Basic Books, 1977), pp.11–38.

28. Kett, p. 221.

29. Gillis, p. 169. But see also Platt, especially p. 135; Kett, chap. 5.

30. See Platt, p. 28.

31. Gillis, pp.137, 170–71. This shift from a class- to age-based explanation of juvenile crime was also reflected in perceptions of homeless youth in the same period. Charles L. Brace, founder of New York's Children's Aid Society, for instance, thought that the growing class of street youth might be eliminated by training in the work-force, particularly in Midwestern communities where labor was needed.

Notes to Chapter 1

See Mark R. Lipschutz, "Runaways in History," *Crime and Delinquency*, July 1977, p. 326; Leanne G. Rivlin and Lynne C. Manzo, "Homeless Children in New York City: A View from the Nineteenth Century," *Children's Environment Quarterly* 5 (1988): 30; Charles Loring Brace, *The Dangerous Classes* (New York: Wynkoop and Hallenbeck, 1880).

32. Kett, p. 257.

33. Kett, p. 256.

34. See Victor L. Strieb, *Juvenile Justice in America* (London: Kennikat Press, 1987), chap. 2, "History and Characteristics of the Juvenile Justice System," p. 5–19; Robert G. Caldwell, "The Juvenile Court: Development and Some Major Problems," *Juvenile Delinquency: A Book of Readings*, ed. Rose Giallombardo (New York: John Wiley and Sons, 1987).

35. Judge Mack, "The Juvenile Court," *Harvard Law Review* 23 (1990), pp. 104–122. Cited in Jack Rothman with Thomas David, *Status Offenders in Los Angeles County; Focus on Runaway and Homeless Youth: A Study and Policy Recommendations* (Los Angeles: University of California, Los Angeles School of Social Work, 1985), p. 28.

36. *Kent v. United States*, in Strieb, pp. 54–55.

37. Cited in D. Steinhart, "The Politics of Status Offender Deinstitutionalization in California," *Neither Angels nor Thieves: Studies in the Deinstitutionalization of Status Offenders* (Washington, D.C.: National Academy Press, 1982), p. 787.

38. Mark R. Lipschutz, "Runaways in History," *Crime and Delinquency*, July 1977, p. 325.

39. See Julia M. Robertson, "Homeless and Runaway Youth: Review of Literature," *Homelessness: The National Perspective*, eds. J.M. Robertson and M. Greenblatt (Prepublication draft: Plenum Publishing Corporation); Marjorie Robertson, "Homeless Youth: An Overview of Recent Literature," *Homeless Children and Youth* (Prepublication draft: Los Angeles: Transaction Press); Rivlin and Manzo; Lipschutz; Dorothy Miller, Roland Miller, Fred Hoffman, and Robert Duggan, *Runaways—Illegal Aliens in Their Own Land: Implications for Service* (New York: Praeger Publishers, 1980).

40. Nancy Fraser and Linda Nicholson, "Social Criticism and Philosophy: An Encounter between Postmodernism and Feminism," *Universal Abandon: The Politics of Postmodernism*, ed. Andrew Ross (Minneapolis: University of Minnesota Press, 1988), pp. 83–104.

41. Rivlin and Manzo, pp. 27–28.

42. Julia Robertson, p. 5.

43. See, for instance, Supervisor Edmund D. Edelman, *The Runaway and Homeless Youth in Los Angeles County: Transcript of Tape-recorded Proceedings* (Plummer Park, California, September 10, 1976).

44. Williams, p. 47.

45. Kett draws on numerous studies to develop this argument, including Hollingshead's study of Elmstown, Plainville. See A.B. Hollingshead, *Elmstown's Youth* (New York: John Wiley and Sons Inc., 1949).

46. I will leave aside a discussion of differences between nations, which were also investigated by social historians. The most extensive treatment of this theme can be found in Gillis. Comparing the differences in orientation between the German and British social institutions developed for adolescence, Gillis emphasizes the differences in class structure and social and political relationships between classes in the two nations as a central dynamic influencing the degree and nature of controls over youth. See chap. 4, "Conformity and Delinquency: The Era of Adolescence, 1900–1950," pp. 133–183.

47. Kett, pp. 246–251.

48. Kett, pp. 246–251.

49. The emerging system of juvenile care included a range of treatment options, such as detention facilities, public training schools, ranches, camps, and "nontraditional institutions," such as private juvenile correctional facilities, child welfare residences, and mental health facilities. P. Lerman, "Trends and Issues in the Deinstitutionalization of Youths in Trouble," Appendix, *United States Senate Ninety-Sixth Congress, Report of the Subcommittee on the Judiciary, Homeless Youth: The Saga of "Pushouts" and "Throwaways" in America* (Washington D.C.: U.S. Government Printing Office, 1980), pp. 155–156.

50. Kett, p. 165.

51. Kett, p. 165.

52. See, for example, Gillis, Kett, and Platt. Compare, however, with William Sharpe and Leonard Wollock, who argue that "the city has given birth to many of the most energetic reform movements, from the social protest and moralizing of Dickens and of Booth and the Salvation Army in London, and Henry Mayhew's less judgemental urban anthropology there, to Jane Addams' settlement houses and Jacob Riis's muckracking masterpieces in Chicago and New York." William Sharpe and Leonard Wollock, *Visions of the Modern City: Essays in History, Art, and Literature* (Baltimore: Johns Hopkins University Press, 1987), p. 8.

53. Soja, p. 56, See also Soja, pp. 56–60

54. Soja, p. 125.

55. Soja, p. 81.

56. "The exclusion of groups, classes, or individuals from the urban is also their exclusion from civilization, if not all of society. The right to the city legitimizes the refusal to allow oneself to be removed from urban reality by discriminatory or segregative organizations" (my translation).

57. Henri Lefebvre, *Espace et politique* (Paris: Éditions Anthropos, 1968), p. 163; Henri Lefebvre, "Space: Social Product and Use Value," *Critical Sociology: European Perspectives*, ed. J.W. Friedberg (New York: Irvington Publishers, 1979), pp. 285–295.

58. Soja, p. 96.

59. See Lawrence Grossberg, "Putting the Pop back into Postmodernism," *Universal Abandon? The Politics of Postmodernism*, ed. Andrew Ross (Minneapolis: University of Minnesota Press, 1988), pp. 167–190.

60. See also Stanley Aronowitz, "Postmodernism and Politics," *Universal Abandon?*, p. 54.

61. See Marshall Berman, "Taking it to the Streets: Conflict and Community in Public Space," *Dissent* (Fall 1986) pp. 476–85; but compare with Michael Rustin, "The Rise and Fall of Public Space," *Dissent* (Fall 1986) pp. 486–494, whose article Berman responds to.

62. Craig Owens expresses this problem well when he argues that when we become simply an "other" among "others," difference is reduced to a vast undifferentiated category to which all marginalized groups can be assimilated, and the path from difference to indifference is very short. See Craig Owens, "The Discourse of Others: Feminists and Post-modernism," *The Anti-Aesthetic: Essays on Postmodern Culture*, ed. H. Foster (Seattle: Bay Press, 1983).

63. Nancy Harstock, "Foucault on Power: A Theory for Women?" *Feminism/ Postmodernism*, ed. Linda J. Nicholson (New York: Routledge and Chapman Hall, 1990), pp. 157–175.

64. Christine Di Stefano, "Dilemmas of Difference: Feminism, Modernity, and Postmodernism," *Feminism/Postmodernism*, pp. 63–82.

65. Roland Barthes, *Mythologies*, trans. Annette Lavers (New York: Hill and Wang, 1957), p. 152.

66. Hal Foster, "Postmodernism: A Preface," *The Anti-Aesthetic: Essays on Postmodern Culture*, ed. H. Foster (Seattle: Bay Press, 1983), pp. xi–xii.

67. Grossberg, p. 176.

68. Grossberg, p. 174.

69. Grossberg, p. 169.

70. See Linda McDowell, "Space, Place and Gender Relations: Part II. Identity, Difference, Feminist Geometries and Geographies," *Progress in Human Geography* 17, 3 (1993), pp. 305–318.

71. See Christian Di Stefano, "Dilemmas of Difference: Feminism, Modernity, and Postmodernism," in *Feminism/Postmodernism*, ed. Linda Nicholson, (London: Routledge, 1990), pp. 63–82.

72. L. Bondi and M. Domosh, "Other Figures in Other Places: On Feminism, Postmodernism and Geography," *Environment and Planning D: Society and Space* 10, (1992) pp. 199–213.

73. Liz Bondi, "Locating Identity Politics," in , *Place and the Politics of Identity*, eds. Michael Keith and Stephen Pile (London and New York: Routledge, 1993), pp. 84–101, p. 98.

74. Neil Smith and Cindi Katz "Grounding Metaphor," in *Place and the Politics of Identity*, pp. 67–83, pgs. 77, 79.

Notes to Chapter 2

75. See Kett; Kenneth Keniston, *Young Radicals: Notes on Committed Youth* (New York: Dell Publishers, 1968), pp. 260–64.

76. Grossberg, p. 168.

CHAPTER 2

1. C.P. Philo, "'The Same and Other': On Geographies, Madness and Outsiders" (unpublished monograph), Cambridge University, Department of Geography, 1986, pp. 49–50.

2. I have adopted this characterization from Blau, who identified ten chronological categories of literature on homelessness. See Joel S. Blau, "The Homeless of New York: A Case Study in Social Welfare Policy," diss. (Ann Arbor, MI: University Microfilms International, 1987), p. 30. See also Gregg Barak, *Gimme Shelter: A Social History of Homelessness in Contemporary America* (New York: Praeger, 1991), p. 22.

3. Kim James Hopper, "A Bed For the Night: Homeless Men in New York City, Past and Present," diss. (Ann Arbor MI: University Microfilms International, 1987); Charles Hoch and Robert Slayton, *New Homeless and Old: Community and the Skid Row Hotel* (Philadelphia: Temple University Press, 1989).

4. See Barak, *Gimme Shelter*.

5. See D. Sibley, *Outsiders in Urban Society* (Oxford: Basil Blackwell, 1981).

6. Philo, p. 51.

7. Edward Soja, *Postmodern Geographies: The Reassertion of Space in Critical Social Theory* (London: Verso, 1989), p. 58.

8. A. Giddens, *The Constitution of Society* (Berkeley: University of California Press, 1984), p. 368.

9. Christine Di Stefano, "Dilemmas of Difference: Feminism, Modernity, and Postmodernism," *Feminism/Postmodernism*, p. 71. see also Genevieve Lloyd, *The Man of Reason: "Male" and "Female" in Western Philosophy* (Minneapolis: University of Minnesota Press, 19xx), p. 105

10. See M.J. Dear and S.M. Taylor, *Not On Our Street* (London: Pion Ltd., 1982); S.M. Taylor, et al., "Predicting Community Reaction to Mental Health Facilities," *Journal of the American Planning Association* Vol. 50 No. 1 (1984) pp. 36–47; Michael Dear and Jennifer Wolch, *Landscapes of Despair: From Deinstitutionalization to Homelessness* (Princeton, NJ: Princeton University Press, 1987).

11. Dear and Wolch, *Landscapes of Despair;* J.R. Wolch and S.R. Gabriel, "Development and Decline of Service-dependent Ghetto," *Urban Geography* 5 (1984); Dear and Taylor, *Not On Our Street*.

12. For Dear and Wolch, this "prepared space" (to borrow from Lloyd) is the inner city. As the authors note, "this drift to the inner city is motivated by hopes and fears that are similar to many groups planning a new move. . . they are not ignorant of the hazards of coping in a new

Notes to Chapter 2

environment . . . some of (their) plans reflect a depressingly accurate realism: they expect to receive an income that is below the poverty line; others expect to be isolated from family and friends." Dear and Wolch, *Landscapes of Despair*, p. 20.

13. Dear and Taylor, *Not On Our Street*.

14. J.R. Wolch, "The Residential Location of the Service-dependent Poor," *Annals of the Association of American Geographers* 70 (1980); Wolch and Gabriel, "Development and Decline."

15. H.M. Bahr, *Skid Row: An Introduction to Disaffiliation* (New York: Oxford University Press, 1973); J. P. Spradley, *You Owe Yourself a Drunk: An Ethnography of Urban Nomads* (Boston: Little, Brown, 1970); C. Foote, "Vagrancy-type Law and its Administration," *Crime and the Legal Process*, ed. W.J. Chambliss (New York: McGraw Hill, 1969); W.J. Chambliss, "A Sociological Analysis of the Law of Vagrancy," *Social Problems* 12 (1964); D.J. Bogue, *Skid Row in American Cities* (Chicago: University of Chicago Press, 1963); E. Wallace, *Skid Row as a Way of Life* (New York: Harper and Row, 1968); E.G. Love, *Subways Are For Sleeping* (New York: Harcourt Brace, 1957); M.R. Henderson, "Acquiring Privacy in Public Places," *Urban Life and Culture* 3 (1975). pp. 446-455

16. Some of the earlier ethnographic literature on tramps and hobos falls into this category as well, including much of what Blau characterizes as the "on-the-road genre of literature on the homeless." Others, such as Nels Anderson and Thomas Minehan, explore the ways that tramps have survived through an intimate knowledge of the moral geography of different towns and cities. Not surprisingly, during the 1920s and the Depression, when homeless people were highly mobile, much of the knowledge of moral geography focused on the differences in general attitude towards hobos as it varied from town to town, as well as an intimate knowledge of seasonal labor markets and different possibilities for day labor in various parts of the country. See, for example, Nels Anderson, *The Hobo: Sociology of the Homeless Man* (Chicago: University of Chicago Press, 1923). That hobos should occupy the marginal spaces of these towns is taken for granted in much of this literature. Minehan, however, points out that space, status, and survival strategies were intricately interlinked : "Stem hitters are ranked in three classes according to what they panhandle and where. Boys and girls who hit the stem (the main-stem, or main-street) for food rank the lowest; boys and girls who hit the back porches are next; boys and girls who hit the stem for money are highest and the highest of all are the ones who hit the houses for cash. The latter occupation takes not only nerve, but brains and personality. The boy or girl successful at it has money and praise." Thomas Minehan, *Boy and Girl Tramps of America* (New York: Farrar & Rinehart, 1934), p. 183, and especially chap. 8, "Their Education."

17. See E.V. Stonequist, *The Marginal Man: A Study in Personality and Culture* (New York: Scribners, 1937); H.M. Bahr, *Disaffiliated Man: Essays and Bibliography on Skid Row, Vagrancy and Outsiders* (Toronto: University of Toronto Press, 1970); J.P. Spradley.

Notes to Chapter 2

18. James Duncan, "Men Without Property: The Tramp's Classification and Use of Urban Space," *Antipode* 11, no. 1 (1979), p. 28.

19. Duncan, p. 24.

20. Preziosi states this most succinctly: "That object of disciplinary desire 'the city'—does powerful work in a wide variety of registers to complement, maintain and perpetuate certain notions about the modern Subject . . . we cannot fail to construe the city as a simulacrum of the self." Donald Preziosi, "Oublier la Citta," *Strategies* 3 (1990), pp. 261–262.

21. Michael Rustin, "The Rise and Fall of Public Space: A Postcapitalist Prospect," *Dissent* 33, no. 4 (1986), pp. 486–494.

22. Philip Kasinitz, "Gentrification and Homelessness: the Single Room Occupant and the Inner City Revival," *Urban Social Review* 17 (1984) pp. 9–14.

23. W.J. Wilson, *Thinking About Crime* (New York: Basic Books, 1975).

24. See Rustin; Marshall Berman, "Taking it to the Streets: Conflict and Community in Public Space," *Dissent* (Fall 1986) pp. 476–485.

25. See Richard Sennett, *The Conscience of the Eye: The Design and Social Life of Cities* (New York: Knopf, 1990).

26. Rosalyn Deutsche, "Men in Space," *Strategies: A Jounal of Theory, Culture, and Politics*, 3, 1990, pp. 130–138; bell hooks, *Black Looks: Race and Representation* (Toronto: Between the Lines, 1992).

27. Exclure de l'urbain des groups, des classes, des individus, c'est aussi les exclure de la civilisation, sinon de la société. Le droit à la ville le refus de se laisser écarter de la realite urbaine par une organisation discriminatoire, ségrégative. Henri Lefebvre, *Espace et politique*, 1968, p. 163.

28. Diana Fuss, *Essentially Speaking* (London and New York: Routledge, 1989), p. 29.

29. Edward Soja and Barbara Hooper, "The Spaces that Difference Makes," in *Place and the Politics of Identity*, eds. Michael Keith and Stephen Pile (London and New York: Routledge, 1993), pp. 183–205.

30. Andrew Mair, "The Homeless and the Post-Industrial City," *Political Geography* 5 (1986), pp. 351–368.

31. P.C. Sexton, "The Life of the Homeless," *Dissent* 30, no.1 (1983), pp. 79–84.

32. Rosalyn Deutsche, "Architecture of the Evicted," *Strategies: A Journal of Theory, Culture and Politics* 3 (1990).

33. Wolch and Gabriel, "Development and Decline"; Dear and Wolch, *Landscapes of Despair*.

34. Kim Hopper, "Whose Lives Are These, Anyway?" *Urban and Social Change Review* 17,2 (1984). Mair makes this connection as well, but accepts the development of such spaces as somehow inevitable.

35. M.E. Hombs and Mitch Snyder, *Homelessness in America: A Forced March to Nowhere* (Washington: Community for Creative Non-Violence, 1983); see also Ellen Baxter and Kim Hopper, *Private Lives/Public Spaces:*

Notes to Chapter 2

Homeless Adults on the Streets of New York City (New York: Community Service Society, 1981); M.R. Henderson.

36. W.C. Baer, "Housing in an Internationalizing Region: Housing Stock Dynamics in Southern California and the Dilemmas of Fair Share," *Environment and Planning D: Society and Space* 4 (1986), pp. 337–349; Jennifer Wolch, "Planning for Service Dependent Populations: A Fair Share Service Distribution Approach," unpublished manuscript, (University of Southern California, School of Urban and Regional Planning, 1987); Michael Dear, "Planning Community-Based Support Systems for the Homeless," unpublished manuscript (University of Southern California, School of Urban and Regional Planning, 1987).

37. Mair, p. 364.

38. See for example A.R Veness, "Home and Homelessness in the United States: Changing Ideas and Realities," *Environment and Planning D: Society and Space* 10 (1992), pp. 445–468.

39. Lawrence Grossberg, "Putting the Pop Back in Postmodernism," *Universal Abandon? The Politics of Postmodernism,* ed. Andrew Ross (Minneapolis: University of Minnesota Press, 1988), p. 169.

40. Stacy Rowe and Jennifer Wolch, "Social Networks in Time and Space: Homeless Women in Skid Row, Los Angeles," unpublished manuscript (University of Southern California, 1989), pp. 20–21.

41. Rowe and Wolch, "Social Networks," p. 12.

42. Rowe and Wolch, "Social Networks," p. 25.

43. These included appearing to be part of a tennis club to use its showers, making private use of the park's publicly available electric lines, banding together in the park to reinforce their tenuous "claim" to this space. See Talmadge Wright and Anita Vermund, "Small Dignities: Local Resistances, Dominant Strategies of Authority, and the Homeless," paper submitted for the 1990 Annual American Sociological Association, Washington, D.C.

44. Wright and Vermund, p. 29.

45. Deutsche, *Strategies,* p. 182.

46. Mair, p. 364.

47. Roland Barthes, *Mythologies,* trans. Annette Lavers (New York: Hill and Wang, 1957), p. 149.

48. M. Gottdiener, "Culture, Ideology, and the Sign of the City," *The City and the Sign,* ed. M. Gottdiener (New York: Columbia University Press, 1986), p. 209.

49. Ibid., p. 209.

50. H.T. Sanders and C.N. Stone, "Development Politics Reconsidered," *Urban Affairs Quarterly* 22 (1987), pp. 521–539; H.T. Sanders and C.N. Stone, "Competing Paradigms: A Rejoinder to Peterson," *Urban Affairs Quarterly* 22 (1987), pp. 548–551.

Notes to Chapter 3

51. Compare, for example, N. Fainstein and S. Fainstein, "Regime Strategies, Communal Resistance and Economic Forces," *Restructuring the City*, ed. Fainstein et al. (New York: Longman, 1983), pp. 245–282.

52. S. Clarke, "More Autonomous Policy Orientations: An Analytical Framework," *The Politics of Urban Development*, eds. H.T. Sanders and C.N. Stone (Kansas: University Press of Kansas, 1987), pp. 105–124.

53. J. Mollenkopf, *The Contested City* (Princeton, New Jersey: Princeton University Press, 1983); C. Stone, "The Study of the Politics of Urban Development," *The Politics of Urban Development*, eds. C. Stone and H.T. Sanders (Kansas: University Press of Kansas, 1987); H.T. Sanders and C.N. Stone, "Competing Paradigms," pp. 548–551.

54. Mollenkopf, pp. 7–8.

55. Clarke, pp. 105–124.

56. Clarke, pp. 105–124.

57. See T.R. Gurr and D.S. King, *The State and the City* (Chicago: University of Chicago Press, 1987).

58. Clarke, pp. 105–124.

59. Clarke, pp. 105–124.

60. Gottdiener, p. 218.

CHAPTER 3

1. I use mythologies in the sense that Barthes does—as depoliticized speech. See Roland Barthes, *Mythologies*, trans. Annette Lavers (New York: Hill and Wang, 1972), p. 143.

2. I have selected this quote from Dear and Wolch's work because it distills, rather succinctly, a particular way of thinking about homelessness. In fact it is not a fair representation of the position generally taken by the authors. See, for instance, Michael Dear and Jennifer Wolch, *Landscapes of Despair: From Deinstitutionalization to Homelessness* (Princeton: Princeton University Press, 1987), pp. 7–21. More representative of this type of mythology is what one scholar appropriately named "the 'Tiny Tim' journalism which occurs every year around Thanksgiving and Christmas." See Madelaine R. Stoner, "An Analysis of Public and Private Sector Provisions for the Homeless," *Urban and Social Change Review* 17,1 (1984), p. 3.

3. See R. Tuber, "The Invisible Women of Skid Row," *Los Angeles Herald Examiner*, January 26, 1984.

4. Imislund goes on to argue, "Society is confronted with men and women whose surface problems appear to be homelessness, or alcohol or drugs, but whose basic emotional discord goes much deeper. Despite the current political rhetoric, it is not a new condition, nor is it the result of different government administrations or economic swings." In fact,

skid rows, which emerged in American cities as a distinct spatial form between 1850 and 1875, have been very sensitive to political and economic crises, with populations increasing dramatically during the depressions of 1973, 1893, and 1929. See Marjorie J. Robertson, et al., *Emergency Shelter For the Homeless In Los Angeles County, Basic Shelter Research Project* (Los Angeles: University of California, Los Angeles, 1984), p. 3.

5. See Barthes, p. 144.

6. This unstable situation stands in contrast to the dominant view of social scientists and service providers in the 1970s, who predicted the demise of skid row and its dependent populations. See Richard Ropers, "The Rise of the New Urban Homeless," *Public Affairs Report* 26, 5 (1985), p. 1.

7. See Dear and Wolch, pp. 255–256.

8. See Barthes, p. 143. "In passing from history to nature, myth acts economically. It abolishes the complexity of human acts, it gives them the simplicity of essences, it does away with dialectics, without any going back beyond what is immediately visible, it organizes a world without contradictions because it is without depth . . . things appear to mean something by themselves."

9. See Dear and Wolch, Chapter 2, "The Social Construction of the Service-Dependent Ghetto," pp. 8–27.

10. Ibid., p. 20.

11. Ibid., p. 21.

12. The authors note that Foucault "omits considerations of how power relations are crystallized and combined into state apparatus or how state institutions act strategically in everyday routines." See Dear and Wolch, p. 11.

13. Here, borrowing from Foucault, Dear and Wolch identify four main practices: (i) enclosure—defining a protected place of treatment; (ii) partitioning—assigning each unit a specific place; (iii) identification of functional sites assigned, for instance, to therapy, administration, or work areas; and (iv) ranking—defining clients in a hierarchy. See Dear and Wolch, p. 18.

14. See Michel Foucault, *Discipline and Punish: The Birth of the Prison*, trans. Alan Sheridan (New York: Vintage Books, 1979), p. 211.

15. Ibid., p. 219.

16. Dear and Wolch argue that deinstitutionalization had the effect of exposing institutional practices to the scrutiny and criticism of the community.

17. Since 1981, federal spending on social service programs has decreased 9% while the national poverty rate has risen approximately 15%.

18. See Edward Soja et al, "Urban Restructuring: An Analysis of Social and Spatial Change in Los Angeles," *Economic Geography* 59, 2 (1983), pp. 195–230.

19. See Michael Dear, "Postmodern Planning," paper presented at the Annual Meeting of the Association of Collegiate Schools of Planning, Atlanta, 1985.

20. Several studies of the subcultures of the homeless support this argument. For examples, see M. Sloss, "The Crisis of Homelessness: Its Dimensions and Its Solutions," *Urban and Social Change Review* 17, 2 (1984), p. 18.

21. While this framework attributes a central role to space in the organization and exercise of relationships of power, it suggests an *infinitely specializing* organization of space, and development of mechanisms of control. For Foucault, this analysis is, in part, directed against an essentialist humanist view of resistance. See Foucault, p. 217. However, Foucault does not deny the possibility of resistance. See Foucault, p. 219.

22. Foucault, p. 211.

23. Stephen Crystal, "Homeless Men and Homeless Women: The Gender Gap," *Urban and Social Change Review* 17, 2 (1984), pp. 2–3.

24. Even skid row faces a series of transformations which should cause us to consider it part of the new geography. These have included the presence of homeless women, families, and political refugees in the area, and the incipient commercial gentrification of adjacent neighborhoods with the introduction of a vast government complex on Spring Street.

25. Michel Foucault, *Power/Knowledge* (New York: Pantheon, 1980), cited in David Harvey, *The Condition Of Postmodernity* (Oxford: Basil Blackwell, 1989), p. 48.

26. Michel Foucault, "Of Other Spaces," *Diacritics* 16:1 Spring (1986), pp. 22–27; 25.

27. See Louis Sahagun, "'Riverbottom' People: Dirt, Debate, Dilemma," *Los Angeles Times*, June 10, 1987.

28. I use the term *tactics* in the sense employed by De Certeau. Michel De Certeau, *The Practice of Everyday Life*, trans. Steven F. Rendall (Los Angeles: University of California Press, 1984), pp. 38–39, later in this chapter.

29. See Stacy Rowe and Jennifer Wolch, "Social Networks in Time and Space: The Case of Homeless Women in Skid Row, Los Angeles," (unpublished manuscript), University of Southern California, 1989.

30. See M.E. Hombs and M. Snyder, *Homelessness in America: The Forced March To Nowhere* (Washington: Community for Creative Non-Violence, 1982).

31. See De Certeau, p. 29.

32. See Erving Goffman, *The Presentation of Self in Everyday Life* (New York: Doubleday, 1959); *Asylums* (New York: Doubleday, 1961); *Behavior in Public Places* (New York: Free Press, 1963); *Strategic Interaction* (London: Basil Blackwell, 1969).

33. I would argue rather that behavior is a social construct in *all* places; what is missing in Goffman's analysis is how the relations of class/race/gender/etc. become spatially sorted, reinforcing or encouraging

different sets of behaviors in different places.

34. J. Rubenstein, *City Police* (New York: Farrar, Straus, and Giroux, 1973), cited in James Duncan, "Men Without Property: The Tramp's Classification and Use of Urban Space," *Antipode* 11,1 (1979), p. 25.

35. Compare Lefebvre on rigid hierarchization of leisure space. Henri Lefebvre, *La survie du capitalisme* (Paris: Éditions Anthropos, 1978), p. 18.

36. See Duncan, p. 27.

37. De Certeau, pp. 36–37.

38. Ibid., pp. 38–39

39. See John Clarke, Stuart Hall, Tony Jefferson, and Brian Roberts, "Subcultures, Cultures and Class: A Theoretical Overview," *Resistance Through Rituals: Youth Subcultures in Post-war Britain*, eds. Stuart Hall and Tony Jefferson (London: Hutchinson & Co., 1976), p. 12.

40. See, for instance, Raymond Ledrut. "If there is an urban semiology, it is dependent on urban anthropology. The changes in the meaning of the city derive not from changes in urban language but from a change in the way of inhabiting of living collective space, due to changes in the cultural and social system." Raymond Ledrut, "Speech and the Silence of the City," *The City and the Sign: An Introduction to Urban Semiotics*, eds. Mark Gottdiener and Alexandros Lagopoulous (New York: Columbia University Press, 1986), p. 123.

41. See Kim Hopper, "Whose Lives are These Anyway?" *Urban and Social Change Review* 17, 2 (1989), p. 12.

42. Andrew Mair, "The Homeless and the Post-Industrial City," *Political Geography* 5 (1986), p. 364.

43. See also Mark Gottdiener, "Culture, Ideology and the Sign of the City," *The City and the Sign: An Introduction to Urban Semiotics*, eds. Mark Gottdiener and Alexandros Lagopoulos (New York: Columbia University Press, 1986), pp. 202–218. Gottdiener argues: ". . . given the polysemous, multi-coded nature of urban life, the need of some groups for a more stable, uniformly conceived representation requires a management of the clash of oppositional environmental typifications. It is important to ask, on the one hand, what groups possess the need for overarching, historically invariant symbols, and on the other what the mechanisms are that are utilized to achieve ideological hegemony. In the former case, it is apparent that the real-estate industry, homeowners associations, chambers of commerce and banks are the most active managers in symbolic generalizations. . . . This is by no means an automatic process of sign conversion. It is contentious and contingent, depending upon the ability of special interest groups to control the symbolic interpretations of processual outcomes in everyday life." Gottdiener, p. 207.

44. See, for instance, Mair.

45. De Certeau, p. 96.

Notes to Chapter 4

46. See De Certeau, p. 96.

47. By 1987, this number had been reduced to approximately 8,000 units, with 1,400 units lost over the decade to demolitions and fires, or unoccupiable while under renovation. *Los Angeles Times*, June 2, 1987.

48. Marjorie J. Robertson et al.

49. *Los Angeles Times*, July 19, 1987.

50. Davis makes a similar argument about the cultural symbolism of the Bonaventure Hotel–see Mike Davis, "Urban Renaissance and the Spirit of Postmodernism," *New Left Review*, no. 151 (1987), pp. 106–113 . What I refer to, however, is a more literal and tactical use of space.

51. *Los Angeles Times*, August 3, 1984.

52. David Harvey, *The Urban Experience* (Baltimore: The Johns Hopkins University Press, 1989), p. 266.

53. Peggy MacMillan, "The Skid Row Sweeps: Staking Out Positions. They're Keeping the Homeless on the Move," *Los Angeles Times*, February 25, 1987.

54. MacMillan, "The Skid Row Sweeps," *Los Angeles Times*, February 25,1987.

55. This represents a qualitatively different use of the spatiotemporal pockets of moral law from that described by Duncan. In this case it does not simply reflect an existing discourse but intends to transform it.

56. "Trek for Justice," *Los Angeles Times*, October 1, 1987.

57. *Los Angeles Times*, October 1, 1987.

58. Ron Bell, thirty-one-year-old unemployed electronics engineer, Riverbottom, Riverside. Quoted in Louis Sahagun, "Riverbottom People: Dirt, Debate, Dilemma," *Los Angeles Times*, June 10, 1987.

CHAPTER 4

1. See Chapter Two.

2. See David Steinhart, "The Politics of Status Offender Deinstitutionalization in California," *Neither Angels Nor Thieves: Studies in Deinstitutionalization of Status Offenders*, eds. Joel F. Handler and Julie Katz (Washington: National Academy Press, 1982), pp. 784–824. This argument can be sustained if we focus exclusively on the "traditional correctional system." See P. Lerman, "Trends and Issues in the Deinstitutionalization of Youths in Trouble," Appendix, *United States Senate Ninety-Sixth Congress, Report of the Subcommittee on the Judiciary, Homeless Youth: The Saga of "Pushouts" and "Throwaways" in America* (Washington: U.S. Government Printing Office, 1980).

3. E. Monkonnen notes that the phrase "dangerous class" . . . appeared in the U.S. in the mid-1840s, and in England slightly earlier . . . In all varieties of the term, the fundamental notion is that this class is an enemy or at

least a threat to society. E. Monkonnen, "Nineteenth-Century Institutions: Dealing with the Urban Underclass," (unpublished), *Social Science Research Council. History of the Urban Underclass.* Of course, one must always be sensitive to the differences between the rhetoric and objectives of institutions and their actual practices (see Rothman). In fact, Strieb argues that while children in premodern times were convicted of crimes under general criminal law, sentences tended to be less severe, juries would often refuse to convict children facing the death penalty and in early English law there was the idea that children under fourteen years of age were presumed incapable of committing a crime. Thus Strieb argues that while there was no separate juvenile court, the law did, even at this point, accept children as a "special class of criminal." See Victor L. Strieb, *Juvenile Justice in America* (London: Kennikat Press, 1987), p. 5.

4. In Los Angeles in the latter half of the 1980s, police began aggressive crackdowns on gang activity, which included such programs as the Gang Related Active Trafficker Suppression program (GRATS). The program instructed the police to "stop and interrogate anyone who they suspect is a gang member, basing their assumptions on their dress or their use of gang hand signals." *Los Angeles Times,* May 8,1988, II, p.1. In M. Davis with S. Ruddick, "Los Angeles: Civil Liberties Between the Hammer and the Rock," *New Left Review* no. 170 (1988), p. 40. In the late 1970s, critical social historians were gently suggesting a more tolerant attitude towards lower-class youth. For instance, Kett argued, "As late as the 1960s major studies continued to confuse gangs and delinquency. One by-product of this confusion was that relatively little attention was paid to the similarities between the behavior of gang youth and that of conventional middle-class young people. Gang members frequently had their own argot and songs. The same could be said of the Boy Scout Manual . . ." Joseph Kett, *Rites of Passage* (New York: Basic Books, 1977), p. 257.

5. See Thomas G. Blomberg, *Juvenile Court and Community Corrections* (New York: University Press of America, 1984), pp. 20–32. A delinquent youth was defined in the state of California at the time as: a person under eighteen found to be begging or receiving alms; in the streets or public places; a vagrant; wandering without home or means of subsistence; without parent or guardian or without proper control; destitute; with unfit home; in the company of criminals; living or being in a house of prostitution; habitually frequenting places where liquors were sold; refusing to obey reasonable parental orders or incorrigible; without proper parents; habitually truant; or habitually using intoxicating liquors. F. Cahn and V. Bary, *Welfare Activities of Federal, State and Local Governments in California 1850–1934* (Los Angeles: University of California Press, 1936).

6. Gordon E. Gonion, "Section 601, W&I Code: A Need for Change," *Youth Authority Quarterly* 26, 2 (1973), pp. 21–31; especially, pp. 25–26.

7. In 1971, for instance, California accounted for 9.8% of the nation's juvenile population, but 31.8 % of all annual admissions to juvenile detention

facilities. Jack Rothman with Thomas David, *Status Offenders in Los Angeles County; Focus on Runaway and Homeless Youth: A Study and Policy Recommendations* (Los Angeles: University of California, Los Angeles School of Social Work, 1985), p. 43.

8. D. Johns and J. Bottcher, *AB 3121 Impact Evaluation: Final Report* (Sacramento: California Youth Authority, 1980), p. 42, cited in Rothman and David.

9. Office of Criminal Justice Planning, *California State Plan for Criminal Justice* (Office of Criminal Justice Planning, 1979),V-J-28–V-J-42. Of course, these youths were not held for the whole year, so the numbers of youths passing through the system per year could be substantially higher than the number of available beds. Although it is not clear that youths were actually jailed for offenses such as smoking, this was legally possible and did contribute to their overall image as "juvenile delinquent."

10. The virtues of incarcerating status offenders were hotly debated during the early 1970s. See David Steinhart, "The Politics of Status Offender Deinstitutionalization," pp. 793–97.

11. See Strieb's discussion of the distinctions between the socialized era of juvenile courts, and the constitutionalized era, pp. 7–13.

12. Strieb, pp. 9–10. This was first anticipated by *Kent v. United States* in 1966, which noted that under the current system, "the child receives the worst of both worlds: . . . he gets neither the protections accorded to adults nor the solicitous care and regenerative treatment postulated for children."

13. Status offenders were classified as 601s, whereas youth who had committed more serious crimes were classified as 602s. For an excellent account of the dynamics leading up to the deinstitutionalization of status offenders in California, see Steinhart, "The Politics of Status-Offender Deinstitutionalization," pp. 784–824.

14. George Saleeby, *Hidden Closets: A Study of Detention Practices in California* (Sacramento: California Youth Authority, 1978).

15. Kett, p. 266. This appears in marked difference to the situation in Britain where both historically and in the current period, the extent of juvenile crime has been overpublicized in a climate of "moral panic." See Stuart Hall et al., *Policing the Crisis: Mugging, the State and Law and Order* (London: Macmillan Education, 1978).

16. In fact, the overall percentage of violent crimes by youth has decreased. The Presidential Youth Issues Forum noted that in 1985 a total of 1.7 million arrests were made (nationwide) of persons under 18; of these, 4.2% had committed violent crimes, representing a 10% decrease in the violent crimes committed by minors in the last ten years. Higher Education Research Institute, *Youth Issues: Background Statements, The Presidential Youth Issues Forum* (Los Angeles: Graduate School of Education, University of California, 1990).

17. Steinhart, "The Politics of Status Offender Deinstitutionalization," p. 797.

18. Ibid., p. 796.

19. Steinhart is careful to argue, however, that following deinstutionalization, there was not—as feared—a tendency to reclassify status offenders as criminal juvenile offenders to circumvent the objectives of deinstitutionalization. He notes, "There was also speculation that minors apprehended for a variety of conducts would no longer receive the benefit of admission to detention on the "soft" Section 601 charge, but would more often be labeled with the Section 602 criminal charge," p. 812. Determinations that might be made with some arbitrariness include whether or not drugs found on a juvenile were carried for the purposes of private consumption or for sale. By the early 1970s, the status offender was defined in the following way: any person under the age of eighteen years who persistently or habitually refuses to obey the reasonable and proper orders of his parents, guardian, custodian, or school authorities, or who is beyond the control of such person; or any person who is habitually truant from school within the meaning of the law of this State, or who from any cause is in danger of leading an idle, dissolute, lewd, or immoral life, is within the jurisdiction of the juvenile court which may adjudge such person to be a ward of the court. Cited in Gonion, "Section 601, W & I Code: A Need for Change," p. 22.

20. David Steinhart, *Private Sector Task Force on Juvenile Justice: Final Report* (San Francisco: The National Council on Crime and Delinquency, TransAmerica Corporation and Chevron Corporation, March 1987), p. 6.

21. This was achieved under AB 3121 (Chapter 1071 of the statutes of 1976). See Rothman with David, p. 44.

22. This trend has developed across the nation to the point that, for example, in the state of Pennsylvania prosecutors are currently attempting to try a nine-year-old boy accused of murder as an adult. The boy would become the youngest person ever tried for murder in an adult court. See Bob Dorgin, "Boy Who Killed at Age Nine May Be Tried as an Adult," *Los Angeles Times*, July 28, 1989.

23. For instance, a youth committed in 1986 for first-degree burglary would have to serve one year before consideration for parole; by 1989, this same youth would have to serve one and a half years. See Paul de Munro, Anne de Munro, and Steve Lerner, *Reforming the California Youth Authority: How to End Crowding, Diversify Treatment, and Protect the Public without Spending More Money* (San Francisco: Commonweal Research Institute, 1988), p. 6.

24. de Munro, de Munro, and Lerner, p. 9. Since its creation in 1941, the Youth Authority Act of California has permitted admission of adult felons up to age twenty-one to its CYA detention centers. See John R. Ellingston, "The Youth Authority Plan and its Development in California," *Youth Authority Quarterly* 20,3 (1967), p. 25.

25. One youth even attempted to escape the CYA with the hope that reconviction to an adult prison would cut his three-year sentence to eighteen months. Ellingston, "The Youth Authority Plan."

Notes to Chapter 4

26. "Hope for Rehabilitation—Outside Prison Walls," *The Christian Science Monitor,* September 30, 1988, p. B2.

27. B. Krisberg, I.M. Schwartz, P. Litsky, and J. Austin, "The Watershed in Juvenile Justice Reform," *Crime and Delinquency,* 32, 1 (1986), pp. 5–38.

28. Krisberg, Schwartz, Litsky, and Austin, p. 9.

29. "Hope for Rehabilitation," *Christian Science Monitor.* Ironically, as the public has become increasingly paralyzed about fears of juvenile crime, rates of violent crime have actually been dropping at the national level, down 10% in 1985 from the 1975 level.

30. See "Forty Years of Service to California (1941–1981)," *California Youth Authority Quarterly* 34,1 (1981), p. 45.

31. de Munro, de Munro, and Lerner, p. 12.

32. Ibid., pp. 3–4.

33. Los Angeles Roundtable for Children, *Policy Analysis for California Education: The Conditions of Children in California* (1983). Cited in Davis with Ruddick, p. 307.

34. Department of Economic Opportunity, *Report by the Advisory Commission of the Department of Economic Opportunity: The Status of Poverty in California 1984–1985* (Sacramento: Department of Economic Opportunity, 1986), pp. 35–37.

35. South Central Organizing Committee, cited in Davis with Ruddick, p. 49.

36. See Paul Bullock, *Youth Training and Employment: From the New Deal to New Federalism* (Los Angeles: Center for Industrial Policy, 1985).

37. See Davis with Ruddick, pp. 50–51.

38. In fact, there were efforts on both sides to attempt to extend either more liberal or more conservative approaches to the juvenile population as a whole. Numerous critical social histories of juvenile law and the child-saving movement argued that the system was an application of middle-class norms to a lower-class population of adolescents who were necessarily more precocious.

39. California Legislature 1970, p. 12; cited in Steinhart "The Politics of Status-Offender Deinstitutionalization," p. 793.

40. Costs of services were estimated by the Department of Finance. Steinhart, "The Politics of Status-Offender Deinstitutionalization," p. 800.

41. Rothman and David, pp. 44–45.

42. Barry Nidorf, Chief Probation Officer, Los Angeles County Probation Department, with twenty-five years' experience in the department, in a public testimony to the Little Hoover Commission, December 13, 1989, notes: "As a result of Proposition 13 in 1978 the Probation Department staff was really cut in half and our caseloads were skyrocketing, and so of necessity we deal with those that pose the greatest danger to the community." (Littletown Commission: Public Hearing on Runaway/ Homeless Youth, Wednesday, December 13, 1983), p. 14.

43. Rothman and David, p. 45.

44. See "Forty Years of Service to California (1941–1981)."

45. Anthony E. Platt, *The Child Savers: The Invention of Delinquency* (Chicago: University of Chicago Press, 1969), p. 61.

46. Steve Lerner, *The CYA Report: Conditions of Life at the California Youth Authority* (San Francisco: Common Knowledge Press, 1984), pp. 62–63.

47. Office of Criminal Justice Planning V-J-28–V-J-42.

48. Steinhart, *Private Sector Task Force on Juvenile Justice*, p. 46.

49. Thomas G. Blomberg, *Juvenile Court and Community Corrections* (New York: University Press of America Inc., 1984), pp. 42–45; Steinhart, *Private Sector Task Force on Juvenile Justice*, p. 46.

50. P. Lerman, *Community Treatment and Social Control: A Critical Analysis of Juvenile Policy* (Chicago: University of Chicago Press, 1975).

51. See Bullock, *Youth Training and Employment.*

52. U.S. Department of Health, Education and Welfare, "Camps for Delinquent Boys: A Guide to Planning," 1960, Foreword, p. 13.

53. Consider these select descriptions of camps and trainings schools: "As one walks through the main control area at El Paso de Robles School, images of a picturesque, peaceful school are viewed. Red brick buildings surround a large grass-covered central area dotted with various trees" (p. 30). "Washington Ridge Camp is located on a 40-acre site at the 3800-ft level in the beautiful Tahoe National Forest" (p. 36). "Nestled among the tall whispering pines of Amador County, Pine Grove Camp has operated continuously as a conservation camp since the days of the Depression" (p. 37). "The Ben Lomond Mountain Camp was established by the Youth Authority in the Santa Cruz Mountains in 1947 . . . A unique aspect of the program from the outset was the tree nursery. Beginning in 1950 as a modest four-acre project producing about one-half million trees for reforestation, the nursery now cultivates 17 1/2 acres which yield up to 5 million seedlings for use by citizens of the state each year. . . . Recreation is a large component of leisure time periods; our activities are wholesome and well-rounded. Camp Fenner Canyon is situated in a beautiful canyon at Valyermo in the Angeles National Forest" (p. 13). See "Forty Years of Service to California (1941–1981)."

54. Andrew Doctoroff, "State Opens its First Detention Camp Exclusively For Girls," *Los Angeles Times*, March 3,1989.

55. D.J. Rothman, *The Discovery of the Asylum* (Boston: Little Brown and Company, 1971), pp. 82–83.

56. Charles Hamson, Deputy Director, Los Angeles County Probation Department, telephone interview, April 19,1991.

57. Charles Hamson, telephone interview, April 19, 1991.

58. See Edward Soja, "Inside Exopolis: Scenes from Orange County," *Variations on a Theme Park: Scenes from the New American City and the End of Public Space*, ed. Michael Sorkin (New York: The Noonday Press, 1992).

Notes to Chapter 4

59. Charles Hamson, telephone interview, April 19, 1991.

60. In 1984–85 it cost about $33,000 per youth per year in juvenile hall and $29,000 per youth per year in California Youth Authority institutions. Steinhart, *Private Sector Task Force on Juvenile Justice*, p. 3. In other states, privatization of correctional services has reduced costs and allowed for a proliferation of different treatment models. In California, state law is at best ambiguous on the extent to which correctional services can be privatized, but there is pressure from some organizations such as the Commonweal Institute to develop alternative placement models.

61. See Steinhart, *Private Sector Task Force on Juvenile Justice*, pp. 69–70.

62. Headquartered in Tucson, Arizona, the program has had approximately 3,000 participants since its founding in 1973, and has among its current 600 clients about 80 youths from California. The bulk of these are from San Diego and Santa Clara Counties and are often referred by probation departments of these counties. "Camp Facilities for Delinquents Faces Charges," *Los Angeles Times*, March 7, 1987. The youngsters in the camp, which admits both delinquent and nondelinquent youth, spend an average of six months in the program, and sometimes up to eighteen months. The program has a $20 million annual budget, and charges about $30,000 a year per youngster. John Hurst, "Delinquents Face Tough Rite of Passage: And a Camp for Troubled Youth Faces Charges of Abuse," *Los Angeles Times*, March 3, 1986, Part 1. Although the program has been heralded as "an economical, effective and humane alternative to prison-like facilities run by the California Youth Authority," it has also been recently plagued by charges of abuse, one of which resulted in the death of a youngster in 1984. Recent investigations have resulted in the withdrawal of youth placed by some counties from California, and the suspension of new placements.

63. Bullock notes that there was yet another impetus for ruralism which had little to do with idealization of premodern youth. Drawing on a study of the Civilian Conservation Corps, he observed that "work created must be widely regarded as useful and productive, but must not be competitive with work regularly performed elsewhere by private industry." Bullock, p. 28.

64. Francis Gil, Recruitment Officer, Conservation Corps, telephone interview, April 11, 1991.

65. Richard Polanco, "Bad Medicine for 'Troubled Teens': Forced Private Hospitalization Is Abuse of Process," *Los Angeles Times*, May 7, 1989, Part V, p. 5.

66. Kurt Shillinger and Cheryl Sullivan, "Treating Kids in the Community Works in Theory, But Not Always in Practice," *The Christian Science Monitor*, September 29, 1988, p. B6.

67. California Youth Authority and Department of Social Services, cited in Shillinger and Sullivan.

68. Steinhart, "The Politics of Status-Offender Deinstitutionalization", p. 787.

69. Harold Shirmen, Program Supervisor, Runaway Adolescent Planning Project, personal interview, April 16, 1991.

70. The State of California disputes these figures, claiming many cases are inactive. See Jonathan Freedman, "California Commentary," *Los Angeles Times*, April 9, 1990, p. B5.

71. Freedman, "California Commentary."

72. Carole Schauffer, Public Interest Attorney, quoted in Freedman. Schauffer is one of the attorneys who recently filed suit against the county.

CHAPTER 5

1. Subcommittee on the Constitution of the Committee on the Judiciary, *United States Senate Ninety-Sixth Congress, Report of the Subcommittee on the Judiciary, Homeless Youth: The Saga of "Pushouts" and "Throwaways" in America* (Washington: U.S. Government Printing Office, 1980). Of course, a certain proportion of these youth belong to both counts.

2. Bruce Torrence, *Hollywood: The First One Hundred Years* (Hollywood: Hollywood Chamber of Commerce & Steve Fiske Enterprises, 1979), p. 247–252.

3. Torrence, p. 264.

4. Dorothy Miller, Donald Miller, Fred Hoffman, Robert Duggan, *Runaways–Illegal Aliens in Their Own Land* (New York: Praeger Publishers, 1980) p. 9.

5. Survival sex may well have been a feature of runaway life in the years before deinstitutionalization, as there are many anecdotal accounts of trading sex for shelter, food, or protection while on the road, even among boy and girl hobos of the 1930s. It is not until the deinstitutionalization of runaways in the mid-1970s and the breakdown in consensus over concepts of youthful criminality and misbehavior (that is, the fall from dominance of the concept of juvenile delinquency) that this practice became recognized, as a distinct strategy for survival.

6. See for example, New York State Council on Children and Families, *Meeting the Needs of Homeless Youth* (Albany, New York: New York State Council on Children and Families, 1984); Van Houten and Golembiewski, *Life Stress as a Predictor of Alcohol Abuse and/or Runaway Behavior* (Washington D.C.: American Youth Work Center, 1978); House of Representatives Subcommittee on Human Resources, Committee on Education and Labor, *The Problem of Runaway and Homeless Youth. Oversight Hearing on Runaway and Homeless Youth Program* (Washington: House of Representatives, Subcommittee on Human Resources, Committee on Education and Labor, May 5, 1982), GPO, pp. 2–13.

Notes to Chapter 5

7. Gary L. Yates, testimony, The Little Hoover Commission on California State Government Organization and Economy, December 13, 1989: Table B. See also Marjorie Robertson, *Homeless Youth in Hollywood: Patterns of Alcohol Use: A Report to the National Institute on Alcohol Abuse and Alcoholism* (Berkeley, CA: Alcohol Research Group, 1989).

8. These interviews were conducted in February 1987 at Teen Canteen with fifteen youths. Two in-depth interviews were taped, the others are drawn from field notes. The youths were often reluctant to talk with tape recorders present. Two agreed to in-depth interviews of about ninety minutes, the others were met in groups and comments were drawn from field notes. Teen Canteen serves the largest percentage of out-of-county and out-of-state homeless and runaway youth of all the Hollywood area services, and provides a good sample for the purpose of exploring the similarities that Hollywood might have with other communities across the country.

9. Miller, et al; Marietta Pursley, "Runaway Youth Situation in Los Angeles County: A General Overview," unpublished document prepared for the United Way Planning Council, 1981.

10. Jason, Teen Canteen, personal interview, February 3, 1988.

11. Jeff, Teen Canteen, personal interview, February 19, 1988.

12. This information is drawn from Division of Adolescent Medicine, Children's Hospital of Los Angeles, *Data Highlights*. October 1, 1988 to June 30, 1989; and Marjorie Robertson, *Homeless Youth in Hollywood: Patterns of Alcohol Use.*

13. A similar refusal is evident in young welfare recipients in Britain. In the mid-1980s, Britain experienced a large-scale migration of unemployed youth to the seaside. They lived in boarding houses and continued to draw their supplementary benefits, in a community that came to be known as Costa del Dole, combining holiday and a search for work. Because of their inappropriate attitude while on unemployment, the Tory government required them to live at home while on assistance or to move from town to town in search for work. Phil Cohen, "Towards Youthopia?" *Marxism Today*, October 1985, p. 35.

14. Kim Brockman, Caseworker, Travelers Aid, personal interview, February 15, 1987; Greg Carlson, Director, Angel's Flight, personal interview, April 9, 1990. Miller, et al. note that the Salvation Army first set up services to runaway youths in its downtown center; Miller et al., p. 199.

15. Mark R. Lipschutz, "Runaways in History," *Crime and Delinquency* (July 1977), p. 330.

16. M. Robertson, R.H. Ropers, and R. Boyer, *The Homeless of Los Angeles County: An Empirical Evaluation* (Basic Shelter Research Project, Document No. 4, 1985); Office of Mayor Tom Bradley, The Community Redevelopment Agency of Los Angeles, Select Committee for Housing and Services for Skid row Residents, *Briefing Book: Preservation of Single Room Occupancy Residential Hotels in the Los Angeles Skid Row Community* (Los Angeles, July 20–24, 1987, Section 3–8), p. 43.

17. Tim, Teen Canteen, personal interview, February 11, 1988.

18. Community Redevelopment Agency of the City of Los Angeles, *Preliminary Report on the Proposed Hollywood Redevelopment Project* (November, 1985), pp. 2–28a.

19. Tim, Teen Canteen, personal interview, February 11, 1988.

20. Personal communication from Marjorie Robertson, October 30, 1987.

21. Robertson, pp. 43–45.

22. Dale Weaver, Director, Teen Canteen, personal interview, April 15, 1991.

23. These firsthand accounts of the punk squatter scene rely heavily on one informant, who was first a member (1978–1980) and later observer (1980–1982) of the punk squatting scene in Hollywood. While he was only "seriously in the scene" during the second of its three incarnations (lamentingly, he said, "too late to be avant-garde, too early to be trendy"), he nevertheless could provide something of an overview, because of the oral histories passed down from the "first generation," and his sustained connections to the scene after he left it. He asked to remain anonymous. I have referred to him as Frank in this account. There are, of course, difficulties in relying on a single interview to describe this scene, and it should be taken as one interpretation rather than a definitive statement. But these difficulties are minimal compared to the difficulty of finding subjects who can give a firsthand account of what went on. Many are dead. Those who went on to something else are often reluctant to discuss their involvement. I did find two others who had survived the scene and admitted to being a part of it, but the first person was unwilling to discuss it, probably because of heavy drug use that was part of the culture, and the second person was willing to talk but because of heavy drug use had a great difficulty recalling what went on there. All the names used in this section have been invented to protect the identities of these people.

24. Miller, et al., p. 124.

25. Scholars of spectacular youth subcultures frequently note the centrality of control over space in sustaining and perpetuating the life of a subculture, and the lack of control over space as a central factor inhibiting the development of a distinctive subculture. See, for instance, Angela McRobbie and Jenny Garber, "Girls in Subcultures: An Exploration," *Resistance Through Rituals: Youth Subcultures in Post-war Britain*, eds. Stuart Hall and Tony Jefferson (London: Hutchinson & Co., 1976), pp. 209–222.

26. F. Thrasher, *The Gang* (Chicago: University of Chicago Press, 1927).

27. John Clarke, Stuart Hall, Tony Jefferson, and Brian Roberts, "Subcultures, Cultures and Class: A Theoretical Overview," *Resistance through Rituals: Youth Subcultures in Post-war Britain*, eds. S. Hall and T. Jefferson (London: Hutchinson & Co., 1976), p. 45. McRobbie and Garber argue in the same book that the lack of control over a common public space has been a central reason for the absence of a distinctive female spectacular youth subculture. See McRobbie and Garber, "Girls and Subcultures: An Exploration."

28. Dick Hebdige, *Subculture: The Meaning of Style* (London: Methuen, 1979), p. 113. Emphasis added.

29. Frank, personal interview, September 22, 1990.

30. Craig Lee and "Shreader," "Los Angeles," *Hard Core California: A History of Punk and New Wave,* eds. Peter Belsito and Bob Davis (Berkeley: The Last Gasp of San Francisco, 1983).

31. Frank, personal interview, September 22, 1990.

32. Lee and "Shreader," p. 30.

33. Richard Alleman, *Movie Lovers' Guide to Hollywood* (New York: Harper and Row, 1985), p. 7.

34. Mindi Levins, caseworker/outreach assistant, Los Angeles Youth Network; former caseworker, Teen Canteen, personal interview, April 10, 1991. "Skinheads—very few come in to get services, they're a gangish group and they depend on each other. We do get a few stragglers— punkers are the same way. There's a whole underground of them. I call them all wannabes that we get, not the real hard core."

35. Frank, personal interview, September 22, 1990.

36. Lee and "Shreader," p. 17.

37. Lee and "Shreader," p. 21.

38. Lee and "Shreader." See also Mike Davis, *City of Quartz* (London: Verso, 1990), p. 45.

39. The amount of commuting to and from gigs in various parts of Los Angeles was considerable, and the strategies sometimes ingenious. According to Frank, the Huntington Beach punks were fairly mobile since they tended to live in their vans, but the punks squatting in Hollywood had neither cars nor vans, and used a number of different strategies for traveling, including occasionally hitching rides in cars that had been "boosted" (i.e., stolen) by people they knew.

40. Frank, personal interview, September 22, 1990.

41. See Chapter 7. See also Edward Soja, "Inside Exopolis: Scenes from Orange County," *Variations on a Theme Park: Scenes from the New American City and the End of Public Space,* ed. Michael Sorkin (New York: The Noonday Press, 1992).

42. Frank, personal interview, September 22, 1990.

43. Ibid., 1990.

44. Ibid., 1990.

45. Ibid., 1990.

46. Dale Weaver, Director, Teen Canteen, personal interview, April 15, 1991. This observation is substantiated by Robertson's survey of homeless street youth in Hollywood. Of the 97 surveyed, Robertson's data suggests that half had more than one "shelter" location within a week of the survey. (Shelter sources included abandoned buildings, streets, public places,

shelters or missions, relatives of friends' homes, nonrelatives' homes, or movie theaters and bus stations). Greg Carlson, Director, Angel's Flight, personal interview, April 9, 1990.

47. This perspective was shared by the former punk I interviewed, and expressed in an article on the history of the punk scene in Los Angeles: Craig Lee and "Shreader," pp. 10–65.

48. Lee and "Shreader," p. 11.

49. Ibid.

50. Frank, personal interview, September 22, 1990.

51. Frank, personal interview, September 22, 1990.

52. Lee and "Shreader," p. 38.

53. Frank, personal interview, September 22, 1990.

54. Frank, personal interview, September 22, 1990.

55. At first they were a little scary 'cause they'd pull up in their vans, a lot of them would live in their vans and you know there'd be like ten of them in this van, and they'd kick the door open at a gig and all come spilling out. . . . Those were really the first hard-core slamming skinheads, that's why we called the dance HB-ing cause we hadn't seen it before these Huntington Beach kids came. Frank, personal interview, September 22, 1990.

56. See Dick Hebdige, *Subculture: The Meaning of Style*, pp. 113–115.

57. John Clarke, "Style," in *Resistance through Rituals: Youth Subcultures in post-war Britain*. The term *bricolage* originates with Claude Lévi–Strauss. Clarke refers to bricolage as "the re–ordering and recontextualization of objects to communicate fresh meaning, within a total system of meanings." C. Lévi-Strauss, *The Savage Mind* (London: Weidenfeld an Nicolson, 1966); C. Lévi-Strauss, *Totemism* (London: Penguin, 1969). Clarke, however, adapts the term *bricolage* to refer not to the construction of myths accepted by society at large, but unofficial styles which are constructed in opposition to the more widely held values of society. Clarke, p. 177.

58. Hebdige, p. 124.

59. Ibid., p. 120.

60. Ibid., p. 120.

61. See Alleman, pp. 180, 188.

62. Lee and "Shreader," p. 47. See Mike Davis, *City of Quartz*, p. 45.

63. This practice was a code to signal to squatters concealed on the park premises that it was safe to appear.

64. This process of naming is itself indicative of a shift in the subculture–a transition from signifying practices which focused primarily on the *slippage of meaning*, a process of disorientation itself, which Barthes describes as a "floating which would not destroy anything, but simply

be content to disorient the Law," to one which became committed to a "*finished meaning.*" This was expressed both in the changing meaning of punk symbols of style (such as the swastika) as well as in the change in spaces used by the squatting punk subculture. On slippage of meaning, see Hebdige, p. 126.

65. Lee and "Shreader."

66. Frank, personal interview, September 22, 1990.

67. Ibid.

68. Lois Lee, *Daily News*, May 17, 1983.

69. See note 5, page 226.

70. Frank, personal interview, September 22, 1990.

71. Ibid.

72. Ibid.

73. Frank, personal interview, September 22, 1990. This shift to the boulevard is confirmed by the Hollywood Police Department, which in a 1987 presentation, talked about punk rockers hanging out on the boulevard and "being obnoxious to tourists."

74. Frank, personal interview, September 22, 1990.

75. Mindi Levins, caseworker/outreach assistant, Los Angeles Youth Network; former caseworker, Teen Canteen, personal interview, April 10, 1991; Gabe Cruks, Director, The Gay and Lesbian Center, personal interview, May 30, 1990; Michael de Paul, caseworker, Covenant House, personal interview, April 16, 1990.

76. Gabe Cruks, personal interview, May 30, 1990.

77. Dale Weaver, Director, Teen Canteen, personal interview, April 15, 1991. See Robertson, p. 108. Robertson's selection criteria limited the sample to youth who were seventeen years old or younger at the time of interview, and had spent the previous night in at a site not normally considered a dwelling—"an emergency shelter, mission or improvised shelter including abandoned buildings, vehicles, public places, parks or beaches." This necessarily excludes a large street population between the ages of eighteen and twenty-three seen by some services, as well as youth involved in survival sex or prostitution who stay in hotels or people's houses. It accounts for the discrepancy between her difficulty in finding subjects, and the large number of street youth seen by outreach workers from The Gay and Lesbian Community Center each year.

78. Frank, personal interview, September 22, 1990. Names have been changed to protect the identities of the people mentioned.

79. Detective Bill Berndt, Los Angeles Police Department, quoted in David Wharton, "Heavy Going: Metal Rockers Stake Out Their Own Turf on Hollywood Boulevard," Los Angeles Times, August 9, 1987. Mindi Levins of the Los Angeles Youth Network notes that heavy metal dominates the day center for LAYN youth, while youth in the shelter tend to be more

oriented towards rap music. Very few punks or skinheads actively seek services.

80. Lee and "Shreader," p. 40.

81. See Wharton, "Heavy Going."

82. Views on this are contradictory and this image has generally been pre-sented as hearsay rather than substantiated by actual visits to the manors. One youth worker I did interview who had actually gone to Erroll Flynn Manor one night noted there were a lot of youth there, both apparently homeless and apparently not, simply partying. This suggests that the image itself has been constructed simply as a way of keeping outsiders away. Greg Carlson, Director, Angel's Flight, personal interview, April 9, 1990; Joe, Teen Canteen, personal interview, February 19, 1988.

83. Greg Carlson, Director, Angel's Flight, personal interview, April 9, 1990; Joe, personal interview, February 19, 1988; and Robertson, *Homeless Youth in Hollywood: Patterns of Alcohol Use.* Of course these figures rep-resent only a "snapshot" of the homeless and runaway population, and may vary from year to year.

84. See Robertson.

85. Dale Weaver, Director, Teen Canteen, personal interview, April 15, 1991.

86. Greg Carlson, Director, Angel's Flight, personal interview, April 9, 1990; Dale Weaver, Director, Teen Canteen, personal interview, April 15, 1991.

87. Frank, personal interview, September 22, 1990.

88. Mindi Levins, caseworker/outreach assistant, Los Angeles Youth Network; former caseworker, Teen Canteen, personal interview, April 10, 1991.

89. Analyzing panhandling strategies of older tramps, Duncan has explored the issue of "moral space" as an explanation for lucrative panhandling within a two-block radius of churches. J. Duncan, "Men Without Property: The Tramp's Classification and Use of Urban Space," *Antipode* 11, 1 (1979). It is possible that the full stomachs and ready change with which customers exit fast-food places make these lucrative spots as well.

90. Information for the map of survival strategies and description in the following paragraph was drawn from Community Redevelopment Agency, *Preliminary Report on the Proposed Hollywood Redevelopment Project,* November 1985 (Map 2–7, Major Social Issues Hollywood 1985: pp. 2–32a), and interviews with Gabe Cruks, May 30, 1990; Mindi Levins, April 10, 1991; and Greg Carlson, April 9, 1990.

91. Children's Hospital, Los Angeles, Presentation of Hollywood Police Department to High Risk Youth, Workshop Series on Resources for Youth in Hollywood, November 1987.

92. Joe, Teen Canteen, personal interview, February 19, 1988.

92. Robertson, p. 68. In this sample approximately 77% of homeless adoles-cents used cannabis, compared to 27% using cocaine. Self-reported

dependence on cannabis was also higher than on cocaine (31% versus 8%).

94. Mindi Levins, "Life on the Streets of Hollywood: Our Youth's Perspectives and Future Projections" (unpublished paper, 1988). Levins was working at Teen Canteen when whe wrote this paper.

95. Jack Rothman and Thomas G. David, *Status-Offenders in Los Angeles County: Focus on Runaway and Homeless Youth. A Study and Policy Recommendations* (Los Angeles: University of California, Los Angeles School of Social Work, 1985), p. 60.

96. Robertson, p. 63.

97. Lois Lee, Director, Children of the Night, in Nicole Yorkin, "Children of the Night," *Los Angeles Herald Examiner*, August 4, 1982.

98. In fact, "real" gangs do form in Hollywood, as youth worker Mindi Levins noted. "The weirdest part of Hollywood is, it seems, that each of the gangs seems to have a little piece of Hollywood—it's supposed to be a Crip turf—the kids we're getting in here (LAYN) are the ones on the outside a little bit who don't have as many support structures in the gang or the ones that want to get out." Mindi Levins, personal interview, April 10, 1991.

99. Greg Carlson, Director, Angels Flight, personal interview, April 9, 1990.

100. For example, where 51% of all street youth interviewed sold illegal drugs, 20.9 % (almost half of these) did so only when homeless; 29.7% of the youth had been paid for sex, but the majority of these (22% of all youth interviewed) had been paid for sex only when homeless; 22% had traded sex for food, but the majority of these (18.7% of all youth interviewed) had done so only when homeless, 10% had traded sex for drugs, but the majority of these (7% of all youth interviewed) had done so only when homeless, 7.9% had posed for sexual photos or movies, but the majority of these (3.4% of all youth interviewed) had done so only when homeless. See Robertson, Table 21, p. 43.

101. Greg Carlson, personal interview, April 9, 1990. Lois Lee noted as early as 1982 that: "You see some teenage girls working on Santa Monica with the boys, and the boys protect them from the pimps. There's a war going on right now on Santa Monica. The pimps are trying to control the boys by beating them up, taking their money, or taking their drugs. That's one of the reasons why many boys now carry weapons. The girls will immediately hook-up with the boys, and some of these kids will stay in a hotel room and whoever makes the money will pay for the room. They substitute this for a family." Lois Lee, interview by Mitchell Fink, *Herald Examiner*, August 4, 1982.

102. A. Hamid (forthcoming) *Beaming Up: Contexts for Smoking Cocaine.* Cited in Lisa Maher, *Women on the Edge of Crime: Crack, Cocaine and the Changing Contexts of Street Level Sex Work in New York City* (Presented at the Joint Meetings of Law and Society Association and Research Committee on the Sociology of Law of the International Sociological Association, Amsterdam, June 26–29, 1991).

103. Maher, *Women on the Edge of Crime.*

103. Michel De Certeau, *The Practice of Everyday Life*, trans. Steven F. Rendall (Los Angeles: University of California Press, 1984), pp. 36–37.

104. It is not simply access to strategic spaces that is important here. Homeless youth still have access to strategic space when they trade sex for accommodation, but these are hardly spaces that they control.

CHAPTER 6

1. Dale Weaver, Director, Teen Canteen, personal interview, April 15, 1991; See also Supervisor Edelman, *The Runaway and Homeless Youth in Los Angeles County: Transcript of Tape-Recorded Proceedings* (Plummer Park, California, September 10, 1976).

2. See William Sharpe and Leonard Wallock, "From 'Great Town' to 'Nonplace Urban Realm': Reading the Modern City," *Visions of the Modern City: Essays in History, Art and Literature* (Baltimore: Johns Hopkins University Press, 1987), p .5.

3. Dale Weaver, personal interview, April 15, 1991.

4. Peter Jackson, *Maps of Meaning: An Introduction to Cultural Geography* (London: Unwin Hyman, 1989), p. 100.

5. See Lawrence Grossberg, "Putting the Pop Back in Post Modernism," *Universal Abandon? The Politics of Post Modernism*, ed. Andrew Ross (Minneapolis: University of Minnesota Press, 1988).

6. Dorothy Miller, Donald Miller, Fred Hoffman, Robert Duggan, *Runaways —Illegal Aliens in Their Own Land* (New York: Praeger Publishers, 1980), p. 149.

7. Miller et al.

8. Miller et al., p. 117.

9. See Miller et al., pp. 179–182.

10. Gabe Cruks, Director, The Gay and Lesbian Center, personal interview, May 30, 1990.

11. Gabe Cruks, personal interview, May 30, 1990. This was not included in the Miller et al., survey.

12. Gabe Cruks, personal interview, May 30, 1990.

13. Larry Shaw, Director, Youth Counselling Services, Hollywood YMCA, personal interview, October 30, 1989.

14. Dale Weaver, personal interview, April 15, 1991.

15. Dale Weaver, personal interview, April 15, 1991.

16. Dale Weaver, personal interview, April 15, 1991.

17. Covenant House was recently publicly criticized for this practice. Children of the Night has also been the focus of unsubstantiated rumors because its founder, Lois Lee, shelters youths in her own home. Christian wilderness camps have also been the subject of investigations, where suspicions of abuse have been confirmed.

18. Gabe Cruks in Kathleen Hendrix, "Sex Charges Don't Shake Faith in Covenant House," Los Angeles Times, February 8, 1990, p. E15.

19. An attempt was made to recover the history of these programs through a telephone survey of the organizations that housed them. Often the organization no longer existed, and when it did, current staff had no idea of programs that had existed fifteen years ago.

20. The hotline and referral service in La Canada/La Crescenta was an example of the former. The Status Offender Detention Alternative (SODA), the county's official project to provide alternatives to detention, exemplified the latter.

21. The Salvation Army in downtown Los Angeles was one organization which housed runaways in the homes of its volunteer members. Others were the Downey Hotline in Downey, and the Youth Crisis Housing Task Force in Van Nuys. See Miller et al., pp. 198, 199, 201. Institute for Scientific Analysis Runaway Resource Guide, "Runaway Youth: How Are They to Be Served?" funded by the Social and Rehabilitation Service of the U.S. Department of Health Education and Welfare (1974) in Miller et al., pp. 199.

22. See Jack Rothman and Thomas David, Status Offenders in Los Angeles County, Focus on Runaway and Homeless Youth: A Study and Policy Recommendations (Los Angeles, University of California School of Social Work, 1985), pp. 46–47.

23. Kim Brockman was one of the outreach workers who began with the Travelers Aid Program to intercept runaways on their way to Hollywood at the downtown Los Angeles Greyhound bus station. She noted that no sooner were the youth were placed in a suburban foster home than they would "run right back to Hollywood." Kim Brockman, personal interview, February 15, 1987.

24. Los Angeles Times, December 26, 1983.

25. Rothman and David, p. 47.

26. Charles Hamson, Deputy Director, Los Angeles County Probation Department, personal interview, April 19, 1991.

27. Goffman, of course, was concerned about the way that individuals negotiate and modify their behavior in front and back regions, and made no attempt to explain how front and back regions themselves emerge or are transformed, especially by groups of people.

28. House of Representatives, Subcommittee on Human Resources, Committee on Education and Labor, Oversight Hearing on Runaway and Homeless Youth Program (Washington: House of Representatives,

Notes to Chapter 6

Subcommittee on Human Resources, Committee on Education and Labor, May 5, 1982), p. 4.

29. Leslie Forbes, Director, Options House, personal interview, April 12, 1991.

30. Sam Yang, youth worker with "The Way In," Salvation Army, personal interview, April 17, 1991.

31. Mindi Levins, caseworker/outreach assistant, Los Angeles Youth Network; former caseworker, Teen Canteen, personal interview, April 10, 1991.

32. The program is funded privately, and its operating ethos has its origins in "Muscular Christianity," as distinct from a therapeutic model using social workers or psychologists. This factor has perhaps enhanced criticism and suspicion of its operating practices from services grounded in a social work approach. The Christian foundations of the program have influenced the development of a policy of "open intake"—no youths in need can be turned away—a policy which, by implication, leads to the sheltering of large numbers of youths rather than the establishment of a small, tightly controlled program.

33. Dale Weaver, Director, Teen Canteen, personal interview, April 15, 1991.

34. Before this, LAYN had rented space from Options House in a residential neighborhood. It ran into difficulties when neighbors complained about the presence of street youth on the lawns and in the neighborhood. Leslie Forbes, Director of Options House, personal interview, April 12, 1991.

35. Mindi Levins, personal interview, April 10, 1991.

36. Dale Weaver, personal interview, April 15, 1991.

37. See *Responding to a Crisis* (Covenant House, Los Angeles, n.d.), p. 8.

38. Under the directorship of Norris Lineweaver, the YMCA made a brief foray into providing services to homeless youths and then backed off, after Lineweaver transferred to another city, deciding it did not have the appropriate resources. This decision is indicative of a broader reorientation of inner-city YMCAs to serve the needs of a new, middle-class clientele. The renovated YMCA in downtown Los Angeles is a case in point. As for the Hollywood YMCA, one disgruntled service provider, Dale Weaver of Teen Canteen, noted, "They used to be, a century ago, a local social service center, and now its just another health club. We had to pay for everything." Teen Canteen rented the use of showers and two beds from the local YMCA.

39. See Edelman, *The Runaway and Homeless Youth in Los Angeles County.*

40. Ethel Narvid, Founder of Options House, personal interview, May 30, 1990.

41. See *Helping Homeless Teens* (Options House, Los Angeles, n.d.)

42. These include Stepping Stone in Santa Monica, and Teen Canteen Drop-In Center in Hollywood.

43. Mindi Levins of LAYN, Greg Carlson of Angel's Flight, and Marjorie Robertson, in an independent study of ninety-seven street youth, have

all reported this phenomenon. The appropriation of family structures in rehabilitative environments for youth is not a novel development. Modeling of affective relationships around family structures was evident in the early reform houses for street youths, such as Rahehouse in Holland, and even in Mettray, Foucault's quintessential marker for the emergence of the carceral archipelago. But in the past one hundred and fifty years, excepting foster homes, familial structures have rarely been used as the central organizing principle for small-scale institutions.

44. This is the case both for Options House and for LAYN.

45. Haig Marikan, Vice Chairman of the Little Hoover Commission, Public Hearing on Runaway/Homeless Youth (Los Angeles, December 13, 1989).

46. Children's Hospital of Los Angeles, *HIV AIDS Prevention Project, LA Street Outreach Minutes*, December 20, 1989, p. 1, 2.

47. Mindi Levins, personal interview, April 10, 1991.

48. See Michael Capaldi, "Pioneer Program for Young Prostitutes: Children of the Night Offers Understanding and Alternatives," *Los Angeles Times*, August 9, 1981.

49. See Chapter 4 of this volume.

50. Leslie Forbes, Director, Options House, personal interview, April 12, 1991.

51. Greg Carlson, Director, Angel's Flight, personal interview, April 9, 1990.

52. Dale Weaver, Director, Teen Canteen, personal interview, April 15, 1991.

53. Mindi Levins, caseworker/outreach assistant, Los Angeles Youth Network; former caseworker, Teen Canteen, personal interview, April 10, 1991.

54. Goffman first introduces this concept in *Behavior in Public Places* (New York: Free Press, 1963), p. 129. He accords police and clergy with the same function.

55. Mindi Levins, personal interview, April 10, 1991.

56. Ibid.

57. Ibid.; Gabe Cruks, Director, The Gay and Lesbian Center, personal interview, May 30, 1990. As this incident happened towards the tail end of my field research, I had in-sufficient time to pursue the issue with interviews of the homeowners' group.

CHAPTER 7

1. Andrew Mair, "The Homeless and the Post-Industrial City," *Political Geography* 5, 1986, pp. 351-368; Philip Kasinitz, "Gentrification and Homelessness: The Single Room Occupant and the Inner City Revival," *Urban Social Change Review* 17 (1984), p. 9.

2. Philip Kasinitz, "Gentrification and Homelessness," p. 9

3. Jean Baudrillard, *Simulations*, trans. by Paul Foss, Paul Patton and Philip Beitchman, (New York: Semiotext(e) Inc., 1983).

4. Susan Ruddick, "The Montreal Citizens' Movement: The Real Politics of the 1990s?" in *Fire in the Hearth*, eds. Mike Davis et al., (London: Verso, 1990), pp. 287-319.

5. See Mark Gottdiener, "Culture, Ideology, and the Sign of the City," in *The City and the Sign: An Introduction to Urban Semiotics*, eds. Mark Gottdiener and Alexandros Lagopoulos (New York: Columbia University Press, 1986), p. 207.

6. This was certainly the case in Hollywood where, in the 1980s, the image of a future Hollywood coalesced around progrowth and no-growth coalitions. Development was fought by middle-class homeowners whose acronym was SHOT—Save Hollywood, Our Town, and recalled images of a small American town about to be engulfed by the modernizing processes of the big city. Brian Moore of SHOT, personal interview, April 16, 1991.

7. Brian Moore, Save Hollywood, Our Town, personal interview, April 16, 1991; Robert Nudelman, Member of the Project Area Committee, Hollywood Redevelopment Plan, personal interview, February 1, 1990.

8. Bruce Torrence, *Hollywood: The First Hundred Years* (Hollywood: Hollywood Chamber of Commerce & Steve Fiske Enterprises, 1979).

9. Carey McWilliams, *Southern California: An Island on the Land* (Santa Barbara: Peregrine Smith Inc., 1979), p. 333.

10. Jean-Luc Evard, "Mickey Maul. Vorden Simulakren," *Aesthetik und Kommunikation* Heft 67/68, p. 134 (my translation).

11. Umberto Eco, *Travels in Hyperreality*, trans. William Weaver (San Diego: Harcourt, 1986), pp. 43-46.

12. Marianne Morino, *The Hollywood Walk of Fame: The Only Guide to the World's Most Famous Stars in the World in the World's Most Famous Sidewalk* (Los Angeles: Ten Speed Press, 1987).

13. Morino, *The Hollywood Walk of Fame*, p.xiii.

14. See Office of Economic Development, City of Los Angeles, *Hollywood Revitalization Plan*, Vol. 3 (Los Angeles, n.d.), p.1.

15. See *Hollywood Revitalization Plan*, Vol. 1, pp. 8, 20.

16. See Office of Economic Development, City of Los Angeles, *Hollywood Revitalization Plan, Environmental Impact Review* (Los Angeles: n.d.), p. 72. High crime rates were still considered a major social problem and a disincentive to private development ten years later. The CRA Preliminary report on Proposed Development noted that, in 1985, four of the nine highest crime reporting districts in the city of Los Angeles fell within the project area.

17. See *Hollywood Revitalization Plan, Environmental Impact Review*, p. E7. Revitalization of the boulevard was still a central concern, but this was

to be driven by the construction of a Regional Retail Center.

18. *Hollywood Revitalization Plan*, Vol. 1, p. 49

19. John Kaliski, Principal Architect, Community Redevelopment Agency, Los Angeles, personal interview, May 19, 1990.

20. Ibid.

21. Blake Grumpecht, "Chamber Chief hopes to polish Hollywood Image," *L.A. Business Journal* August 14, 1989.

22. John Kaliski, personal interview, May 19 ,1990.

23. Pierre Bourdieu, *Outline of a Theory of Practice* (Cambridge: Cambridge University Press, 1977).

24. Elizabeth Ewen, ""Citylights: Immigrant Women and the Rise of the Movies," *Signs* 5,3 (1980),, Supplement, Women and the American City, pp. 545-567.

25. Bourdieu, p. 80.

26. See Sharon Zukin., *Landscapes of Power: From Detroit to Disneyland*, (Berkeley: University of California Press, 1991).

27. Sharon Zukin, *Loft Living* (Baltimore, Johns Hopkins University Press, 1988), p. 439.

28. Pierre Bourdieu, *Distinction: A Social Critique of the Judgement of Taste* (London: Routledge and Kegan Paul, 1984); Scott Lash and John Urry, *The End of Organized Capitalism* (Oxford: Basil Blackwell, 1987), p. 292.

29. Mark Royden Mitchell, "Fantasy Seen: Hollywood Fiction Since West," *Los Angeles in Fiction: A Collection of Original Essays*, ed. David Fine (Albuquerque: University of New Mexico Press, 1984), p.148.

30. See Robert Shields, *Places on the Margin: Alternative Geographies of Modernity* (New York: Routledge, 1991), p. 285.

31. See Halcyon Ltd., *Hollywood Boulevard Retail Tenant Inventory and Office and Retail Market Analysis and Street Comparable Memorandum*. See also David Wharton, "Heavy Going: Metal Rockers Stake out Their own Turf on Hollywood Boulevard," *Los Angeles Times*, August 9, 1987.

32. See Sarah E. Foster, "Urban Gorilla: When Redevelopment Strikes," *Reason*, January 1988; See also Halcyon Ltd. The Halcyon reports tend to confirm this analysis. Retailing on the boulevard was characterized by an expansion of tenants geared exclusively to the "T-shirt" subsegment of the tourist market.

33. One survey of approximately 1,270 individuals found the major tourist clientele were relatively young, and in their twenties (48%), predominantly male (70%) and relatively lower-income, with over 50% earning less than $25,000, and 30% earning less than $15,000 per year. IBI Group, prepared for the Community Redevelopment Agency of the City of Los Angeles, *Draft Report of Resident and Shopper/Visitor Survey* (1987).

34. Halcyon Ltd., *Hollywood Boulevard Retail Tenant Inventory*, p. 18.

35. See Brendan J. Gleason and Jennifer Wolch, "Homelessness and the Politics of Turf: The Case of Venice, California," unpublished manuscript, University of Southern California, Los Angeles Homelessness Project, 1989.

36. Dave Palermo, "Bums take the Rap: Hollywood Curfew gets Mixed Reviews," *Los Angeles Times,* August 11, 1986.

37. N. Fainstein and S. Fainstein, "Regime Strategies, Communal Resistance and Economic Forces," *Restructuring the City,* eds. Fainstein et al. (New York: Longman, 1983), pp. 278, 254. The authors argue that these are a relatively constant set of fault lines which have remained relatively unchanged since the 1950s and include (1) a division within the business and middle class; (2) allocation of public investment between core and peripheral areas, (3) allocation of state expenditures for capital accumulation versus social consumption; and (4) treatment modalities and resource allocations between and within lower-income neighborhoods.

38. This shelter was managed under a separate sister organization which had scarcely been founded when the Hollywood Revitalization Plan and its committee were scuttled.

39. Other occupants of this middle ground included Hollywood's Historic Preservation Group.

40. I would like to thank Roger Keil for drawing out this implication. See Roger Keil, "Weltstalt—Städt der Welt: Internationalisierung und Lokale Politik in Los Angeles," diss., Johann Wolfgang Goethe Universitat, Frankfurt am Main, 1991.

41. Rusty Flinton, Executive Director, Hollywood Revitalization Committee, personal interview, May 16, 1990.

42. Halcyon Ltd., Real Estate Advisors, Development Consultants, Project and Asset Managers, noted: "What is negative (in Hollywood) is the mix and quality of retail merchandise and restaurants. . . . In the absence of admission-related tourist attractions, tourist (*sic*) must be given an alternative vehicle for a unique experience. This experience must be able to transcend the tourist domain and have an allure for the local market. . . . A location with an established identity provides the ideal environment for this type of concept," p. 53. They continue: "Upgrading the residential component of any urban revitalization area is of paramount importance to the ultimate success or failure of redevelopment. A neighborhood community can determine the fate of an urban commercial area by virtue of its ability to create an identity for such an area." Halcyon Ltd. *Office and Retail Market Analysis and Street Comparable Memorandum.*

43. See Chapter 6 of this volume.

44. The establishment of a Project Area Committee is a necessary part of the redevelopment process under the California Community Redevelopment Act of 1948. The committee is a representative body of the locally elected community whose role it is to comment on the redevelopment plan in its stages of development.

Notes to Conclusion

45. Fran Offenhauser, Hollywood Historic Preservation Association, personal interview, May 16, 1990; Rusty Flinton, Executive Director, Hollywood Revitalization Committee, personal interview, May 16, 1990.

46. Ethel Narvid, Founder, Options House, personal interview, May 30, 1990.

47. David Ferrell, "Woo wants Changes in Hollywood Renewal," *Los Angeles Times,* December 9, 1987. Robert Nudelman, Member of the Project Area Committee, Hollywood Redevelopment Plan, personal interview, February 1, 1990.

48. Dale Weaver, Director, Teen Canteen, personal interview, April 15, 1991.

49. Kenneth J. Fannucchi, "Council O.K.'s $922 Million Hollywood Revitalization," *Los Angeles Times,* May 1, 1986.

50. Dale Weaver, personal interview, April 15, 1991.

51. This was most forcefully expressed in Homeowners Associations' critiques of the proposed galaxy project, featuring a concept of food court which in the eyes of critics "evoke(d) the image of fast-food stands where foot-weary tourists relax between purchases of souvenir T-shirts, personalized baseball caps and plastic ashtrays. . . . Would I, neighbors or associates, be drawn to establishments within this project? Would I recommend this to my out-of-town guests? Unfortunately the answer to each question is a resounding NO. Robert A. Higgins, President, Whitley Heights Civic Association, letter to Mayor Tom Bradley, June 17, 1988.

52. David W. Myers,"Suit Could Postpone Hollywood Project," *Los Angeles Times,* April 26, 1987.

53. Whitley Heights Civic Association, Hollywood Heights Association, Outpost Estates, Hollywoodland Homeowners Association, Hollywood Heritage, Hollywood Project Area Committee, Melrose Hill Homeowners Association, and Hollywood Boulevard Merchants' Association, letter to Mayor Tom Bradley, June 17, 1988.

54. Dean Murphy, "Woo Names New Panel for Hollywood Redevelopment," *Los Angeles Times,* August 4, 1989.

55. Community Redevelopment Agency, City of Los Angeles, *Hollywood Social Needs Plan* (1990).

CONCLUSION

1. Bret Easton Ellis, *Less Than Zero* (New York: Simon and Schuster, 1985).

2. Robert Shields, *Places on the Margin: Alternative Geographies of Modernity* (London: Routledge, 1991), pp. 29-31.

3. Shields, p. 263.

4. James Duncan, "Men Without Property: The Tramp's Classification and Use of Space," *Antipode* 11, no.1 (1979): 24–34.

Notes to Conclusion

5. Nancy Harstock, "Foucault on Power: A Theory for Women?" in *Feminism/Postmodernism*, ed. Linda J. Nicholson (New York: Routledge, 1990).

6. Nancy Harstock, p. 171.

7. De Certeau describes tactics as a calculated action determined by the absence of proper locus. See Chapters Two and Three of this volume.

8. See Dick Hebdige, *Subculture: The Meaning of Style.* (London: Methuen, 1979), p. 121.

9. Ernesto Laclau and Chantal Mouffe, *Hegemony and Socialist Strategy: Towards a Radical Democratic Politics*, trans. Winston Moore and Paul Cammack. (London: Verso, 1985). Shields makes a similiar argument when he notes the existence of a "cartography of fractures which emphasizes the relations between differently valorized sites and spaces, sutured together under masks of unity," p. 278.

10. See Merya Folch-Serra, "Place, Voice and Space: Mikhail Bahktin's Dialogical Landscape," *Environment and Planning D: Society and Space* 8 (1990): 258.

11. Roland Barthes, *Mythologies* pp. 109-158.

12. Barnor Hesse, "Black to the Front and Black Again," in *Place and the Politics of Identity*, eds. Michael Keith and Stephen Pile (London and New York: Routledge, 1993) pp. 162–182.

BIBLIOGRAPHY

BOOKS AND ARTICLES

Abrams, M. *The Teenage Consumer.* London: Routledge and Kegan Paul, 1959.

Addams, Jane. *The Spirit of Youth and the City Streets.* Chicago: University of Illinois Press, 1972.

Alleman, Richard. *Movie Lovers' Guide to Hollywood.* New York: Harper and Row, 1985.

Anderson, Nels. *The Hobo: Sociology of the Homeless Man.* Chicago: University of Chicago Press, 1923.

Aronowitz, Stanley. "PostModernism and Politics." *Universal Abandon? The Politics of PostModernism,* ed. Andrew Ross. Minneapolis: University of Minnesota Press, 1988: 46–62.

Baer, W.C. "Housing in an Internationalizing Region: Housing Stock Dynamics in Southern California and the Dilemmas of Fair Share." *Environment and Planning D: Society and Space* 4, 1986: 337–349.

Bahr, H.M. *Disaffiliated Man: Essays and Bibliography on Skid Row, Vagrancy and Outsiders.* Toronto: University of Toronto Press, 1970.

———. *Skid Row: An Introduction to Disaffiliation.* New York: Oxford University Press, 1973.

Bibliography

Barak, Gregg. *Gimme Shelter: A Social History of Homelessness in Contemporary America*. New York: Praeger, 1991.

Barthes, Roland. *Mythologies*, trans. Annette Lavers. New York: Hill and Wang, 1972.

Baudrillard, Jean. *Simulations,* trans. Paul Foss, Paul Patten, and Philip Beitchman. New York: Semiotext(e) Inc., 1983.

Baxter, Ellen and Kim Hopper. *Private Lives/Public Spaces: Homeless Adults on the Streets of New York City*. New York: Community Service Society, 1981.

Berger, John. *The Look of Things*. New York: Viking Press, 1974.

Berman, Marshall. *All that Is Solid Melts into Air: The Experience of Modernity*. New York: Penguin, 1982.

——. "The Signs in the Street: A Response to Perry Anderson." *New Left Review*, NLR 44, (1984): 114–123.

——. "Taking it to the Streets: Conflict and Community in Public Space." *Dissent* (Fall 1986): 476–85.

Blau, Joel S. "The Homeless of New York: A Case Study in Social Welfare Policy." Diss., Ann Arbor, MI: University Microfilms International, 1987.

Blomberg, Thomas G. *Juvenile Court and Community Corrections*. New York: University Press of America, 1984.

Blonsky, Marshall. *On Signs*. Baltimore: The Johns Hopkins University Press, 1985

Bogue, D.J. *Skid Row in American Cities*. Chicago: University of Chicago Press, 1963.

Bondi, Liz. "Locating Identity Politics." in *Place and the Politics of Identity*. eds. Michael Keith and Stephen Pile. London and New York, Routledge 1993: 84–101.

Bondi, I. and M. Domosh. "Other Figures in Other Places: Feminism, Post-Modernism and Geography." *Environment and Planning D: Society and Space* 10, 199–213.

Bourdieu, Pierre. *Distinction: A Social Critique of the Judgement of Taste*. London: Routledge and Kegan Paul, 1984.

Bourdieu, Pierre. *Outline of a Theory of Practice*. Cambridge: Cambridge University Press, 1979.

Brake, Mike. *The Sociology of Youth Culture and Youth Subcultures: Sex and Drugs and Rock 'n' Roll?* London: Routledge and Kegan Paul, 1980.

Bullock, Paul. *Youth Training and Employment: From the New Deal to New Federalism*. Los Angeles: Center for Industrial Policy, 1985.

Cahn, F. and V. Bary. *Welfare Activities of Federal, State and Local Governments in California 1850–1934*. Los Angeles: University of California Press, 1936.

Caldwell, Robert G. "The Juvenile Court: Development and Some Major Problems." *Juvenile Delinquency: A Book of Readings*, ed. Rose Giallambardo. New York: John Wiley and Sons, 1987.

Books and Articles

Chambliss, W.J. "A Sociological Analysis of the Law of Vagrancy." *Social Problems* 12 (1964): 67–77.

Clarke, John. "Style." *Resistance through Rituals: Youth Subcultures in Post-war Britain*, eds. Stuart Hall and Tony Jefferson. London: Hutchinson & Co., 1976: 175–191.

Clarke, John, Stuart Hall, Tony Jefferson, and Brian Roberts. "Subcultures, Cultures and Class: A Theoretical Overview." *Resistance Through Rituals. Youth Subcultures in Post-war Britain*, eds. Stuart Hall and Tony Jefferson. London: Hutchinson & Co., 1975: 9–74.

Clarke, S. "More Autonomous Policy Orientations: An Analytical Framework." *The Politics of Urban Development*, eds. H.T. Sanders and C.N. Stone. Kansas: University Press of Kansas, 1987: 105–124.

Clifford, James. *The Predicament of Culture: Twentieth-century Ethnography, Literature and Art*. Cambridge: Harvard University Press, 1988.

Cohen, Phil. "Towards Youthopia?" *Marxism Today*, October 1985: 33–37.

Coleman, J.S. *The Adolescent Society*. New York: Free Press, 1961.

Crystal, Stephen. "Homeless Men and Homeless Women: The Gender Gap." *Urban and Social Change Review* 17, no. 2, (1984): p. 9

Davis, Mike with Susan Ruddick. "Los Angeles: Civil Liberties Between the Hammer and the Rock." *New Left Review*, no. 170, 1988: 37–61.

Davis, Mike. "Urban Renaissance and the Spirit of Post Modernism." *New Left Review NLR* 151 (1987): 106–113.

Davis, Mike. *City of Quartz. Excavating the Future in Los Angeles*. London: Verso, 1990.

De Certeau, Michel. *The Practice of Everyday Life*, trans. Steven F. Rendall. Los Angeles: University of California Press, 1984.

———. "Practices of Space." in *On Signs*, ed. Marshall Blonsky. Baltimore: Johns Hopkins University Press, 1985: 122–145.

de Munro, Paul, Anne de Munro and Steve Lerner. *Reforming the California Youth Authority: How to End Crowding, Diversify Treatment, and Protect the Public without Spending More Money*. San Francisco: Commonweal Research Institute, 1988.

Dear, M.J. and S.M. Taylor. *Not On Our Street*. London: Pion Ltd., 1982.

Dear, Michael and Jennifer Wolch. *Landscapes of Despair: From Deinstitutionalization to Homelessness*. Princeton: Princeton University Press, 1987.

Dear, Michael. "Planning Community-Based Support Systems for the Homeless." Unpublished manuscript, University of Southern California, School of Urban and Regional Planning, 1987.

———. "Postmodern Planning." Paper presented at the Annual Meeting of the Association of Collegiate Schools of Planning, Atlanta, 1985.

Deutsche, Rosalyn. "Architecture of the Evicted." *Strategies: A Journal of Theory, Culture and Politics* 3 (1990): 159–183.

Bibliography

——. "Men in Space." *Strategies: A Journal of Theory Culture and Politics.* 3 (1990): 130–138

Di Stefano, Christine. "Dilemmas of Difference: Feminism, Modernity, and PostModernism." *Feminism/PostModernism*, ed. Linda J. Nicholson. New York: Routledge, Chapman and Hall, 1990: 63–82.

Duncan, James. "Men Without Property: The Tramp's Classification and Use of Urban Space." *Antipode* 11, no. 1 (1979): 24–34.

Ellingston, John R. "The Youth Authority Plan and its Development in California." *Youth Authority Quarterly* 20, no. 3, (1967).

Ellis, Brett Easton, *Less Than Zero.* New York: Simon and Shuster, 1985.

Evard, Jean-Luc. "Mickey Maul. Voden Simulakren." *Aesthetik und Kommunikation,* Heft 67/68, 1990.

Ewen, Elizabeth. "City Lights: Immigrant Women and the Rise of the Movies." *Signs* 5, no. 3 (Spring 1980) Supplement. Women and the American City 545–567.

Fainstein, N. and S. Fainstein. "Regime Strategies, Communal Resistance and Economic Forces." *Restructuring the City*, ed. Fainstein et al. New York: Longman, 1983: 245–282.

Folch-Serra, Merya. "Place,Voice and Space: Mikhail Bakhtin's Dialogical Landscape." *Environment and Planning D: Society and Space* 8, 1990: 255–274.

Foote, C. "Vagrancy-type Law and its Administration." *Crime and the Legal Process,* ed. W.J. Chambliss. New York: McGraw Hill, 1969: 295-329.

Foster, Hal. "PostModernism: A Preface." in *The Anti-Aesthetic: Essays on PostModern Culture*, ed. H. Foster. Washington: Bay Press, 1983: ix-xvi.

Foster, Sarah E. "Urban Gorilla: When Redevelopment Strikes." *Reason* January 1988.

Foucault, Michel. "Of Other Spaces," *Diacritics,* 16, no. 1, (Spring 1986): 22–27.

——. *Power/Knowledge: Selected Interviews and Other Writings 1972–1977,* ed. Colin Gordon, New York: Pantheon, 1980.

——. *Discipline and Punish: The Birth of the Prison*, trans. Alan Sheridan. New York: Vintage Books, 1979.

Fraser, Nancy and Linda Nicholson. "Social Criticism and Philosophy: An Encounter between Postmodernism and Feminism." *Universal Abandon? The Politics of PostModernism*, ed. Andrew Ross. Minneapolis: University of Minnesota Press, 1988: 83–104.

Fuss, Diana. *Essentially Speaking.* London and New York: Routledge, 1989.

Giddens, Anthony. *The Constitution of Society.* Berkeley: University of California Press, 1984.

Books and Articles

Gillis, John R. *Youth and History: Transition and Change in European Age Relations 1770–Present*. New York: Academic Press, 1981.

Gleason, Brendan J. and Jennifer Wolch. "Homelessness and the Politics of Turf: The Case of Venice, California." Unpublished manuscript, University of Southern California, Los Angeles Homelessness Project, 1989.

Goffman, Erving. *The Presentation of Self in Everyday Life*. New York: Doubleday, 1959.

——. *Asylums*. New York: Doubleday, 1961.

——. *Behavior in Public Places*. New York: Free Press, 1963.

——. *Strategic Interaction*. London: Basil Blackwell, 1969.

Gonion, Gordon E. "Section 601, W & I Code: A Need for Change." *Youth Authority Quarterly* 26.2, 1973: 21–31.

Gottdiener, Mark. "Culture, Ideology, and the Sign of the City." *The City and the Sign: An Introduction to Urban Semiotics*, eds. Mark Gottdiener and Alexandros Lagopoulos. New York: Columbia University Press, 1986: 202–218.

——, "Recapturing the Center: A Semiotic Analysis of Shopping Malls." *The City and the Sign: An Introduction to Urban Semiotics*, eds. Mark Gottdiener and Alexandros Lagopoulos. New York: Columbia University Press,1986: 288–327.

Grossberg, Lawrence. "Putting the Pop Back in PostModernism." *Universal Abandon? The Politics of PostModernism*, ed. Andrew Ross. Minneapolis: University of Minnesota Press, 1988: 167–190.

Grumpecht, Blake. "Chamber Chief Hopes to Polish Hollywood Image." *L.A. Business Journal*, August 14, 1989.

Gurr, T.R. and D.S. King. *The State and the City*. Chicago: University of Chicago Press, 1987.

Hall, Stuart et al. *Policing the Crisis: Mugging, the State and Law and Order*. London: Macmillan Education, 1978.

Harstock, Nancy. "Foucault on Power: A Theory for Women?" *Feminism/ PostModernism*, ed. Linda J. Nicholson. New York: Routledge, Chapman and Hall, 1990: 157-175.

Harvey, David. *The Urban Experience*. Baltimore: Johns Hopkins University Press, 1989.

Hebdige, Dick. *Subculture: The Meaning of Style*. London: Methuen and Co., 1979.

Henderson, M.R. "Acquiring Privacy in Public Places." *Urban Life and Culture* 3, 1975: 446–455.

Hesse, Barnor. "Black to the Front and Black Again." in *Place and the Politics of Identity*. eds., Michael Keith and Stephen Pile. London and New York: Routledge, 1993: 162–182.

Bibliography

Higher Education Research Institute. *Youth Issues: Background Statements, The Presidential Youth Issues Forum.* Los Angeles: Graduate School of Education, University of California, 1990.

Hoch, Charles and Robert Slayton. *New Homeless and Old: Community and the Skid Row Hotel.* Philadelphia: Temple University Press, 1989.

Hollingshead, A.B. *Elmstown's Youth.* New York: John Wiley and Sons Inc., 1949.

Hombs, M.E. and Mitch Snyder. *Homelessness in America: A Forced March to Nowhere.* Washington: Community for Creative Non-Violence, 1983.

hooks, bell. *Black Looks: Race and Representation.* Toronto: Between the Lines, 1992: 165–179.

Hopper, Kim James. "Whose Lives Are These, Anyway?." *Urban and Social Change Review* 17, no. 2 (1984): 12–13.

———. "A Bed For the Night: Homeless Men in New York City, Past and Present." Diss., Ann Arbor MI: University Microfilms International, 1987.

Jackson, Peter. *Maps of Meaning: An Introduction to Cultural Geography.* London: Unwin Hyman, 1989.

Judge Mack. "The Juvenile Court." *Harvard Law Review* 23 (1990):104–122. Cited in Jack Rothman with Thomas David, *Status-Offenders in Los Angeles County; Focus on Runaway and Homeless Youth: A Study and Policy Recommendations.* Los Angeles: University of California, Los Angeles School of Social Work, 1985.

Keil, Roger. "Stadt der Welt: Internationalisierung und Lokale Politik in Los Angeles." Diss. Johann Wolfgang Goethe Universitat, Frankfurt am Main, 1991.

Kasinitz, Philip. "Gentrification and Homelessness: The Single Room Occupant and the Inner City Revival." *Urban Social Change Review* 17, (1984): 9–14.

Keniston, Kenneth. *The Uncommitted Youth: Alienated Youth in Society.* New York: Dell, 1965.

———. *Young Radicals: Notes on Committed Youth.* New York: Dell Publishers, 1968.

Kett, Joseph. *Rites of Passage.* New York: Basic Books, 1977.

Krisberg, B., I.M. Schwartz, P. Litsky and J. Austin. "The Watershed in Juvenile Justice Reform." *Crime and Delinquency* 32, no. 1 (1986): 5–38.

Lacan, Jaques. "Sign, Symbol and Imaging." *On Signs.* ed. Marshall Blonsky. Baltimore: The John Hopkins University Press, 1985: 203–210.

Laclau, Ernesto and Chantal Mouffe. *Hegemony and Socialist Strategy: Towards a Radical Democratic Politics,* trans. Winston Moore and Paul Cammack. London: Verso, 1985.

Laclau, Ernesto. "Populist Rupture and Discourse," trans. Jim Grady. Montreal: Department of Literary Studies and Philosophy, University of Quebec, 1977.

Books and Articles

Laclau, Ernesto. "Building a New Left: An Interview with Ernesto Laclau." *Strategies: A Journal of Theory, Culture and Politics*, 1 (Fall 1988): 10–28.

Lash, Scott and John Urry. *The End of Organized Capitalism*. Oxford: Basil Blackwell, 1987.

Ledrut, Raymond. "Speech and the Silence of the City." *The City and the Sign: An Introduction to Urban Semiotics*, eds. Mark Gottdiener and Alexandros Lagopoulous. New York: Columbia University Press, 1986: 114–134.

Lee, Craig and "Shreader." "Los Angeles." *Hard Core California: A History of Punk and New Wave*, eds. Peter Belsito and Bob Davis. Berkeley: The Last Gasp of San Francisco, 1983.

Lefebvre, Henri. *La survie du capitalisme, la reproduction des rapports de production*. Paris: Éditions Anthropos, 1973.

———. *Espace et politique*. Paris: Editions Anthropos, 1968.

———. "Space: Social Product and Use Value." *Critical Sociology: European Perspectives*, ed. J.W. Friedberg. New York: Irvington Publishers, 1979: 285–295.

———. *Une Pensée Devenue Monde: Faut-il Abandonner Marx?* Paris: Fayard, 1980.

———. *Le Droit à la Ville*. Paris: Editions Anthropos, 1968.

———. *The Production of Space*. Oxford and Cambridge: Basil Blackwell, 1991.

Lerman, P. *Community Treatment and Social Control: A Critical Analysis of Juvenile Policy*. Chicago: University of Chicago Press, 1975.

Lerner, Steve. *The CYA Report: Conditions of Life at the California Youth Authority*. San Francisco: Common Knowledge Press, 1984.

Levi-Strauss, Claude. *The Savage Mind*. London: Weidenfeld and Nicolson, 1966.

———. *Totemism*. London: Penguin, 1969.

Lipietz, Alain. "The Structuration of Space: The Problem of Land and Social Policy" *Regions in Crisis*, eds. J. Carney, R. Hudson, and J. Lewis. London: Croom Helm, 1980: 288–327.

Lipschutz, Mark R. "Runaways in History." *Crime and Delinquency* (July 1977): 321–332.

Lloyd, Genevieve. *The Man of Reason: "Male" and "Female" in Western Philosophy*. Minneapolis: University of Minnesota Press, 1984.

Loring Brace, Charles. *The Dangerous Classes*. New York: Wynkoop and Hallenbeck, 1880.

Love, E.G. *Subways Are For Sleeping*. New York: Harcourt Brace, 1957.

Maher, Lisa. *Women on the Edge of Crime: Crack, Cocaine and the Changing Contexts of Street Level Sex Work in New York City*. Presented at the Joint Meetings of Law and Society Association and Research Committee on the Sociology of Law of the International Sociological Association, Amsterdam, June 26–29, 1991.

Bibliography

Mair, Andrew. "The Homeless and the Post-Industrial City." *Political Geography* 5 (1986): 351–368.

McDowell, Linda. "Space, Place and Gender Relations. Part II. Identity, Difference, Feminist Geometrics and Geographies." *Progress in Human Geography* 17, no. 3 (1993): 305–318.

McRobbie, Angela and Jenny Garber. "Girls and Subcultures: An Exploration." *Resistance Through Rituals: Youth Subcultures in Post-war Britain*, eds. Stuart Hall and Tony Jefferson. London: Hutchinson & Co., 1976: 209–222.

McWilliams, Carey. *Southern California: An Island on the Land*. Santa Barbara: Peregrine Smith Inc., 1979.

Miller, Dorothy, Donald Miller, Fred Hoffman, Robert Duggan. *Runaways—Illegal Aliens in Their Own Land*. New York: Praeger Publishers, 1980.

Millison, Martin Bruce. "Shopping Center Society: The Effects of Peer Norms, Structure and Security on Adolescent Behavior at Regional Shopping Malls." Diss., University of Pennsylvania, 1974.

Minehan, Thomas. *Boy and Girl Tramps of America*. New York: Farrar & Rinehart, 1934.

Mollenkopf, J. *The Contested City*. Princeton, NJ: Princeton University Press, 1983.

Monkonnen, E. "Nineteenth Century Institutions: Dealing with the Urban Underclass." *Social Science Research Council. History of the Urban Underclass*. Unpublished ms.

Morgan, D.H.J. *Social Theory and the Family*. London: Routledge and Kegan Paul, 1975.

Morino, Marianne. *The Hollywood Walk of Fame: The Only Guide to the World's Most Famous Stars in the World in the World's Most Famous Sidewalk*. Los Angeles: Ten Speed Press, 1987.

Murdock, Graham and Robin McCron. "Youth and Class: The Career of a Confusion." *Working Class Youth Culture*, eds. Geoff Mungham and Geoff Pearson. London: Routledge and Kegan Paul, 1976: 10–26.

Musgrove, Frank. *Youth and the Social Order*. Bloomington IN: University of Indiana Press, 1965.

———, "The Problems of Youth and the Social Structure." *Youth and Society* 11 (1969): 38–58.

Owens, Craig. "The Discourse of Others: Feminists and Postmodernism." in *The Anti-Aesthetic: Essays on Post-Modern Culture*, ed. H. Foster. Washington: Bay Press, 1983: 57–82.

Parsons, Talcott. "Age and Sex in the Social Structure of the United States." *Personality in Nature, Society and Culture*, eds. Clyde Kluckhohn and H.A. Murray. New York: Alfred A. Knopf, 1949: 269–281.

Philo, C.P. "'The Same and Other': On Geographies, Madness and Outsiders." Unpublished monograph, University of Cambridge, Department of Geography, 1986.

Books and Articles

Pinkey, Tony, "Introduction," *The Politics of Modernism: Against the New Conformists.* Raymond Williams, ed. Tony Pinkey. London: Verso, 1989.

Platt, Anthony E. *The Child Savers: The Invention of Delinquency.* Chicago: University of Chicago Press, 1969.

Preziosi, Donald. "Oublier la Citta." *Strategies* 3 (1990): 260–267.

Rivlin, Leanne G. and Lynne C. Manzo. "Homeless Children in New York City: A View from the Nineteenth Century." *Children's Environment Quarterly* 5 (1988): 26–33.

Robertson, Julia M. "Homeless and Runaway Youth: Review of Literature." *Homelessness: The National Perspective*, eds. J.M. Robertson and M. Greenblatt. Prepublication draft: Plenum Publishing Corporation.

Robertson, Marjorie, et al. *Emergency Shelter for the Homeless in Los Angeles County, Basic Shelter Research Project.* Los Angeles: University of California, Los Angeles, 1984.

Robertson, Marjorie. "Homeless Youth: An Overview of Recent Literature." *Homeless Children and Youth.* Prepublication draft. Los Angeles: Transaction Press .

Rodman, Hyman. "Talcott Parsons's View of the Changing American Family." *Marriage, Family and Society*, ed. Hyman Rodman. New York: Random House, 1967: 262–286.

Ropers, Richard. "The Rise of the New Urban Homeless." *Public Affairs Report* 26, no. 5 (1985).

Rothman, D.J. *The Discovery of the Asylum.* Boston: Little Brown and Company, 1971.

Rothman, Jack and Thomas David. *Status-Offenders in Los Angeles County, Focus on Runaway and Homeless Youth: A Study and Policy Recommendations.* Los Angeles: University of California School of Social Work, 1985.

Rowe, Stacy and Jennifer Wolch. "Social Networks in Time and Space: The Case of Homeless Women in Skid Row, Los Angeles." Unpublished manuscript, University of Southern California, 1989.

Royden Mitchell, Mark. "Fantasy Seen: Hollywood Fiction Since West." *Los Angeles in Fiction: A Collection of Original Essays*, ed. David Fine. Albuquerque: University of New Mexico Press, 1984: 147–168.

Rubenstein, J. *City Police.* New York: Farrar, Straus, Giroux, 1973.

Ruddick, Susan. "The Montreal Citizens' Movement: The Realpolitik of the 1990s?" eds. Mike Davis et al. *Fire in the Hearth.* London: Verso, 1990: 287–317.

Rustin, Michael. "The Rise and Fall of Public Space: A Postcapitalist Prospect." *Dissent* 33, no. 4 (1986): 486–494.

Sanders, H.T. and C. N. Stone. "Development Politics Reconsidered." *Urban Affairs Quarterly* 22 (1987): 521 - 539.

Sayer, Andrew. *Method in Social Sciences: A Realist Approach.* London: Hutchinson & Co., 1984.

Bibliography

———, "Competing Paradigms: A Rejoinder to Peterson." *Urban Affairs Quarterly* 22, 1987: 548–551.

Sennett, Richard. *The Conscience of the Eye: The Design and Social Life of Cities.* New York: Knopf, 1990.

Sexton, P.C. "The Life of the Homeless." *Dissent* 30, no. 1 (1983): 79–84.

Sharpe, William and Leonard Wallock. "From 'Great Town' to 'Nonplace Urban Realm': Reading the Modern City." *Visions of the Modern City: Essays in History, Art and Literature*, eds. William Sharpe and Leonard Wallock. Baltimore: Johns Hopkins University Press, 1987.

Shields, Robert. *Places on the Margin: Alternative Geographies of Modernity.* London: Routledge, 1991.

Sibley, D. *Outsiders in Urban Society.* Oxford: Basil Blackwell, 1981.

Sloss, M. "The Crisis of Homelessness: Its Dimensions and Its Solutions." *Urban and Social Change Review* 17, no. 2 (1984): 18–20.

Smith, Neil and Cindi Katz. "Grounding Metaphor." *Place and the Politics of Identity*, eds. Michael Keith and Stephen Pile. London and New York: Routledge, 1993: 67–83.

Soja, Edward W. *Postmodern Geographies: The Reassertion of Space in Critical Social Theory.* London: Verso, 1989.

———. "Inside Exopolis: Scenes from Orange County." *Variations on a Theme Park: Scenes from the New American City and the End of Public Space*, ed. Michael Sorkin. New York: The Noonday Press, 1992: 94-122.

Soja, Edward W. et al., "Urban Restructuring: An Analysis of Social and Spatial Change in Los Angeles." *Economic Geography* 59, no. 2 (1983): 195–230.

Soja, Edward and Barbara Hooper. "The Space that Difference Makes." *Place and the Politics of Identity*, eds. Michael Keith and Stephen Pile. London and New York: Routledge, 1993: 183–205

Spradley, J.P. *You Owe Yourself a Drunk: An Ethnography of Urban Nomads.* Boston: Little, Brown, 1970.

Steinhart, D. "The Politics of Status-Offender Deinstitutionalization in California." *Neither Angels nor Thieves: Studies in the Deinstitutionalization of Status Offenders*, eds. Joel F. Handler and Julie Katz. Washington, D.C.: National Academy Press, 1982: 784–824.

Stone, C. "The Study of the Politics of Urban Development." *The Politics of Urban Development*, eds. C. Stone and H.T. Sanders. Kansas: University Press of Kansas, 1987.

Stonequist, E.V. *The Marginal Man: A Study in Personality and Culture.* New York: Scribners, 1937.

Stoner, Madelaine R. "An Analysis of Public and Private Sector Provisions for the Homeless." *Urban and Social Change Review* 17, no. 1 (1984): 3–8.

Strieb, Victor L. *Juvenile Justice in America.* London: Kennikat Press, 1987.

Taylor, S.M., et al. "Predicting Community Reaction to Mental Health Facilities." *Journal of the American Planning Association* 50 (1984): 36–47.

Reports and Government Documents

Thrasher, F. *The Gang*. Chicago: University of Chicago Press, 1927.

Torrence, Bruce. *Hollywood: The First Hundred Years*. Hollywood: Hollywood Chamber of Commerce & Steve Fiske Enterprises, 1979.

Veness, A.R. "Home and Homelessness in the United States: Changing Ideas and Realities." *Environmental and Planning D: Society and Space* 10 (1992): 445–468.

Van Houten and Golembiewski. *Life Stress as a Predictor of Alcohol Abuse and/or Runaway Behavior*. Washington, D.C.: American Youth Work Center, 1978.

Wallace, E. *Skid Row as a Way of Life*. New York: Harper and Row, 1968.

Williams, Raymond. *The Politics of Modernism: Against the New Conformists*. ed. Tony Pinkey New York: Verso, 1989.

Wilson, W.J. *Thinking About Crime*. New York: Basic Books, 1975.

Wolch, J.R. and S.R. Gabriel. "Development and Decline of the Service-dependent Ghetto." *Urban Geography* 5 (1984): 111–129.

Wolch, J.R. "The Residential Location of the Service-dependent Poor." *Annals of the Association of American Geographers* 70 (1980): 330–341.

Wolch, Jennifer. "Planning for Service Dependent Populations: A Fair Share Service Distribution Approach." Unpublished manuscript, University of Southern California, School of Urban and Regional Planning, 1987.

Wright, Talmadge and Anita Vermund. "Small Dignities: Local Resistances, Dominant Strategies of Authority, and the Homeless." Draft Paper submitted for the 1990 Annual American Sociological Association, Washington D.C.

Zukin, Sharon. *Loft Living*. Baltimore: Johns Hopkins University Press,1988.

Zukin, Sharon. *Landscapes of Power. from Detroit to Disneyland*. Berkeley, University of California Press, 1991.

REPORTS AND GOVERNMENT DOCUMENTS

"Forty Years of Service to California (1941-1981)." *California Youth Authority Quarterly* 34.1, 1981.

City of Los Angeles. Community Redevelopment Agency. *Hollywood Boulevard District Urban Design Plan*. Los Angeles: City of Los Angeles, 1990.

———. Community Redevelopment Agency. *Hollywood Social Needs Plan*. Los Angeles: City of Los Angeles, 1990.

———. Community Redevelopment Agency. *Preliminary Draft Report on the Hollywood Urban Design Plan*. Los Angeles: City of Los Angeles, 1988.

———. Community Redevelopment Agency. *Preliminary Report on the Proposed Hollywood Redevelopment Project*. Los Angeles: City of Los Angeles, 1985.

Bibliography

————. Community Redevelopment Agency. *Preliminary Report on the Proposed Hollywood Redevelopment Project.* Los Angeles: City of Los Angeles, 1985. Map 2-7. Major Social Issues, Hollywood 1985: 2-32a.

Data Highlights. October 1, 1988 to June 30, 1989. Los Angeles: Children's Hospital of Los Angeles, Division of Adolescent Medicine.

Department of Economic Opportunity. *Report by the Advisory Commission of the Department of Economic Opportunity: The Status of Poverty in California 1984–1985.* Sacramento: Department of Economic Opportunity, 1986.

Halcyon Ltd. *Hollywood Boulevard Tenant Retail Inventory.* Los Angeles: City of Los Angeles Community Redevelopment Agency, 1988.

————. in Association with the IBI Group. *Office and Retail Market Analysis and Street Comparable Memorandum.* Los Angeles: City of Los Angeles Community Redevelopment Agency, 1988.

Helping Homeless Teens, Options House, Los Angeles, n.d.

HIV Aids Prevention Project, LA Street Outreach. Minutes of meeting, December 20, 1989. Los Angeles: Children's Hospital of Los Angeles.

IBI Group. *Draft Report of Resident and Shopper/Visitor Survey.* Los Angeles: City of Los Angeles Community Redevelopment Agency, 1987.

Johns, D. and J. Bottcher. *AB 3121 Impact Evaluation: Final Report.* Sacramento: California Youth Authority, 1980.

Kotin, Regan and Mouchly Inc., in joint venture with the Planning Group Inc. *Baseline Market Assessment Proposed Hollywood Redevelopment Project Area Volume I.* Los Angeles: City of Los Angeles Community Redevelopment Agency, 1984.

Levins, Mindi. "Life on the Streets of Hollywood: Our Youth's Perspectives and Future Projections." Unpublished paper, 1988.

Marikan, Haig, Vice Chairman. *Little Hoover Commission: Public Hearing on Runaway/Homeless Youth.* Los Angeles: December 13, 1989.

New York State Council on Children and Families. *Meeting the Needs of Homeless Youth.* Albany, NY: New York State Council on Children and Families, 1984.

Office of Economic Development, City of Los Angeles. *Hollywood Revitalization Plan, Environmental Impact Review.* Los Angeles: n.d.

————. *Hollywood Revitalization Plan, Volume Three.* Los Angeles: n.d.

Office of Mayor Tom Bradley, Community Redevelopment Agency of Los Angeles, Select Committee for Housing and Services for Skid Row Residents. *Briefing Book: Preservation of Single Room Occupancy Residential Hotels in the Los Angeles Skid Row Community.* Los Angeles: City of Los Angeles Community Redevelopment Agency, July 20–24, 1987.

Policy Analysis for California Education: The Conditions of Children in California. Los Angeles: Los Angeles Roundtable for Children, 1983.

Presentation of Hollywood Police Department to High Risk Youth: Workshop Series on Resources for Youth in Hollywood. November 1987. Los Angeles: Children's Hospital of Los Angeles.

Reports and Government Documents

Pursley, Marietta. "Runaway Youth Situation in Los Angeles County: A General Overview." Los Angeles: United Way Planning Council, Unpublished document, 1981.

Responding to a Crisis. Covenant House, Los Angeles, n.d.

Robertson, M., R.H. Ropers, and R. Boyer. *The Homeless of Los Angeles County: An Empirical Evaluation.* Basic Shelter Research Project, Document No. 4, 1985. Psychiatric Epidemiology Program, School of Public Health, UCLA.

Robertson, Marjorie. *Homeless Youth in Hollywood. Patterns of Alcohol Use: A Report to the National Institute on Alcohol Abuse and Alcoholism.* Berkeley, CA: Alcohol Research Group, 1989.

Rothman, Jack and Thomas G. David. *Status-Offenders in Los Angeles County: Focus on Runaway and Homeless Youth, A Study and Policy Recommendations,* Los Angeles: Bush Program in Child and Family Policy, University of California Department of Children's Services, Los Angeles County, 1985.

Saleeby, George. *Hidden Closets: A Study of Detention Practices in California.* Sacramento: California Youth Authority, 1978.

State of California. Office of Criminal Justice Planning. *California State Plan for Criminal Justice.* City: Office of Criminal Justice Planning, 1979.

Steinhart, David. *Private Sector Task Force on Juvenile Justice: Final Report.* San Francisco: The National Council on Crime and Delinquency, Transamerica Corporation and Chevron Corporation, March 1987.

Supervisor Edmund D. Edelman. *The Runaway and Homeless Youth in Los Angeles County: Transcript of Tape-Recorded Proceedings.* Plummer Park, CA: September 10, 1976.

United States Department of Health Education and Welfare. Institute for Scientific Analysis. Runaway Resource Guide. *Runaway Youth: How Are They to Be Served?* San Francisco: Social and Rehabilitation Service of the U.S. Department of Health Education and Welfare,1974.

United States House of Representatives Subcommittee on Human Resources, Committee on Education and Labor. *The Problem of Runaway and Homeless Youth. Oversight Hearing on Runaway and Homeless Youth Program.* 97th Congress, 2nd session. Washington: GPO, 1982.

United States. Senate. Subcommittee on the Judiciary. P. Lerman. "Trends and Issues in the Deinstitutionalization of Youths in Trouble." Appendix. *Report of the Subcommittee on the Judiciary, Homeless Youth: The Saga of "Pushouts" and "Throwaways" in America.* 96th Congress, 2nd Session. Washington: GPO, 1980.

Whitley Heights Civic Association, Hollywood Heights Association, Outpost Estates, Hollywoodland Homeowners Association, Hollywood Heritage, Hollywood Project Area Committee, Melrose Hill Homeowners Association

Bibliography

ˇnd Hollywood Boulevard Merchants Association. Letter to Mayor Tom
adley. June 17, 1988.

ﾍtes, Gary L. T.estimony, *Little Hoover Commission on California State
overnment Organization and Economy.* Los Angeles: State of California,
ﾍcember 13, 1989.

:WSPAPER ARTICLES

ﾍmp Facilities for Delinquents Faces Charges." *Los Angeles Times,* March
7, 1987.

Capaldi, Michael. "Pioneer Program for Young Prostitutes: Children of the
Night Offers Understanding and Alternatives." *Los Angeles Times,* August 9,
1981.

Doctoroff, Andrew. "State Opens its First Detention Camp Exclusively For
Girls." *Los Angeles Times,* March 3, 1989.

Dorgin, Bob. "Boy Who Killed at Age Nine May Be Tried as an Adult."
Los Angeles Times, July 28, 1989.

Fannucchi, Kenneth J. "Council O.K.'s $922 Million Hollywood Revitalization."
Los Angeles Times, May 1, 1986.

Ferrell, David. "Woo Wants Changes in Hollywood Renewal." *Los Angeles
Times,* December 9, 1987.

Freedman, Jonathan. "California Commentary." *Los Angeles Times,* April 9,
1990: B5.

Hendrix, Kathleen. "Sex Charges Don't Shake Faith in Covenant House."
Los Angeles Times, February 8, 1990: E15.

"Hope for Rehabilitation—Outside Prison Walls." *The Christian Science
Monitor,* September 1988: B2.

Hurst, John. "Delinquents Face Tough Rite of Passage: And a Camp for
Troubled Youth Faces Charges of Abuse." *Los Angeles Times,* March 3, 1986:
Part 1.

Los Angeles Times, July 19, 1987.

Los Angeles Times, June 2, 1987.

Los Angeles Times, Dec 26, 1983.

Los Angeles Times, May 8, 1988, II.

MacMillan, Peggy. "The Skid Row Sweeps: Staking Out Positions. They're
Keeping the Homeless on the Move." *Los Angeles Times,* February 25, 1987.

Murphy, Dean. "Woo Names New Panel for Hollywood Redevelopment."
Los Angeles Times, August 4, 1989.

Interviews

Myers, David W. "Suit Could Postpone Hollywood Project." *Los Angeles Times,* April 26, 1987.

Palermo, Dave. "Bums take the Rap: Hollywood Curfew gets Mixed Reviews." *Los Angeles Times,* August 11, 1986.

Polanco, Richard. "Bad Medicine for 'Troubled Teens': Forced Private Hospitalization is Abuse of Process." *Los Angeles Times,* May 7, 1989: Part V: 5.

Sahagun, Louis. "'Riverbottom' People: Dirt, Debate, Dilemma." *Los Angeles Times,* June 10,1987.

Shillinger, Kurt and Cheryl Sullivan. "Treating Kids in the Community Works in Theory, But Not Always in Practice." *The Christian Science Monitor* 29, September 29, 1988: B6.

Tuber, R. "The Invisible Women of Skid Row." *Los Angeles Herald Examiner,* January 26, 1984.

Wharton, David. "Heavy Going: Metal Rockers Stake out Their own Turf on Hollywood Boulevard." *Los Angeles Times,* August 9, 1987.

Yorkin, Nicole. "Children of the Night." *Los Angeles Herald Examiner,* August 4, 1982.

INTERVIEWS

Berg, Lester. Social Needs Committee, Community Redevelopment Agency. Personal interview. April 4, 1991.

Brockman, Kim. Travelers Aid. Personal interview. February 15, 1987.

Carlson, Greg. Director, Angel's Flight. Personal interview. April 9, 1990.

Cruks, Gabe. Director, Gay and Lesbian Center. Personal interview. May 30, 1991.

de Paul, Michael. Caseworker, Covenant House. Personal interview. April 16, 1990.

Flinton, Rusty. Executive Director, Hollywood Revitalization Committee. Personal interview. May 16, 1990.

Forbes, Leslie. Director, Options House. Personal interview. April 12, 1991.

Frank. Personal interview. September 22, 1990.

Gil, Francis. Recruitment Officer, Conservation Corps. Telephone interview. April 11, 1991.

Hamson, Charles. Deputy Director Los Angeles County Probation Department. Telephone interview. April 19, 1991.

Joe. Teen Canteen. Personal interview. February 19, 1988.

Kaliski, John. Principal Architect, Community Redevelopment Agency, City of Los Angeles. Personal interview. May 19, 1990.

Bibliography

Lee, Lois. Personal interview by Mitchell Fink, *Herald Examiner*, August, 1982.

Levins, Mindi. Caseworker/Outreach Assistant, Los Angeles Youth Network; former Caseworker, Teen Canteen. Personal interview. April 10, 1991.

Moore, Brian. Save Hollywood Our Town. Personal interview. April 16, 1991.

Narvid, Ethel. Founder, Options House. Personal interview. May 30, 1990.

Nudelman, Robert. Member, Project Area Committee, Hollywood Redevelopment Plan. Personal interview. February 1, 1990.

Offenhauser, Fran. Hollywood Historic Preservation Association. Personal interview. May 16, 1990.

Shaw, Larry. Director, Youth Counseling Services, Hollywood YMCA. Personal interview. October 30, 1989.

Shirmen, Harold. Program Supervisor, Runaway Adolescent Planning Project. Personal interview. April 16, 1991.

Tim, Teen Canteen. Personal interview. February 11, 1988.

Weaver, Dale. Director, Teen Canteen. Personal interview. April 15, 1991.

Yang, Sam. Youth worker, The Way In, Salvation Army. Personal interview. April 17, 1991.

Yates, Gary. Director, Children's Hospital Los Angeles. Telephone interview. May 25, 1990.